Critique, Subversion, and Chinese Philosophy

Also available from Bloomsbury

Chinese Philosophy of History, by Dawid Rogacz
Imagination: Cross-Cultural Philosophical Analyses, edited by Hans-Georg Moeller and Andrew K. Whitehead
Landscape and Travelling East and West, edited by Hans-Georg Moeller and Andrew K. Whitehead
Michael Slote Encountering Chinese Philosophy, edited by Yong Huang
Transcendence and Non-Naturalism in Early Chinese Thought, by Joshua R. Brown and Alexus McLeod
Wisdom and Philosophy: Contemporary and Comparative Approaches, edited by Hans-Georg Moeller and Andrew K. Whitehead

Critique, Subversion, and Chinese Philosophy

Sociopolitical, Conceptual, and Methodological Challenges

Edited by
Hans-Georg Moeller and Andrew K. Whitehead

BLOOMSBURY ACADEMIC
LONDON • NEW YORK • OXFORD • NEW DELHI • SYDNEY

BLOOMSBURY ACADEMIC
Bloomsbury Publishing Plc
50 Bedford Square, London, WC1B 3DP, UK
1385 Broadway, New York, NY 10018, USA
29 Earlsfort Terrace, Dublin 2, Ireland

BLOOMSBURY, BLOOMSBURY ACADEMIC and the Diana logo are trademarks of Bloomsbury Publishing Plc

First published in Great Britain 2021
This paperback edition published 2022

Copyright © Hans-Georg Moeller, Andrew K. Whitehead and Contributors, 2021

Hans-Georg Moeller and Andrew K. Whitehead have asserted their right under the Copyright, Designs and Patents Act, 1988, to be identified as Editors of this work.

Cover design by Rebecca Heselton
Cover image © unsplash

All rights reserved. No part of this publication may be reproduced or transmitted in any form or by any means, electronic or mechanical, including photocopying, recording, or any information storage or retrieval system, without prior permission in writing from the publishers.

Bloomsbury Publishing Plc does not have any control over, or responsibility for, any third-party websites referred to or in this book. All internet addresses given in this book were correct at the time of going to press. The author and publisher regret any inconvenience caused if addresses have changed or sites have ceased to exist, but can accept no responsibility for any such changes.

A catalogue record for this book is available from the British Library.

Library of Congress Cataloging-in-Publication Data
Names: Moeller, Hans-Georg, 1964– editor. | Whitehead, Andrew K., editor.
Title: Critique, subversion, and Chinese philosophy :
socio-political, conceptual, and methodological challenges /
edited by Hans-Georg Moeller and Andrew K. Whitehead.
Description: London ; New York : Bloomsbury Academic, 2020. |
Includes bibliographical references and index.
Identifiers: LCCN 2020027581 (print) | LCCN 2020027582 (ebook) |
ISBN 9781350115842 (hardback) | ISBN 9781350115859 (ebook) |
ISBN 9781350115866 (epub)
Subjects: LCSH: Philosophy, Chinese. | Analysis (Philosophy)–China. |
Contradiction.Classification: LCC B126 .C75 2020 (print) |
LCC B126 (ebook) | DDC 181/.11–dc23
LC record available at https://lccn.loc.gov/2020027581
LC ebook record available at https://lccn.loc.gov/2020027582

ISBN: HB: 978-1-3501-1584-2
PB: 978-1-3501-9140-2
ePDF: 978-1-3501-1585-9
eBook: 978-1-3501-1586-6

Typeset by Newgen KnowledgeWorks Pvt. Ltd., Chennai, India

To find out more about our authors and books visit www.bloomsbury.com and sign up for our newsletters.

Contents

1. Introduction: Conflict, Contradiction, Reconciliation: (Dis-)harmonious Critique in Chinese Philosophies, *Hans-Georg Moeller and Andrew K. Whitehead* — 1

Part 1 Critique as Method — 7

2. Pedagogical Self-Subversion and Critical Becoming in Early Confucian Philosophy, *Geir Sigurðsson* — 9

3. Crisis and Critique: Zhuangzi's Philosophical Turning Point, *Hans-Georg Moeller and Paul J. D'Ambrosio* — 21

4. Otherwise than God and Man: Subverting Purpose and Knowledge in Zhuangzi's Perspectival Mirror, *Brook Ziporyn* — 35

5. Confucius's Irony: Silent Subversion and Critique in the *Analects*, *Dimitra Amarantidou* — 57

6. Efficacious Subversion: Argument by Relegation in Chan Buddhism, *Andrew K. Whitehead* — 69

7. Scolding the Buddhas, Abusing the Patriarchs: An Outlook on the Subversive Hermeneutics of Chan, through Case Four of the *Blue Cliff Record*, *Rudi Capra* — 77

Part 2 Sociopolitical Subversion — 87

8. To Become the King of All under Heaven: Mengzi as a Strategist of Regime Subversion, *Ting-mien Lee* — 89

9. A Daoist Critique of the *Huaxia* Civilization Project, *Daniel Sarafinas* — 99

10. Li Zehou's Critique of Marx through the Lens of Kantian Philosophy, or the Transcendental Illusion of Class Struggle, *Jana S. Rošker* — 113

11. Kundao 坤道, Daring Odyssey: Female Daoists' Discontentment and Challenge to Confucian Womanhood, *Robin R. Wang* — 125

Part 3 Critiques of Concepts and Ideas 137

12 Critique and Subversion: Rethinking Yang Zhu's Conception of "Self," *Ellen Y. Zhang* 139

13 Subversive Cosmology in the *Zhuangzi*: On the Dispensability of Ritual, *Manuel Rivera Espinoza* 153

14 Dai Zhen's Critique of Song Confucian Ideology, *Robert A. Carleo III* 167

15 What Is Critique and What Does It Subvert? Epistemic Intransparency in the Critique of Modern Society, *Ady Van den Stock* 181

List of Contributors 193
Index 197

1

Introduction: Conflict, Contradiction, Reconciliation: (Dis-)harmonious Critique in Chinese Philosophies

Hans-Georg Moeller and Andrew K. Whitehead

To someone who studied philosophy at a university in mainland China in the 1980s, the development of Chinese thought would have seemed like an endless chain of critiques and subversions. At the time, most textbooks and overviews of the history of philosophy still applied the framework of dialectical materialism quite rigidly. Accordingly, socioeconomic contradictions were regarded as the "base structure" of society and the ensuing class struggles as determining all intellectual developments. Some schools of thought, such as the Legalists and Daoists, were located within the progressive, materialist camp opposing feudal structures, while other schools, most prominently the Confucians, were seen as reactionary idealists whose ideology served the function of legitimizing oppressive social hierarchies and maintaining exploitative modes of production.

In the wake of the reform politics and modernizations initiated in 1978, China underwent rapid changes which eventually swept away traditional Marxist and Maoist modes of thought. China's 1990s should prove dialectical materialism correct, albeit in a most ironic way: Indeed, the shift toward a new mode of production, namely capitalism, once more brought about fundamental changes in philosophical thought—this time, however, these changes resulted in an almost complete demise of old-school dialectical materialism in mainstream Chinese philosophy. Since the 1990s, the philosophical discourse in mainland China has replaced emphasis on conflict and contradiction with emphasis on unity and, especially, harmony (*hexie* 和谐)—which has become a major buzzword in the present decade. If, for instance, one points out today at an academic conference in mainland China that early Daoist texts tend to harshly criticize their Confucian counterparts, one is soon likely to be reminded that in the end Daoists and Confucians nevertheless pursue more or less the same goals.

In philosophy, the current focus on harmony is sometimes implicitly or explicitly connected with the traditional motto of the "unity of the three teachings" (*sanjiao heyi* 三教合, referring to Confucianism, Daoism, and Buddhism), the roots of which can be traced back to the sixth century CE (Gentz 2011). The *sanjiao heyi* discourse typically suggests that differences between the main Chinese intellectual and religious traditions are outweighed by an ultimate spiritual coherence. In fact, however, there has hardly ever been "any successful attempt at creating a harmonious system of Chinese religions in which all three religions have equal positions" (Gentz 2011: 540). As Gentz (2011) demonstrates, those who have claimed the "unity of the three teachings" mostly concluded that one of the teachings was more equal than the others. Today, this role is once more ascribed to Confucianism. Confucian "culture" is often presented as the centerpiece of Chinese civilization, and Daoism, Buddhism, and other philosophies or religions appear as supporting ornaments on its fringes. Such a "Confucian-centrism" is not only prevalent among representatives of Chinese philosophy in "greater China" or the "sinophone" world, but also among many leading Western scholars of Chinese thought.

In effect, however, a philosophy that emphasizes harmony over contradiction is just as critical and subversive as a philosophy that takes the opposite stance. Both sides of the dispute critique one another. Critique is first and foremost a philosophical method and not tied to any specific doctrine, position, or argument. Arguably, it is the philosophical method per se. Philosophical thinking and writing is intrinsically critical.

In the context of explaining the art of dialectics in book seven of Plato's *Republic*, Socrates points out that contradictions in our sense perceptions "summon the intellect" (523b; Bloom 1991: 202). A finger seems soft to our senses when we first touch it, but when we press harder and get to the bone, it seems hard. This simple example illustrates a first meaning of critique and subversion. One perception ("hard") negates another ("soft"). Thereby the senses subvert themselves. They disclose their own limitations. They cannot tell us if a finger is soft or hard. Because of this subversion, we can no longer rely only on immediate sense data and must try something in addition. The intellect needs to get to work and reaches a different level of consciousness that transcends the senses. It critiques the available sense data and analyzes them in order to arrive at a more complex understanding of the concept or the "idea" of a finger that can entail both softness and hardness at the same time. Critique, in this sense, is for both Plato and Hegel the engine of thought that drives the development or building (*Bildung*, as Hegel would say) of the mind.

Kant further specified the significance of critique as method. For him, philosophy consists in a systematic reflection of the mind, as "reason," on itself. Critical thinking, in this sense, does not take knowledge about "things" in a dogmatic sense at face value, but tries to identify the conditions that allow knowledge of them to arise in the first place. After Kant, philosophical critique no longer simply asks: Is this so? Instead, it tries to "deconstruct" the underlying structures that make claims about things appear plausible or true. For Kant, such structures were the "a priori" conditions of reason, but for the thinkers that practiced critical philosophy after him, these structures could be, for instance, historical, psychological, social, linguistic, or economic—as was the case for Marx.

Critique consists by no means merely in criticisms—in saying that something is wrong or bad, and that something else instead is true or good. Rather, critique questions the simplicity of such claims; it questions why we believe what we believe or know what we know. Importantly, critique is therefore also self-critique. Wherever philosophy is practiced, in the ancient world or in present-day China or the "West," critique and self-critique are very much at its heart.

The chapters collected in this volume investigate the possibility of a defined notion of critique in Chinese philosophical history, offering a resounding and emphatic affirmation to the idea that critique has been operating in a number of different, sophisticated ways across a wide array of texts and traditions. They discuss critique as method, instances of sociopolitical subversion, and practices of critiquing concepts and ideas.

Contributors cover topics such as Critical Confucianism, feminist critiques in Daoist writings, and Chinese philosophical encounters with thinkers such as Marx and Kant. Offering original philosophical contributions, the authors look at ideas and arguments attributed to Confucius, Zhuangzi, and the Chan master Mazu Daoyi alongside the works of Plato and Husserl. They thus provide new ways of understanding how critique connects to philosophy and underline the need to reemphasize precisely this in how we practice and what we mean by philosophy today.

Two caveats deserve to be mentioned here. First, early Chinese texts are typically composite works drawing from numerous sources and often reflect diverse viewpoints and philosophical orientations. Scholarship therefore warns us to not overly personalize early Chinese philosophers and the texts ascribed to them. To give just two examples: Confucius's words, like those of Socrates, were written down after his death, and it is impossible to assess today in how far the texts in which these words are found represent his "original" ideas. The text that bears the name *Zhuangzi*, on the other hand, is a collection of materials that has been revised and edited over the course of many centuries. Rather than being a coherent treatise going back to one person and one specific time in history, it is a multilayered and "polyphonic" text.

Second, the history of Chinese philosophy is so long and complex that it is impossible to present a comprehensive or even representative collection of critical and subversive positions and voices it includes. Our collection, reflecting the respective areas of expertise of its contributors, focuses on the Confucian, Daoist, and Buddhist traditions and includes only few chapters (those by Rosker, van den Stock, and Wang) focusing on contemporary contexts. We apologize for the limitations of our volume and encourage others to help filling its lacunae in the future.

The chapters of the first part of this volume approach the topic of critique in terms of methodology, drawing on sources from Confucianism, Daoism, and Chan Buddhism, with a focus on different instances of critique and its various forms in early Chinese philosophical texts.

In Chapter 2, Geir Sigurðsson rethinks the process of learning in terms of "pedagogical self-subversion," using Confucianism as his chief reference point in understanding this process as one of critical becoming, as a process of critique. He finds that there is an increasing tendency in current scholarship toward a more open-minded analysis of Confucian philosophy in which its critical elements become significant. Sigurðsson develops his reading of Confucian texts as philosophies of education in service to a "transformative self-critical attitude."

Hans-Georg Moeller and Paul J. D'Ambrosio, in their co-authored chapter "Crisis and Critique: Zhuangzi's Philosophical Turning Point," seek out the crucial turning point in the *Zhuangzi*, philosophically understood as the "existential or intellectual experience of the imminent collapse of what has been taken for granted, and the subsequent emergence of a different viewpoint" (p. 21). In reflecting on the story of the poaching at Diaoling, the authors take it to be an allegorical expression "of a crisis that brought about the critical method of the *Zhuangzi*."

Brook Ziporyn draws our attention to Zhuangzi, and to what Ziporyn calls Zhuangzi's "perspectival mirror." This is a mirror that has "its own position, its own perspective, enabling it to 'overcome,' rather than reflect, whatever stands before it, and to do so without harming either itself or what it responds to" (p. 53). As such, it helps appreciate what he calls Zhuangzi's "Atheistic Apophatic Mysticism." Ziporyn shows how the mirror both subverts that which stands before it, as well as how it subversively works against the authority of any given perspective as capable of offering genuine reflection. Referring back to an array of passages from the Zhuangzi, Ziporyn is able to highlight the isomorphism between "the unknowing knowings of Heaven and unknowing knowings of man," ultimately showing what he calls the "distinctive Zhuangzian form" of atheist apophatic mysticism (p. 54).

In Chapter 5, Dimitra Amarantidou works through her reading of Confucius as a figure "often portrayed as ironically critical towards the attitudes and deeds of others, as well as his own" (p. 57). She works to highlight how and why Confucius develops an ironic attitude, finding that his linguistic expressions of paradoxicality are made requisite by a world of change.

Andrew K. Whitehead, writing on the use of argument by relegation in Chan Buddhism, argues for the value of investigating alternative forms of argumentation in the contemporary climate of misinformation, especially those arguments which begin from and force radically different questions and establish radically different premises from which argumentative positions can ensue. Turning to the "performative argumentative showings" of the Chan masters, Whitehead offers new insights concerning the various forms of argumentation which might be considered relegational.

In his chapter "Scolding the Buddhas, Abusing the Patriarchs: An Outlook on the Subversive Hermeneutics of Chan, through Case Four of the Blue Cliff Record," Rudi Capra discusses the "self-negating dialectics of Chan pedagogy." Turning to the logic of negation, and its function at both the level of narrative as well as meta-narrative, Capra rethinks the reflexive self-undermining of Chan masters in their teachings in support of his reading of Chan hermeneutics as a subversive tool.

The second part of this volume presents a number of cases of sociopolitical subversion throughout the history of Chinese philosophy. Authors discuss historical instances of critique and subversion in the works of Mengzi, Zhuangzi, Li Zehou, and a number of female Daoists, showcasing the role that critique plays in their works.

In Chapter 8, Ting-mien Lee turns to the figure of Mengzi, reconsidering his work as one of strategic subversion, taking him to be describable as a "strategist and theorist of regime subversion." In order to do so, she considers the "intimate relationship and salient resonance between today's widely studied classical 'philosophical texts' and classical 'military texts'" (p. 89).

Daniel Sarafinas's contribution offers a critique of the *Huaxia* civilization project from a Zhuangzian perspective. Sarafinas understands the *huaxia* civilization project as the process by which the *huaxia* identity was created, and notes that "the *Zhuangzi*'s critique of *huaxia* civilization identity is provided primarily through the vantage point of barbarian-sages" (p. 101).

Jana S. Rošker turns our attention to critique in contemporary China, looking to the works of Li Zehou in relation to his critique of Marx in the second half of the twentieth century. Rošker assesses this critique as one operating through the lens of Kantian "transcendental illusions," arguing that Li works to synthesize Marxist and Kantian theories with those which are traditionally Chinese "in order to create a theoretical model of modernization," a model based in the works of Hegel, Marx, Kant, and Confucius.

In Chapter 11, Robin R. Wang uncovers an "invisible resistance to the Confucian ideal womanhood" in the form of female Daoists, the *Kundao* (the Way of Femininity). She discusses how it is that although "the Daodejing has not been used politically, socially or economically to advance women's interests and benefits, nevertheless, it has carved out an intellectual and physical space for women in practice" (p. 128). Turning to concrete textual and personal examples, Wang calls for us to "reorient our epistemic, social, cultural, and personal framework related to the identity of the woman" (p. 131).

The third part of the volume looks at a variety of cases in which there are critiques of concepts and ideas. Authors present instances of critique against specific notions or ideologies, such as the self or differing definitions of principle, or cosmology as such.

In her chapter "Critique and Subversion: Rethinking Yang Zhu's Conception of 'Self,'" Ellen Y. Zhang challenges existent representations of the proto-Daoist figure Yang Zhu, working to explicate "Yang's conception of self in terms of self-ownership and self-preservation, showing that his individualistic argument functions as a critique and subversion of the mainstream tradition in Pre-Han China, which values the interest of the empire over individual persons" (p. 140).

In Chapter 13, Manuel Rivera reminds us of the important role played by ritual-centered cosmologies in working to evaluate Zhuangzian cosmology in such a way as to account for its subversive character. Rivera concludes that the second chapter of the Zhuangzi effectively subverts both steering agencies and hierarchical differentiations, two central notions of ritual-centered cosmologies.

Robert Carleo III, in his chapter "Dai Zhen's Critique of Song Confucian Ideology," focuses on the eighteenth-century thinker's critique of the Song Confucian interpretation of principle. He finds that Dai subverted "both the orthodox Confucian doctrine of his time as well as the orthodox method of scholarship of his time, and made a lasting contribution to Confucian ethical and political theory in so doing" (p. 178).

Chapter 15 by Ady Van den Stock turns back, offering a select genealogy of critique in modern society, working to establish how critique is effective in subversion. Tracing a development from Kant through to social-systems theorists such as Niklas Luhmann, Van den Stock finds that there is a need for us to criticize, if only out of a bodhisattva-like compassion, in the face of ontological indeterminacy accompanying the "ontological significance of our epistemic stance to the world."

The editors would like to thank all of those who have helped make this volume possible. In particular, we would like to thank Harriette Grissom for her invaluable assistance in preparing the final versions of the text. We would also like to thank the University of Macau for finances in support of editing as well as Helen Saunders and Colleen Coalter of Bloomsbury Publishing for their patience and support.

References

Bloom, Allan, trans. (1991), *The Republic of Plato*. New York: Basic Books.
Gentz, Joachim (2011), "Rational Choice and the Chinese Discourse on the Unity of the Three Religions (*sanjiao heyi* 三教合一)." *Religion* 41(4): 535–46.

Part One

Critique as Method

2

Pedagogical Self-Subversion and Critical Becoming in Early Confucian Philosophy

Geir Sigurðsson

Introduction: Historical Traditions and Philosophical Interpretations

Throughout its long and complex history, Confucianism has taken on many diverse guises. The most influential is undoubtedly its role as state ideology in Imperial China for about two millennia. Even within this particular role, a manifold of differing tendencies can be found. Some of the more unfortunate ones can be described as authoritarianism, sexism, dogmatism, and an overkill of conservatism. Certainly, these tendencies were not present at all times and in every respect, but they were arguably the main hallmarks of the Confucian ideology during the last two centuries of imperial rule, for which reason they are still today strongly associated with Confucianism in general.

Historical contingencies are often decisive for the emergence of image. This applies, I believe, very much to the dominant image of Confucianism today. In the nineteenth century, arguably during its least open, creative, and attractive phase, Confucianism began to be measured against the cultural components of the scientifically advanced and successful Euro-American colonialists, with whom the Chinese clashed. It is therefore not surprising that this main ideology of Imperial China has tended to be considered as the negative "other" of positively regarded social and cultural aspects of nineteenth-century Western culture, such as Christianity, Enlightenment philosophy, and systematic scientific rational endeavors.

While such an appraisal is not entirely unjustifiable with regard to the particular nature of Confucian state ideology at the time, it can be highly misleading when applied without qualification to its many other manifestations and features. In other historical periods, for instance, during most of the Tang and the Song, the Confucian state ideology was in many ways quite effective and successful. Furthermore, when understood as a cultural tradition, Confucianism may have a number of positive elements for, say, family cohesion and social stability. One of the points I am trying to make is that we may be throwing the baby out with the bathwater by refusing to familiarize ourselves with what Confucianism has to offer, simply because of the rather poor condition in which it found itself shortly before its collapse as a state ideology.

Another and more important point with regard to this discussion is that if we are seeking to make a tradition of thought viable for our times, we can also allow ourselves to more or less pass over some manifestations of the tradition in question and focus instead on others that better suit our purposes. I would contend, for instance, that we can offer a philosophical interpretation of a Confucian text without being in any way constrained by how it has been understood and translated into practice in actual history by actual people.

This is far from saying that previous interpretations are irrelevant, for they can of course be both illuminating and helpful. Furthermore, there is every reason to be fully aware of problematic or objectionable components of the philosophy in question, precisely because an important part of our engagement with it is to find ways to alleviate or eradicate such components. In the case of some ideologies or systems of thought this may prove impossible, because their objectionable aspects are such essential features of the overall structure that they cannot be eradicated without at the same time demolishing the entire system. Other systems, conversely, may turn out to contain problematic features that at the same time are in contradiction or at least serious tension with their overall character. In such cases, it becomes extremely urgent to rid them of their flaws, because it will help to bring out their essential features more clearly. One way to go about this is simply to present a version of the thought tradition in which the problematic elements are downplayed or even eliminated entirely. It then remains to be seen whether the resulting version can still be considered a part of that tradition or whether it has to be taken as too different from it to remain an instance of it. In some cases, in fact, such an approach can also reveal that the problematic features that have manifested themselves in history are in fact largely inconsistent with the thought tradition in question. This hermeneutic-pragmatic approach, as I would like to call it, seeks to be responsible by understanding the philosophy in question contextually and holistically, but at the same time it has the underlying agenda of making it useful and applicable.[1]

All these considerations are highly relevant to this investigation, because its aim is precisely to show that the Confucian philosophy as expressed in some of its earliest texts contains a strong critical element that is indispensable for its self-consistency. At the same time, however, it has not been customary to associate Confucianism with a critical spirit, probably (I suspect) because of the dogmatic and conservative route that it took, or was pushed into taking, from the latter part of the Ming dynasty onwards.[2] In the twentieth century it became, on the contrary, all the more common to consider Confucianism in a Marxist fashion as a reactionary ideology and Confucius as "an apologist for a feudal code of ethics" (Hansen 1976: 203–4). Moreover, the rote-learning character of the Chinese and other East Asian education systems, which is undeniably a remnant of the Confucian ideological past and can even be traced back to certain elements in the Confucian philosophy of education, has also produced such an antagonistic view of Confucianism that even implausible sayings have been attributed to the Master himself by serious scholars, for example: "Confucius asserted that students would better spend their time absorbing ideas from experts than thinking independently" (Brookfield 2012: 217).[3]

Recent publications indicate that such views and similar ones are changing, and that as an increasingly open-minded analysis of the Confucian philosophy takes place, more and more scholars are discovering the critical elements in Confucianism, most notably in the texts belonging to the pre-imperial period (see Lam 2014; Sigurðsson 2017; Tan 2017). However, looking primarily at the earliest texts may simply be the beginning of a more extensive discovery in later ones as well.

In my own engagement with the Confucian philosophy in recent years, I have focused in particular on interpreting it as a philosophy of education or even a philosophy of life, in so far as education is understood as the continuous aim of human living. This interpretation does not necessarily exclude the possibility of understanding Confucianism differently, as, say, a political philosophy or even a religiously oriented clan ideology. Nor do I deny with my interpretation that the Confucian tradition, and even its philosophy as such, is problematical in a number of ways. All I intend is to advocate that more attention be given to its educational aspect, which involves continuous self-improvement with the never-fully-realizable aim of forming a community or society in which people are able to find fulfillment as integrated individual beings *qua* social beings. Understanding the Confucian philosophy first and foremost as a philosophy of education, I contend, is among the most productive and fruitful understandings of it for contemporary times (Sigurðsson 2015). There is much to be gained from it by adopting such a focus.

I shall begin with a general discussion of the critical spirit of the Confucian philosophy by looking into some relevant passages in the early literature. I will then move more specifically to the Confucian philosophy of education and elaborate on what I take to be its central and indispensable method, a highly critical one, which I refer to as "self-subversive critique" or, alternatively, a "transformative self-critical attitude."

Critical Spirit of the Confucian Philosophy

What is the point of being critical? Why would philosophers and educationalists generally attach so much value to presiding over a critical spirit? An important reason is that it prevents one from being deceived or misled. In Western philosophy and culture, a critical spirit is simultaneously the spirit of individuality, autonomy, and truthfulness or verity. Being critical means taking nothing for granted, scrutinizing every aspect of the issue in question and accepting it only when we ourselves have seen or been presented with adequate support of it. A critical individual is independent and in control. He or she is capable of verifying claims and assertions in his or her surroundings, and can therefore act on the basis of true knowledge.

In a certain sense, critical thinking is the hallmark of Western philosophy. The Presocratics were understood as the first philosophers due to their rejection of religious or supernatural explanations and their reliance on reason and critical approaches, though, admittedly, many of their suggestions were quite fantastic. Subsequently, Socrates and Plato introduced the distinction between sophistry and philosophy, rhetoric and reason, and dogmatic thinking and critical thinking, though they did not formulate it in all these terms. Ever since, philosophy has been the champion of the latter concept in each of the three pairs, perhaps culminating in the Enlightenment philosophy, which was explicitly associated with reason, truth, autonomy, individuality, and so forth, all of which are meant to rest upon a critical method.

As is well known, the origin of Chinese philosophy is quite different from that of Greek philosophy. In pre-Qin China there was a much greater sense of urgency due to the anomic state of her accelerating disintegration. Certainly, the contrasting social situations in China and Greece do not explain all the differences between their philosophies, but they partially shed light on them. In ancient China, critical thinking both manifests itself differently and plays a different role than it has in Europe, but it is still fully present. To the early Confucians, who are the focus of this discussion, critical thinking was not primarily meant to tease out truths for the sake of enhancing our understanding of the natural world, though such aims or similar ones may have been found with other schools of thought, most notably the Mohist thinkers. It was rather a guard against deliberate deception through the use of language, which was probably rampant in the volatile political and social circumstances of Confucius's day; or, as he is recorded to have said himself: "I detest when glib speakers overturn states and clans" (*Analects* 2006–20: 17.18).[4]

Thus, a critical attitude was precisely meant to prevent one from being deceived or misled by smooth operators with questionable agendas. Those who can be considered wise are those who can see through or unmask them, and thus do not let themselves be confused (or see *Analects* 2006–20: 14.28). Overall, in fact, Confucius frequently expresses his distrust of speech. The correspondence or consistency between what human beings say and what they do seems to have concerned him more than anything, comparable to the epistemological certainty of knowledge. He said: "Initially, in my dealings with others, I listened to their words and believed that they would act accordingly. Now, in my dealings with others, I listen to their words but observe their actions" (5.10). He therefore often underscores the priority of action to speech; for example, he says: "The ancients were wary of speaking as they would be ashamed if they themselves would not live up to what they said" (4.22); or "The exemplary person desires to be slow to speak but quick to act" (4.24). Being "slow to speak," as he puts it, is further presented as one meaning of the highest Confucian virtue, or "humanness" (*ren* 仁), because effecting *ren* is difficult and one should therefore be careful when speaking of it (12.3). To rave about one's future intentions requires little effort, but to genuinely accomplish what one intends to do may turn out to be more demanding than it initially seems. This is why we should be careful in our speech and not say more than is necessary, as we do not know whether we will be capable of living up to our promises.

It is for this reason that he emphasizes in particular the notion of *xin* 信, "trust" or "to be true to one's words." Thus, it is not *truth* in the usual (Western) philosophical sense of the word that is the object of concern, but rather *trust* between human beings. Trust is regarded as a precondition for a functional society. If there is no level of trust in society, it is entirely dysfunctional and rather something close to Thomas Hobbes's "state of nature," which as a matter of fact may in some ways be quite descriptive of the situation in ancient China during the chaotic Warring States Period. Thus, someone who is not trustworthy, or generally does not make good on his/her word (*xin* 信), is simply incapable of functioning in a social context, not unlike a broken carriage that is unable to drive: "If anyone doesn't make good on his word, I don't understand how such a person can function at all. If a large carriage lacks a linchpin in the yoke, and a small carriage lacks a linchpin in the crossbar, how can they be made to move at all?" (*Analects* 2006–20: 2.22).

Closely related to *xin* is *zhengming* 正名, or "using names appropriately." In a manner similar to *xin*, *zhengming* implies that words ought to be properly applied in the right situation at the right time, that they should be taken seriously, and thus it emphasizes the conformity between speech and action. Among Confucius's most notable (and notorious) expressions on *zhengming* is that "a prince should act as a prince, a minister should act as a minister, a father should act as a father and a son should act as a son" (*Analects* 2006–20: 12.11). It is interesting that this expression is often taken as a clear indication of how conservative or even reactionary Confucius was. It is argued, for instance, in an authoritative *History of Chinese Philosophy* edited by Ren Jiyu, that "Confucius believed that reality ought not to have changed, and intends to make use of names (stipulations of Zhou rituals) in order to correct aspects of 'reality' that have already changed or are in a process of change" (1966: 68). More recently, Ge Rongjin has similarly claimed that with his *zhengming* theory, Confucius "attempts to correct actual situations that have undergone changes by means of old names" (2001: 386). But if this is the case, the question seems to arise, why is he not being more specific in this regard? If his intention were to "rectify," that is, to reclaim or reinstate what it used to mean to be a prince, minister, and so forth, then one would expect him to stipulate or fill in what that exactly means. And yet, he seems to deliberately avoid doing so.

The primary reason for this, I believe, is that Confucius and his earliest followers were highly conscious of seeking consistency with their understanding of world operations, of their cosmology, or as I prefer to call it, "daology."[5] A detailed discussion of this underlying daology is beyond the scope of this chapter, but what matters most for the present purposes is that everything is immersed in a continuous flow of time and change. One consequence of such a worldview is that there cannot be any eternal and fixed truths applicable in all situations, since everything is always changing. If such a worldview is conscious or even latently underpinning one's approach to things, it will encourage and even push for maintaining an open mind and considering all possibilities in each circumstance, since the changes in both social and natural surroundings are to a significant degree indeterminate and unforeseeable. In light of this, it is not possible to specify in detail what the roles of a prince, minister, and so forth should be. It depends on the unfolding of ever-changing circumstances. Moreover, and no less importantly, instead of being told what such roles should be like, we should discover them for ourselves. We should critically engage with what it means to occupy such roles. Indeed, it is very much our responsibility as carriers of the cultural tradition to move it forward, to readjust it, or even to redefine it: "Human beings are able to broaden the *dao*; *dao* does not broaden human beings" (*Analects* 2006–20: 15.29).

It is in light of this that Confucius emphasizes, after discussing the steadfastness of some outstanding personalities of the past, that "I, however, differ from all these, for I have no 'must not' or 'must'" (*Analects* 2006–20: 18.8). The point is that he doesn't limit himself to conventional rules, but is flexible at all times and adapts to the variations specific to any situation. A general principle does not and cannot apply to all situations. On the contrary, individuals are precisely compelled to constantly engage in the demanding task of carefully assessing each situation and making decisions on this basis. This is what "education" really means in the Confucian sense: to use every situation in daily life as a learning experience.

The worldview of continuous change also explains why a notion of "truth" comparable with the one found in Western discourse is really not present. Certainly, we should not confuse this with a claim that there is no such thing as truth in the Confucian world. The absence of a nominalized truth, especially one with a capital T, does not at all mean that "untruth" was unheard of. Confucius's critical attitude to speech versus action is precisely aimed at deliberate lies and deception, as already discussed. In the context of interpersonal relations, though, trust may function as its near counterpart. However, the notion of "appropriateness" (*yi* 義) can also function in much the same way as truth does in Western discourse. The difference is that appropriateness is context-dependent and has no fixed or unchanging content. It represents precisely that which the Confucian philosophy demands of each and every individual: to evaluate and assess each and every situation and find appropriate "solutions" or "responses" to it. It is a learning process that trains a deep sense for the situation. Thus, as related in the *Mengzi*:

> Exemplary persons study the way profoundly and intensively because they wish to get it on their own. Getting it on their own, they dwell in it calmly; dwelling in it calmly, they have profound faith in it; having profound faith in it, they draw from its source wherever they turn. This is why the exemplary persons wish to get it on their own. (2006–2020: Li Lou II, 42)

Roland Barnett has criticized the dominant concept of critical thinking in contemporary Euro-American culture for being too narrow and called instead for a larger emphasis on "critique in context"; he suggests that the narrow concept of "critical thinking" be replaced with the "wider concept of critical being." Such a concept encompasses reflectivity and imagination: "Reflection and critical evaluation … have to contain moments of the creation of imaginary alternatives. Reflexivity has to offer resources for continuing development" (Barnett 1997: 6–7). I believe that the entire Confucian framework surrounding "appropriateness" comes intriguingly close to meeting Barnett's demand. In the Confucian philosophy, we can hardly think of appropriateness without its association with "ritual propriety" or *li* 禮. With some simplification, ritual propriety functions as the embodiment of the cultural tradition and the source of both stability and meaningful continuity, while appropriateness may be seen as a mediating and even critical factor that "adapts" *li* to the constantly evolving configurations. Continuity, it should be noted, is necessarily temporal continuity, thus implying inescapable change.

Xunzi expresses this symbiotic relationship between *yi* and *li* quite clearly:

> The way [*dao* 道] of the ancient kings consisted in exalting humanness [*ren* 仁] whereby they sought to hit the mark [*zhong* 中] in enacting it. What is meant by hitting the mark? I say that it consists in *li* and *yi*. The way that I am speaking of

is not the way of heaven, nor the way of earth, but the way followed by the human being and embodied in the conduct of the exemplary person [*junzi* 君子]. (Xunzi 2006–20: 8.8)

Elsewhere he says that "*yi* is to pattern [*li* 理], hence proper action follows" (27.21). *Yi* is thus the mediator between the greater and always-evolving pattern of things, *li* 理, and the traditional patterns of human conduct, *li* 禮. Thus, it is a "critical sensibility" which is needed for cultural adaptation and development—to hit the mark or *zhong* 中. Its role is to ensure appropriate changes in social patterns responding to the process of change that is always at play in the greater patterns of nature. Without such social changes and adaptations, the tradition stagnates and ceases to be a source of human flourishing, which could be taken as an understanding of *ren* 仁, the guiding light of a vibrant tradition.

Charlene Tan (2017) has proposed a reading and interpretation of critical thinking in Confucianism that I believe resonates with mine. She portrays critical thinking in Confucianism as a form of *judgment* that is formed through the combination of ritual propriety (*li* 禮), "the totality of normative behaviours that are accompanied by corresponding attitudes and values" as she describes it (Tan 2017: 334), and *yi*, what is appropriate (336). She emphasizes that the Confucian kind of critical thinking goes well beyond "deductive and inductive reasoning, syllogistic argumentation and causal thinking" (339), though it might very well avail itself of such tools, methods, and approaches.[6] The point is that it is a much wider kind of critical thinking, including "the historical, situated, complex and inter-connected nature of worldviews and problem-situations" (339) in a way close to Barnett's call for "critique in context" or "critical being." I agree with Tan that the Confucian version of critical thinking includes an ethical dimension that may "include one's attitudes, motives and disposition" (Tan 2017: 338–9). To this I would add that the focus is on action, on what is being done, which is why it is closer to "critical being" than "critical thinking." However, considering that the critical attitude is also a transformative way, as will be clear in the following section, it might be more appropriate to refer to it as "critical becoming."

Pedagogical Self-subversion

Learning requires not only an attitude of openness, but more importantly the awareness and acceptance that one's ideas may be wrong or can at least be improved. The less one is ready to admit one's own fallibility, the less likely it is that one will learn something new or modify one's ideas according to the actual state of affairs.

European philosophy is in fact grounded in such a self-skeptical attitude, introduced by Socrates, who, as the story goes, discovered that he was wiser than others "to this small extent, that I do not think I know what I do not know" (Plato 1997: 21d). Socrates famously criticized the members of his community for a lack of humility with regard to knowledge; they would tend to claim full knowledge about certain areas, especially those in which they were meant to be experts. Socrates, on the other hand, while not retreating to radical skepticism or Pyrrhonism, assumes a self-critical attitude as a precondition for openness to learning something new. At the same time, of course, this is a clear contrast to dogmatic thinking. A dogmatic person claiming to have grasped the truth is unlikely to spot the flaws in his or her views and thus to overcome them. On the contrary, someone who is open to the possibility that her beliefs may be incorrect is more receptive to new evidence. She is happy to subvert herself and her beliefs for the sake of gaining new knowledge or understanding.

Confucius presents a quite similar way of thinking in his conversation with his disciple Zilu: "Shall I teach you what wisdom is? Knowing what one knows and realizing when one doesn't know, this is wisdom" (*Analects* 2006–20: 2.17). Since, in the Confucian tradition, there is explicitly no final end point in the process of acquiring knowledge and improving understanding, wisdom essentially consists in an attitude of being always ready to acquire new learning. This vision is reinforced in Xunzi, who begins his magnum opus with his succinct but pregnant statement that "Learning must never be halted" (Xunzi 2006–20: 1.1).

Besides the contextual critique, I believe that this disposition should count as the other Confucian contribution to the enrichment of the notion of critical thinking. Elsewhere I have referred to it as a "transformative self-critical attitude" (Sigurðsson 2017), but it could also be termed "pedagogical self-subversion." This profoundly reflexive dimension is strongly emphasized by the early Confucians. Certainly, as already pointed out, such a dimension is far from being alien to the Western traditions and can, for instance, be identified rather clearly in the Socratic approach. But it seems that the emphasis on critical self-reflection in the Western understanding of critical thinking has been more or less downplayed in recent centuries, possibly as a consequence of the rise of radical individualism, but perhaps also because of the emphasis on the epistemological quest for absolute certainty in the modern era.

As is to be expected from the Confucian world, pedagogical self-subversion is not an aim in itself. It is an attitude, a mindset, or disposition that facilitates improvement, betterment, self-cultivation. It is the way to strive for the ongoing and never wholly attainable end of transforming oneself to become fully human, which involves, as Rodney Taylor has put it, recognizing "one's moral obligations to both oneself and others, obligations that force one to transcend self-centered activity, that from the Confucian perspective create the basis for the problems we all encounter in the world" (1998: 95). Thus, to reiterate a point made by Charlene Tan, one that I have already mentioned, it is a critical outlook that takes into account not only logical consistency but also an ethical and normative dimension. To this I would add that the ethical dimension is largely seen as a pedagogical process in which our initial and exclusive concern for our own ego as young children is gradually overcome to become a concern for other persons as we grow. Adopting such concern is a learning process, which must be carefully attended to.

Now one might think that overcoming of egocentric concerns requires some kind of self-effacement, a disregard for oneself. But such an effort would be much closer to the classical approach of gaining objectivity by ostensibly detaching oneself from the object. The Confucian approach is really quite the reverse. It involves a strong sense of reflexivity whereby the agent's self is considered *just as* important as any other component of the overall situation to be critiqued. This is a crucial aspect of pedagogical self-subversion. The point is that we, as agents, are always causal or influencing elements in the overall situation. There is no fixed or independent objectivity out there to be "discovered," not least because of our own approaches, values, and projections. Therefore, it is not sufficient to critically scrutinize the external object only. Our own perspective of that object is in a strong sense a part of the object itself, because it affects the way we experience it and how it becomes meaningful to us.

Xunzi says about a wise man in the conduct of official duties: "when he is adequate, he considers situations in which he might be inadequate. When progressing smoothly, he reflects on any rash action he might take" (Xunzi 2006–20: 7.6). The focus here is on being always attentive, prepared for changes, and, last but not least, maintaining oneself in the mode of learning or self-improvement, which involves self-subversion in the sense that we must be ready to revise our views and opinions.

In a similar manner, Confucius has little patience for those who are unwilling to examine themselves: "Oh my! I haven't yet met anyone, who, when identifying his own excesses, is ready to critique himself" (*Analects* 2006–20: 5.27). And: "When meeting excellent people, think how to become equal to them; when meeting unexceptional people, turn inward and examine yourself" (4.17). Any experience, any association with others, is taken as an opportunity to improve oneself: "When in the company of only two others, I am certain to find a teacher. Realizing where they excel, I follow them; realizing where they do not excel, I mend my own ways" (7.22).

In a daological world in which every situation is unique and changing, there can be no absolute principles, but only rules of thumb or rather vague guiding lights. Human life is portrayed as the challenge of being continuously in novel situations. Such situations are rarely dramatically different from each other, and we can build much on our previous experiences, but they *do* vary at least slightly and in some cases quite considerably, which ought to prompt us to be prepared to approach things afresh. The ultimate aim is not to seek truth, but to find agreeable or appropriate ways to come to terms with all those who have a stake in the issue in each case. This requires flexibility, openness, and a trained judgment. Such training is an ongoing task, which is why Confucianism makes tough demands on individuals to engage themselves in constant critical assessment, appraisal, and scrutiny of whatever they are dealing with in every single moment. It is obviously important to follow the rules of logic, but that may not be the right—or rather appropriate—way to proceed in all circumstances. The parties to any given situation, their position, circumstances, and (last but not least) feelings must also be taken into consideration. There must be a sophisticated "sense" for the situation and the configuration of all its elements. Therefore, what may be remotely close to functioning as a principle is "empathy" or "reciprocity," as expressed in the following conversation between Zigong, Confucius's disciple, and the Master himself: "Zigong asked: 'Is there a single expression that can be applied in one's entire life?' The Master responds: 'There is "reciprocity" (*shu* 恕): do not impose on others what you yourself do not want'" (*Analects* 2006–20: 15.24).

Finally, several passages stress the importance of being mindful of oneself in solitude. Being a social being is not merely a game; the world is not a stage and the people merely actors. Our roles and responsibilities are not simply played out, although we may of course need to play them in order to learn them through practice.

They are, in the final instance, lived, which is why we cannot simply cast them entirely aside when it suits us. We must be mindful of ourselves when alone. Book 10 of the *Analects* contains detailed descriptions of Confucius's behavior in various formal and nonformal situations, including his comportment while eating and sleeping, and even the way in which he mounts his carriage.

The point is that even when in solitude, one must not let one's guard fall. The training must never be neglected, as Xunzi emphasizes at the very beginning of his voluminous work. To be able to transform oneself into a responsible, socialized individual, one must maintain a constantly self-critical and disciplined attitude, so that the transformation occurs in one's character, but not simply on the surface as a slick ability to go through the motions. To become a human being, or rather to be a human becoming, is a deep learning process which requires continuous self-subversion and self-overcoming.

Conclusion

Early Confucianism contains clear, extensive, and unique critical traits. The early Confucian teachings emphasize a contextual critique, and, with their stress on action and overall social and individual development, they encompass a concept of "critical becoming" that is considerably wider than tends to be the case in contemporary Euro-American culture. Learning to be human is necessarily a critical task, but one that demands a continuous assessment of circumstances, configurations, and situations in which the self is also an integral part that must be critiqued no less than other components. Certainly, the "uniqueness" of the Confucian critique is limited, as an entirely comparable approach can be found in earlier Western philosophy, notably with the ancient Greeks and in particular with Socrates. However, it seems to have been neither sustained in the evolution of Western culture nor at all emphasized in the works of later thinkers. The critical endeavor was turned outwards toward external objects and, at the same time, the reflexive move was left out of the picture.

Moreover, it appears that this crucial feature of the Confucian philosophy has been largely ignored by later interpreters, not least by those who tend to cling to an image of Confucianism as dogmatic and reactionary. This is unfortunate, as "pedagogical self-subversion" is among those features of the Confucian philosophy from which our contemporary culture has much to gain. Ironically, the failure to notice it stems precisely from the inability to apply it.

Notes

1 See Sigurðsson (2015: 5–10), where I discuss this approach in more detail, without, however, explicitly associating it with a hermeneutic-pragmatic combination of approaches.
2 Many factors contributed to the constrained circumstances of the Confucian literati from about the fifteenth century onwards. I have attempted to provide a brief overview of these in Sigurðsson (2010), but see also Zhu (1990: 125–7).

3   Tan (2017: 331–2) refers to a number of sources which state "that critical thinking is under-developed or suppressed in Confucianism and Confucian Heritage Cultures such as China, Japan and South Korea."
4   Translations of Chinese sources are all mine.
5   I find the neologism "daology" a better term for the ancient Chinese worldview than the usual "cosmology," as it makes clearer that the constantly evolving whole is operating within a relational yin-yang explanatory framework. In short, I consider daology to consist of three main features: continuous change, "absolute" relationality, and pragmatically envisaged human-nature integration. I discuss this in somewhat more detail in Sigurðsson (2020: 23–8).
6   Elsewhere I have provided examples from the early Confucian literature where use is made of (typical "Western") logical argumentation, logical fallacies, and so forth, to make a point (Sigurðsson 2017: 137). See also Lam (2014), who provides other such examples.

References

Analects (2006–20), Chinese Text Project. https://ctext.org/analects.
Barnett, Roland (1997), *Higher Education: A Critical Business*. Buckingham: The Society for Research into Higher Education and Open University Press.
Brookfield, Stephen D. (2012), *Teaching for Critical Thinking. Tools and Techniques to Help Students Question Their Assumptions*. San Francisco, CA: Jossey-Bass.
Ge Rongjin 葛榮晉 (2001), *Zhongguo zhexue fanchou tonglun* 中國哲學範疇通論. Beijing: Shoudu shifan daxue chubanshe.
Hansen, Chad (1976), "Review of *Confucius: The Secular as Sacred*, by Herbert Fingarette." *Journal of Chinese Philosophy* 3(2): 197–204.
Lam, Chi Ming (2014), "Confucian Rationalism." *Educational Philosophy and Theory* 46(13): 1450–61.
Mengzi (2006–20), Chinese Text Project. https://ctext.org/mengzi.
Plato (1997), "Apology." In *Complete Works*, edited by John M. Cooper, translated by G. M. A. Grube, 17–36. Indianapolis: Hackett.
Ren Jiyu 任繼愈, ed. (1966), *Zhongguo zhexue shi* 中國哲學史, vol. 1. Beijing: Renmin chubanshe.
Sigurðsson, Geir (2010), "Towards a Creative China: Education in China." In *The Irish Asia Strategy and Its China Relations* 爱尔兰的亚洲战备与中爱关系 *1999–2009*, edited by Fan Hong and Jörn-Carsten Gottwald, 61–79. Amsterdam: Rozenberg.
Sigurðsson, Geir (2015), *Confucian Propriety and Ritual Learning: A Philosophical Interpretation*. Albany: State University of New York Press.
Sigurðsson, Geir (2017), "Transformative Critique: What Confucianism Can Contribute to Contemporary Education." *Studies in Philosophy and Education* 36: 131–46.
Sigurðsson, Geir (2020), "Confucian Philosophy as a Universal Account of Integrated Living: A Contemporary Interpretation." In *Differences in Identity in Global Philosophy and Religion: A Cross-Cultural Approach*, edited by Russell Manning and Sarah Flavel, 21–40. London: Bloomsbury.
Tan, Charlene (2017), "A Confucian Conception of Critical Thinking." *Journal of Philosophy of Education* 51(1): 331–43.

Taylor, Rodney L. (1998), "The Religious Character of the Confucian Tradition." *Philosophy East and West* 48(1): 80–107.
Xunzi (2006–20), *Xunzi*. Chinese Text Project. https://ctext.org/xunzi.
Zhu Weizheng (1990), *Coming Out of the Middle Ages*, translated by R. Hayhoe. Armonk: M.E. Sharpe.

3

Crisis and Critique: Zhuangzi's Philosophical Turning Point

Hans-Georg Moeller and Paul J. D'Ambrosio

"Finding Its Feet in Its Absolute Disruption": The Critical Turning Point as the Philosophical Event

The notions of critique and crisis stem from the same Greek linguistic root: κρίνω (krínō), meaning to "pick out," "decide," or "judge." In the same vein, in contemporary English "to criticize" something means to judge it and to decide on its merits and flaws. In connection with this notion of "decisiveness," a crisis is a moment in time when the "hour of judgment" arrives and it comes to a decision on life and death, on continued existence or annihilation. Accordingly, the English word "critical" was originally a medical term indicating the decisive period of a disease which one would either survive to recover, or not. Until today, the word has retained this meaning of a crucial turning point, next to designating a reflective attitude or mindset.

Philosophically, too, critique is rooted in crisis—in the existential or intellectual experience of the imminent collapse of what has been taken for granted, and the subsequent emergence of a different viewpoint—of thought or life—which, so to speak, puts things in perspective. It may even be said that philosophy itself, at its core, is the practice of critique grounded in the fundamental breakdown of the common, non-philosophical or uncritical, assumption of certainty and of being secure (indeed this is exactly what we think philosophy is). The experience of such a crisis is thus, in a sense, the "event," that is, the moment of the *e-venire*, or, literally, of the "coming out," that gives rise to philosophy, or at least to philosophy in the mode of critique.

This essay focuses eventually on a story from the *Zhuangzi* 莊子 that beautifully illustrates the emergence of critique out of crisis in the form of an allegory. However, before discussing this story in detail, it may be helpful to see how two key philosophers who shaped modern Western thought, Kant and Hegel, also conceived of philosophy as critique, and how this conception is tied to an intellectual conversion that profoundly subverts an established outlook on life or reality.

In the preface to his *Prolegomena to Any Future Metaphysics*, Kant famously expressed his indebtedness to David Hume by pointing out that the latter "interrupted my dogmatic slumber and gave a completely different direction to my enquiries in the field of philosophy" (Kant 2004: 67). In this memorable sentence, Kant combines within very few words the imagery of a conversion with the imagery of awakening. By joining these two standard metaphors for an intellectual epiphany, he identifies the transition from dogmatism to critique as the truly critical turning point in his personal philosophical development.

Waking up from his slumber, Kant now realizes that, prior to Hume, philosophy and especially metaphysics had been trapped in "dogmatism," that is, in the attempt to deduce truth from the analysis of a set of propositions which were taken to be certain, or beyond doubt, or, to speak with Descartes, which served as the Archimedean point for providing an adequate account of the world as it is. In his *Lectures on Metaphysics* (*Metaphysik Mongrovius* 29: 772) Kant said:

> A treatment of science is dogmatic when it does not trouble to investigate from which powers of mind a cognition arises, but rather lays down as a basis certain general and accepted propositions and infers the rest from them. (Kant 2001: 134)

Kant explicitly defines the critical method in relation to, and in distinction from, the dogmatic method (*Metaphysik Mongrovius* 29: 938):

> (1) The dogmatic method is when I take some cognitions as unprovable propositions as a basis and build the others upon that. (2) The critical [method] when I investigate the principles themselves according to the way they came about, from which power of mind they arose, and according to their possibility, how they could have arisen *a priori*. (Kant 2001: 285)

The radical shift from dogmatism to critique in philosophy outlined by Kant results in taking on a "completely different" perspective: rather than looking at the world as an objective reality that can be described by a complete and final philosophical account, in the form of propositions outlining the principles of this reality, thinking now turns toward an analysis of the very "powers of mind" that allow for the emergence of such propositions and the objective reality they refer to in the first place.

As is well known, Kant uses another famous analogy to highlight the enormity of this methodological shift by equating it with the Copernican turn in astronomy. Kant claims to revolutionize the human worldview as dramatically as Copernicus, only that his own turn goes even deeper and does not merely change the way in which we do physics and see the world physically, but rather alters the way in which we do metaphysics and see the world metaphysically. In the *Critique of Pure Reason* (Bxvi) Kant explains:

> Up to now it has been assumed that all our cognition must conform to the objects; but all attempts to find out something about them a priori through concepts that would extend our cognition have, on this presupposition, come to nothing. (Kant 1998: 110)

These words describe the "scandal" (in Kant's own terminology in the *Critique of Pure Reason*, p. Bxl) of philosophy. The dogmatic assumption that we can "find out something" about the "objects" in the world through traditional (dogmatic) metaphysical concepts has "come to nothing." All our previous metaphysical efforts have been completely in vain, and thus we have seen the world wrong—we have seen it as in a dream or slumber. To continue this way of thinking would mean the sure demise of philosophy—it would be replaced by physics and other natural sciences which have been doing a much better job than philosophy in describing the world objectively. Thus, in this moment of crisis, a radical philosophical turn is necessary to ensure the survival of philosophy as metaphysics (*Critique of Pure Reason* Bxvi–xvii):

> Hence let us once try whether we do not get farther with the problems of metaphysics by assuming that the objects must conform to our cognition. ... This would be just like the first thoughts of Copernicus, who, when he did not make good progress in the explanation of the celestial motions if he assumed that the entire celestial host revolves around the observer, tried to see if he might not have greater success if he made the observer revolve and left the stars at rest. (Kant 1998: 110)

In order to resolve the crisis of philosophy, to rescue it from its "almost ridiculous" (Kant 2004: 63) backwardness and from vanishing into total insignificance, we need to change our approach to reality. Using stark imagery, Kant speaks of the need for reason to once more "dismantle" the tower it has built and "to see what its foundations might be like" (2004: 64). Instead of assuming that our cognition must conform to the object, we need to assume the opposite, namely that the objects must conform to our cognition. In analogy to Copernicus, Kant asks us to change our conception of the relation between the observer and the observed. What really "revolves"—where the action is, so to speak—is not the observed object, but in fact the observing mind. We can leave the objects of observation (the "things," in analogy to the stars for Copernicus) "at rest" and instead focus our analysis on the observer.

Critical thinking, for Kant, is a thinking that no longer looks primarily at the "objects" but at the cognitive conditions, or the "powers of mind," which look at the objects and make it possible for them to be seen. Instead of trying to observe the unobservable "things in themselves," we must, and can, only observe how things are observed. We must observe the observer, or, to speak in terms of Niklas Luhmann, shift from first-order observation to second-order observation. Thereby we can become truly critical: we can see what can be seen (and how it is seen), and what cannot be seen (and why not).

For Kant, the crisis of philosophy was rooted in dogmatism and, for him, critique was the only way forward. Here, it is important to understand how critique is distinct from mere criticism. A mere criticism of metaphysical dogmas would result in the replacement of old dogmas with new ones. The point of critique, however, is a radical shift in perspective which does not seek, as dogmatism does, to set our cognition straight so that we finally see the world correctly, but to identify the very structures of cognition that inform our views of the world. It wants to understand how we see the world rather than how the world is "in itself." In this sense, critique implies a *constructivist* shift—and it is necessitated by a dogmatic crisis, a crisis that does not threaten to subvert specific dogmas, but dogmatism as such.

The connection between a crisis of reason and its subsequent shift toward an altogether different, namely, thoroughly critical, approach is equally (or even more) foundational for Hegel's understanding of philosophy. For Kant, the crisis, once overcome through (his own) critique, is resolved, and a "secure path of science" (1998: Bxviii) is found which ought to be taken, as he believed, by "any future metaphysics." For Hegel, however, the crisis was not the result of an erroneous philosophical orientation that could be corrected once and for all. For him, the crisis of reason was, to the contrary, its inbuilt engine, driving it forward. Cognition and its objects are interrelated moments of an ongoing process rather than, as for Kant, related to one another through an "a priori" structure that is by definition transcendental, and thus not subject to change. For Hegel, the "powers of mind" are not static; they give rise to their own constant growth, that is, to the development of consciousness, or spiritual maturation, or *Bildung*.

The *Phenomenology of Spirit* was supposed to provide a conceptual and "scientific" account of this developmental process; but it did this, more often than not, in a rather poetic fashion. It depicts the story of the mind as a "spiritual history" (or *Geistesgeschichte*) on both the individual and collective level. Both personal intellectual growth and the history of humankind consist of a series of spiritual self- and world-constructions that collapse through the realization of contradictions. These destructive collapses serve at the same time as constructive learning experiences informing new spiritual self- and world-formations. The early Greek worldview and way of life (*Sittlichkeit*), for instance, along with its metaphysics, its religion, its ethics, and its art, has eventually lost its *Wirklichkeit* (actuality)—it does not *work* (*wirken*) for us anymore, it has lost its spell. We no longer believe in the Greek gods or metaphysical theories, and we no longer create art in the way the Greeks did. However, the collapse of the Greek world has been a critical experience for us. While we are today no longer Greek, the specific or determinate negation of the Greek world has eventually brought about the specific worldviews and practices of the post-Greek world. We are all necessarily post-Greek now.

As with Kant's critique, a true crisis is not resolved by a mere replacement of what has turned out to be wrong, or a no-longer sustainable dogma or truth, by another and presumably better one that works on the same plane as the previous. Central to true *Bildung* is the complete "dismantling," to use Kant's image again, of the tower of knowledge that was built (along with its temples and other social institutions, one might add), in order "to see what its foundations might be like." One of the many terms that Hegel uses for such a critique (he hardly ever uses "critique" as such) is *Insichgehen* or, as Terry Pinkard (Hegel 2018) translates it, "taking-the-inward-turn." Consciousness reacts to its crisis not by "mopping-up" operations—to use Thomas Kuhn's language—that simply modify its descriptions of the objective world, but by a "paradigm shift" that takes the inward turn and now sees how and why it took to be true what it now can no longer take to be so. Once it understands why it believed what it believed, it reaches a new stage of development. It now not only sees what it saw but also sees through its own seeing. By seeing our former beliefs "in perspective," we reach a more complex level of consciousness, and, most importantly, a higher degree of self-consciousness by understanding that we believed what we believed not only because of *it* but also because of *us*.

At the end of the *Phenomenology*, Hegel describes this process in his typically obscure, but also beautiful, and almost religious (Protestant), diction:

> The negative is the negative of itself. … While its consummation consists in spirit's completely knowing what it is, in spirit knowing its substance, this knowing is its taking-the-inward-turn in which spirit forsakes its existence and gives its shape over to recollection. In taking-the-inward-turn, spirit is absorbed into the night of its self-consciousness, but its vanished existence is preserved in that night, and this sublated existence—the existence which was prior but is now new born from knowing—is the new existence, a new world, and a new shape of spirit. (Hegel 2018: 466)

The negation of a worldview, or of a religion, or metaphysics, or ethics, or of an art or a way of life, is a complete self-negation that we do not survive unchanged. We emerge "new born" and into a "new world" because we took the inward turn, and made our world view "vanish" and enter the "night of its self-consciousness" by completely deconstructing its foundations—precisely because we found its foundations *in ourselves*.

It is important to recognize that for Hegel, unlike Kant, crisis and critique are perpetual moments of the "living spirit" rather than a one-time event that leads to the discovery of a transcendental grounding. For Hegel, a philosophy of the spirit is as much an epistemology (a philosophy of cognition) as it is an existential philosophy (or a "phenomenology"). Crisis and critique are not merely abstract mental processes, they are matters of life and death, as the following passage from the preface of the *Phenomenology* (among many others) dramatically illustrates:

> Death, if that is what we wish to call that non-actuality, is the most fearful thing of all, and to keep and hold fast to what is dead requires only the greatest force. … However, the life of spirit is not a life that is fearing death and austerely saving itself from ruin; rather, it bears death calmly, and in death, it sustains itself. Spirit only wins its truth by finding its feet in its absolute disruption. Spirit is not this power which, as the positive, avoids looking at the negative, as is the case when we say of something that it is nothing, or that it is false, and then, being done with it, go off on our own way on to something else. No, spirit is this power only by looking the negative in the face and lingering with it. This lingering is the magical power that converts it into being. (Hegel 2018: 20–1)

To survive or sustain oneself in a moment of "absolute disruption" and collapse is to survive the death of one's world view and way of life. Hegel translates the Christian *dogma* of the immortality of the soul into a principle of *critical* philosophy: Spirit's immortality, taken in a secular sense, lies not in getting rid of a mortal body while entering spiritually unchanged into an eternal paradise. Instead, spirit is "finding one's feet" in taking on a truly critical, and thus "life-changing," perspective on itself, by "looking the negative in the face and lingering with it." Again, the imagery indicates an observation of observation—or second-order observation. Precisely upon this shift of perspective from dogma to critique depends on the continued life of the spirit. This very shift, Hegel famously explains in the *Phenomenology*, is the "*dialectical* movement which consciousness practices in its own self …, is properly what is called experience." (Hegel 2018: 57, emphasis in the original). This experience, the emergence of critique out of crisis is, for Hegel, unlike for Kant, not a "secure path" but rather a "bacchanalian revel" (Hegel 2018: 29) filled with critical moments of "despair" (*Verzweiflung*).

Critical Exposure: Eating and Being Eaten, Seeing and Being Seen

In his brief introductory comments on the story of Zhuang Zhou's "poaching at Diaoling 雕陵" (*Zhuangzi* section 20: 8[1]), A. C. Graham (2001) remarks that it is one of only three narratives in the whole book (next to the famous butterfly dream episode in 2: 14 and the story of the fish on the road in 26: 2)[2] which call the Daoist master by his personal name Zhuang Zhou 莊周. Graham thus speculates that these stories suggest "a stage in his life before he earned the honorific suffix" *zi* 子, or "Master" (Graham 2001: 117), and that, taken together, they may be seen as clues for reconstructing an intellectual biography of Zhuang Zhou. Such a reconstruction, given the lack of other reliable indicators that would support it, is historically highly speculative. However, Graham's observation of the quite rare use of the personal name Zhuang Zhou in these stories is obviously correct and can be regarded as significant for their philosophical interpretation. It makes sense to assume that they all, in different ways, depict crucial *experiences* (in the Hegelian sense of "dialectical movements" mentioned above) that gave rise to the development of core philosophical ideas expressed elsewhere in the book. And, as this chapter intends to show, it specifically makes sense to regard the story of the poaching at Diaoling, with Graham, as an allegorical expression of an existential and philosophical "crisis" (Graham 2001: 118)—that is, of a crisis that brought about the critical method of the *Zhuangzi*.

The rather well-known story (see the appendix for the Chinese text and a translation) depicts (a young?) Zhuang Zhou rambling around (*you* 遊) (on this central philosophical metaphor in the *Zhuangzi*, see Moeller and D'Ambrosio 2017: 164–70) in the hunting grounds of a place called Diaoling. A huge bird flies by, strikes Zhuang Zhou's face with its wings, and then sits down on a tree. While Zhuang Zhou sets out to shoot it, he sees that the bird is just about to prey on a mantis which in turn is just about to catch a cicada. Suddenly realizing this scene, Zhuang Zhou expresses his dismay about the brutality of the natural food chain and runs away in shock—only to find out that the gamekeeper is chasing him for attempting to poach in the preserve. The second part of the story consists of a short dialogue between Zhuang Zhou and someone who seems to be a student of his. After the incident, Zhuang Zhou had retreated into solitude for three days—or even three months, depending on the reading of the text—and the student asks him for the reason why. Zhuang Zhou somewhat cryptically replies: "I stuck to my identity, oblivious to my appearance. I looked into muddy water, confused about the clear pool. Also, I've heard the masters' saying: 'Entering into the conventional is to follow the conventional.'" Then he briefly reports to the student what had happened in Diaoling.

Before philosophically analyzing the narrative, it is important to emphasize that it is told, like so many stories in the *Zhuangzi*, in a quite humorous manner. It begins with a description of a bizarrely oversized bird. Creatures out of proportion are found several times in the book, and most famously right at the beginning in the pseudo-mythological tale of the giant fish Kun 鯤, who transforms into the equally giant bird Peng 鵬. The unnamed monster bird in the poaching story, however, is introduced in a much less reverent way than Kun/Peng: It awkwardly hits Zhuang Zhou in the face without even noticing it. Such a clumsy encounter is a typical, comical motif. Moreover, the big bird is described as rather lazy. Zhuang Zhou wonders why, despite its massive wings, it does not fly away, but takes a rest. The scene of the four creatures about to devour or to kill one another is, to be sure, tense and rather serious, specifically when Zhuang Zhou explicitly reflects on the perennial drama of eating and being eaten illustrated by it. However, the tension is resolved at the end in an almost cartoon-like fashion when the gamekeeper runs after the fleeing Zhuang Zhou, cursing him loudly.

Humor is based on playing with incongruity, and this is exactly what the story does. The giant bird is quite dopey; its large eyes do not see well, and it does not make good use of its huge wings. The character of Zhuang Zhou is comically subverted in the story—seemingly the hunter at the top of the food chain, he becomes, only a moment later, the hunted himself. The authority figure of the gamekeeper also appears in the form of a caricature when depicted in his angry pursuit. These humorous incongruities all serve to distance the reader from the three protagonists—there is no hero or master that one can identify with; rather than wise men, everyone is, to some extent, a fool.

The story does not end comically, however. Zhuang Zhou's retreat in frustration is not funny, and neither is the dialogue with his student. Or is it? After all, at the end Zhuang Zhou retells the most grotesque elements of the story in a laconic way: the clumsy encounter between himself and the big bird, and the cartoon-like chase. Thereby the story intertwines comical imagery with philosophical reflection and allusion. The humorous elements that are freely mixed into an allegory of crisis, intellectual despair, and mutual killing make it a sort of philosophical tragic-comedy. The core Daoist theme of the perpetually ongoing transformation of life into death and vice versa—the "transformation of things" (*wu hua* 物化) as the *Zhuangzi* paradigmatically calls it (for instance, in the butterfly dream story in 2: 14)—clearly provides the philosophical framework of the story. The tragic-comical "genre" of the story connects the theme of the "transformation of things" with the fluid alteration between the emotions of elation and anguish—or joy and sorrow.

Zhuang Zhou's initial philosophical insight, expressed with a sense of worry or gloom (*chu ran* 怵然) when noticing that the three animals are literally feeding off each other, is that "creatures certainly trouble one another; one kind calls upon another" (物固相累，二類相召也). This is commonly understood as lamenting the "Darwinian" characteristics of the state of nature, or, to put it in the words of chapter 5 of the *Laozi* 老子: "Heaven and earth are not humane. They regard the ten thousand things as straw dogs." (天地不仁，以萬物為芻狗.) Nature is a relentless and unsentimental cycle of killing and being killed for the sake of survival. This insight, though grave and indeed emotionally unsettling, is nevertheless neither highly original nor, as such, already "critical." The truly critical moment of the story consists in the sudden realization, illustrated through the scene of the gamekeeper chasing Zhuang Zhou and yelling at him, that Zhuang Zhou himself is not merely wisely comprehending and explaining the cruelty within or behind the "transformation of things" from the outside, but, importantly, that he himself is in the very midst of this transformation. This is the event of the actual crisis—the realization of oneself "being caught" and of one's imminent downfall. Thereby a somewhat commonplace truism is dramatically turned into a personal experience. This experience, in turn, thoroughly subverts the previous, merely provisional, insight and adds a decisive turn to it. The point that matters most is now no longer that "creatures certainly trouble one another," but that "I am living a predatory life—I am a beast of prey and preyed on by other such beasts."

In other words, Zhuang Zhou's moment of crisis brings about a critical change of perspective. The initial "objective" insight into the cruel nature of the transformation of things is revealed, so to speak, as a mere "dogma"—that is as a "certain general and accepted proposition" which yet lacks reflection on the "subjective" conditions under which it is being produced. Crisis, however, initiates critique and subverts such "dogmatism." In the narrative, the experience of crisis drastically alters the orientation of Zhuang Zhou's understanding; it makes him "take the inward turn," as the second half of the story shows, which depicts Zhuang Zhou as returning from an extensive retreat period.

Before discussing this inward turn in more detail, it is important to outline more clearly the specific "phenomenological" characteristics of the crisis that the story depicts. In fact, it shows multiple crises, not only the crisis of Zhuang Zhou but also those of the three animals. The smallest one, the cicada, "had just found a beautiful patch of shade" (*fang de mei yin* 方得美蔭), and, while making itself comfortable, literally "forgot about its body" (*wang qi shen* 忘其身), or, as this phrase can be translated here as well, it was "oblivious to its appearance." Feeling perfectly at leisure, it neglected any concern for its own safety, disregarded its natural environment with all its predators, and, crucially, displayed itself carelessly to them. It *made itself vulnerable by self-exposure*. The paradoxical logic of self-exposure is a main narrative theme of the story. The three animals and Zhuang Zhou all become comfortable with themselves, they become who they really are, so to speak, and thereby, unwittingly, they show themselves to their environment and are about to be eaten by their natural enemies.

The dialectical relation between "doing one's thing" and, through this very self-display, undermining one's safety and inviting one's destruction by others is expressed in slight variation in what can be conceived of as the "chorus" in the story. In the case of each animal, and, at the end of the narrative, in the words of the main protagonist Zhuang Zhou, the dialectics of self-revelation, exposure, and annihilation is explicitly stressed: when the cicada made itself comfortable, it forgot about its body and could be preyed on by the mantis; when the mantis was focused on her catch, it forgot about its form, or "exterior" (*xing* 形), and could be eaten by the bird; when the bird zoomed in on the mantis, it forgot about its here and now, or "self-manifestation" (*zhen* 真), and could be shot by Zhuang Zhou. And, of course, Zhuang Zhou too, when stepping out as a hunter, similarly forgot about his body, or "appearance" (*shen*身), and was caught by the gamekeeper.

The intense and repeated descriptions of the dialectical relationship between self-manifestation, self-exposure, and destruction by one's "natural enemies" create a very specific account of the moment of crisis. Concretely, crisis looms as soon as we identify ourselves most comfortably with ourselves—so much so that we venture to present ourselves openly. Public self-presentation and exposure to others is, at the same time, the culmination of our "selfhood" and the moment when its dialectical deconstruction in society begins. The moment when we "get on the scene" is the moment when we expose ourselves to criticism and critique, and thereby the moment when the dialectical annihilation of our self by our "peers" begins.

Such an understanding of the story shifts its philosophical significance from the "metaphysical" level of existential analysis that is concerned with larger issues of life and death and the "transformation of things" in nature to an existential analysis of *life in society*. Such a social reading of the narrative is invited by the text itself when, in the dialogue with his student in the second part of the story, Zhuang Zhou quotes an obscure saying by unspecified masters: "Entering into the conventional is to follow the conventional" (入其俗，從其俗). This can be interpreted as signaling that Zhuang Zhou's inward turn (not that different from Hegel's) did not so much consist of a reflection on the metaphysical or biological aspects of nature, but on the social conditions of thinking and communicating with others. Seen in this way, the story turns out to be an allegory concerned with a critique of the absurd (taking into account its humorous elements) and dialectical conditions of human interaction—and, more specifically, of intellectual or philosophical debates.[3]

An allegorical reading of the story as an illustration of the dialectics of self-exposure in society, and, in this context, of philosophical crisis and critique, is supported by the semantics it applies. Although the mutual killing and eating of natural creatures is certainly the main narrative motif of the story, the vocabulary and the actual plot center much more on the subject of seeing or not seeing others, and on being seen by them. Zhuang Zhou *sees* (*du*睹) a big bird, but the big bird, despite its huge *eyes* (*mu*目), does not *look about* (*du* 覩). Then Zhuang Zhou *sees* (*du*睹) how the animals prey on one another; all *looking* (*jian*見) at their prey, and precisely because of this falling prey to someone else whom they cannot see. Eventually, Zhuang Zhou reflects on his own "blindness" by employing a metaphor of vision: "I looked into muddy water, misled about the clear pool." (觀於濁水而迷於清淵.)

The story thus combines the notion of exposing oneself with the notion of having someone else in view as an object of prey, or "following" (*cong* 從) them.[4] Allegorically, this illustrates how we define ourselves or assume an identity in society. We assume our place and position by taking on a specific *perspective*. We become what we are, in part, by what we focus on or are occupied with. The mantis is defined by its focus on the cicada, and the huge bird by its focus on the mantis. A beast of prey is defined, in part, by and through its prey. Its visual focus becomes an existential determination. The ways in which creatures are seeing the world simultaneously becomes the way in which they are being seen by others—others whom they themselves sometimes do not see, and cannot see, precisely because they are looking at something else.

The chain of observation of the three animals and two humans is a chain of first-order observation. Each observer is looking at an object. This very observation results in a blind spot. The animals in this story do not see how they appear to those behind their backs, those that are outside their focus. Only Zhuang Zhou, the human, realizes this feature of first-order observation, and thereby already moves toward second-order observation. He sees what others see and what they do not see. Thereby he observes the very conditions of their seeing. However, at first, he does not draw the "autological" conclusion that the conditions of observation are also informing his own seeing. Only when chased by the gamekeeper does he realize, we are led to assume, that his second-order observation of the sequence of first-order observations in front of him was itself also a first-order observation. The decisive critical step from first-order observation to second-order observation is not the realization of the blind spot of others, but of one's own inevitable blind spot.[5] Taking the inward turn, Zhuang Zhou finally understands that there is no "Archimedean point" from which an objective or total reality can be seen. Every observation is contingent upon certain conditions. These conditions, in turn, present a blind spot that can be observed by others. Through our observation we construct the world as we see it—and thereby ourselves. Others see us as we see the world—and thereby they see our blind spots which provide them with an angle of attack. The truly critical insight consists of the realization that our worldview, and thus both we and our world, is based on a mode of observation, or "on powers of mind" as conditions of its possibility—and in the subsequent realization, that presenting ourselves under these conditions is precisely what makes us vulnerable to others.

The critical insight into the contingency of any worldview, and into the blind spot that comes with it, leads, first, to the well-known "perspectivism" that is found throughout the text. No point of view is ultimate or *letztbegründet* (founded on an ultimate grounding). As Richard Rorty would say: there are no final vocabularies. Especially the second chapter of the *Zhuangzi* expounds the constructivist framework on which dogmatic assertions of "what is the case" or "what is right" (*shi* 是), as well as their corresponding denials (*fei* 非) are built, and thus their dialectical interconnectedness which conditions, and limits, their validity:

> Hence we have the rights and wrongs of the Confucians and Mohists, each affirming what the other negates and negating what the other affirms. ... There is no being that is not "that." There is no being that is not "this." But one cannot be seeing these from the perspective of "that": one knows them only from "this" [i.e. from one's own perspective]. Thus, we can say "That" emerges from "this," and "this" follows from "that." This is the theory of the simultaneous generation of "this" and "that." But by the same token, their simultaneous generation is their simultaneous destruction, and vice versa. Simultaneous affirmability is simultaneous negatability, and vice versa. What is circumstantially right is also circumstantially wrong, and vice versa. Thus, the Sage does not proceed from any one of them alone but instead lets them all bask in the broad daylight of heaven. And that too is only a case of going by the rightness of the present "this." (Ziporyn 2009: 11–12; *Zhuangzi* 2: 4–5)

The visual metaphor ("But one cannot be seeing these from the perspective of 'that': one knows them only from 'this'") as well as the metaphor of "generation" and "destruction" (or "life" [*sheng* 生] and "death" [*si* 死] as the text literally says) of this central passage mirrors the metaphor employed in the story of the poaching at Diaoling. Thereby, the "theory of the simultaneous generation of 'this' and 'that'" (*bi shi fang sheng zhi shuo* 彼是方生之說), which is also the theory of their simultaneous destruction (*fang si* 方死), can be regarded as the theoretical counterpart to that narrative. Importantly, the theory explicitly acknowledges its own blind spot: "And that too is only a case of going by the rightness of the present 'this.'" The Daoism of the *Zhuangzi*, stemming from an experience of crisis, is just not merely a negation of the "rights and wrongs of the Confucians and Mohists," but a truly critical reflection on the conditions of their dogmatic disputes by which they expose themselves to one another, and by which they thus mutually limit and subvert their validity.

Second, the "theory of the simultaneous generation of 'this' and 'that'" leads, on an existential level, to what we have called elsewhere the mode of "genuine pretending" (Moeller and D'Ambrosio 2017). Given the dialectically conditioned and constructed nature of any "position" we take on, either socially or philosophically, we come to realize that our existential and intellectual identifications are *inevitably contingent*. Understanding this contingency does not eliminate out blind spots, but confirms them. Our genuine self-exposure or "self-manifestations" (*zhen* 真), as the allegory of the poaching of Diaoling once states, is necessarily contingent upon a pretense that we assume, and simultaneously, and provisionally, forget about. Critical philosophy reflects on the necessary pretense that conditions and informs the appearance of any such exposed or manifested genuineness. It is the condition of exposure that allows us to see and be seen, and metaphorically, to eat and be eaten.

Translation

Zhuang Zhou was rambling around in the game preserve at Diaoling. He saw a strange magpie, coming from the south. Its wings were wide, about seven *chi;* and its eyes were large, about one *cun*. It struck Zhou's forehead, and then rested in a chestnut grove. Zhuang Zhou thought: "What kind of bird is this? Its wings are huge, but it does not fly on. Its eyes are big, but it does not look about." He hitched up his robe and quickened his steps, and with crossbow at the ready waited to aim. He saw a cicada which had just found a beautiful patch of shade, oblivious to its appearance. A mantis hiding behind the leaves grabbed at it. It looked at its catch, oblivious to its exterior. The strange magpie had followed it and was preying on it. It looked at its prey, oblivious to its self-manifestation. Zhuang Zhou thought worryingly: "Oh, creatures certainly trouble one another; one kind calls upon another." As he threw down his crossbow and ran away, the game keeper came running behind, cursing him.

When Zhuang Zhou had returned, he was gloomy for three days. Lin Qie had followed him and asked: "Why have you been gloomy for so long, Master?" Zhuang Zhou said: "I stuck to my identity, oblivious to my appearance. I looked into muddy water, confused about the clear pool. Also, I've heard the masters' saying: 'Entering into the conventional is to follow the conventional.' Now, when rambling around in Diaoling, I was oblivious to my appearance. A strange magpie struck my forehead. Rambling around in the chestnut grove, it was oblivious to its self-manifestation. In the chestnut grove, the game keeper took me for a poacher, and therefore I have been gloomy."

(This translation follows in part Graham 2001: 118.)

> 莊周遊乎雕陵之樊，睹一異鵲自南方來者，翼廣七尺，目大運寸，感周之顙而集於栗林。莊周曰：「此何鳥哉？翼殷不逝，目大不覩。」褰裳躩步，執彈而留之。睹一蟬方得美蔭而忘其身；螳蜋執翳而搏之，見得而忘其形；異鵲從而利之，見利而忘其真。莊周怵然曰：「噫！物固相累，二類相召也。」捐彈而反走，虞人逐而誶之。
>
> 莊周反入，三月不庭。藺且從而問之：「夫子何為頃間甚不庭乎？」莊周曰：「吾守形而忘身，觀於濁水而迷於清淵。且吾聞諸夫子曰：『入其俗，從其俗。』今吾遊於雕陵而忘吾身，異鵲感吾顙，遊於栗林而忘真，栗林虞人以吾為戮，吾所以不庭也。」

Notes

1 References to sections of the *Zhuangzi* in this chapter follow the widely used database www.ctext.org/zhuangzi.
2 The personal name Zhuang Zhou is also mentioned in the critical account of his writings in the final chapter of the book (33: 6).
3 According to Chen Guying 陳鼓應, connecting with a standard reading, the philosophical message of the story is about not getting lost in disputes and thereby "confusingly forgetting" (*mi wang* 迷忘) one's "genuine tendencies" (*zhen xing* 真性) (Chen 2008: 578).
4 The magpie is said to "follow" the mantis, Zhuang Zhou's student "follows" Zhuang Zhou, and Zhuang Zhou, it seems, considers himself "following" the conventional.
5 Niklas Luhmann described the "autological" realization with a metaphor that is somewhat reminiscent of the story of the poaching at Dialoing: "In this way, the epistemologist him/herself becomes a rat in the labyrinth and has to reflect on the position from which he/she observes the other rats" (Luhmann 2006: 250).

References

Chen Guying陳鼓應 (2008), *Lao-Zhuang xin lun* 老莊新論 (*New Theories on Laozi and Zhuangzi*). Beijing: Commercial Press.
Graham, A. C. (2001), *Chuang-Tzu: The Inner Chapters*. Indianapolis: Hackett.
Hegel, G. W. F. (2018), *The Phenomenology of Spirit*, translated by Terry Pinkard. Cambridge: Cambridge University Press.
Kant, Immanuel (1998), *Critique of Pure Reason*, edited by Paul Guyer and Allen E. Wood. Cambridge: Cambridge University Press.

Kant, Immanuel (2001), *Lectures on Metaphysics*, translated by Karl Ameriks and Steve Naragon. Cambridge: Cambridge University Press.
Kant, Immanuel (2004), *Prolegomena to Any Future Metaphysics That Will Be Able to Present Itself as Science*, translated by Peter G. Lucas and Günter Zöller. Oxford: Oxford University Press.
Luhmann, Niklas (2006), "Cognition as Construction." In *Luhmann Explained: From Souls to Systems*, edited by Hans-Georg Moeller, 241–60. Chicago: Open Court.
Moeller, Hans-Georg, and Paul D'Ambrosio (2017), *Genuine Pretending: On the Philosophy of the Zhuangzi*. New York: Columbia University Press.
Zhuangzi. www.ctext.org/zhuangzi.
Ziporyn, Brook (2009), *Zhuangzi: The Essential Writings*. Indianapolis: Hackett.

4

Otherwise than God and Man: Subverting Purpose and Knowledge in Zhuangzi's Perspectival Mirror

Brook Ziporyn

Strange to say, there have been certain people in human history who seem to think that it is good to cease to try to be good. They may even have thought that it is good not to *know* what is good, or that it is good not to know what is *so*, including whether it is good to be good or not. Stated that way, this is not just "strange to say" but plainly self-contradictory and paradoxical. Nevertheless, imagine someone who thinks the best thing a human being can do is stop trying to know what is so and what is good—to cease being guided by his own knowing and willing. Imagine that he abandons any attempt to come to any definite knowledge about what the ultimate nature of reality is, about what is ultimately true, and also (paradoxically) about what is ultimately best, about where beings (including himself) come from and about where they are going, about what is ultimate and about what is foundational. This would be someone who embraces *non-knowing*—both of what is so and what is right, and of what the *purpose* of his own experiences and actions are—as opening the way to the "highest" (scare quotes to acknowledge the paradox) attainable state of human beings. This person might regard that "highest state," attainable only through non-knowing, to be something like "intellectual rigor" or else something like "emotional tranquility." In both of those cases, I would call this person a "skeptic."

But imagine someone of this stripe who imagines the "highest" human state, which is brought by non-knowing, as something more, dramatically unlike all other human experiences, who reports that this results not merely in intellectual cleanliness, or a state of relative calm or ataraxia, or the dropping of unsolvable dilemmas that disturb his peace of mind, but rather in some kind of ecstasy of new virtuosities that are very unlike ordinary, non-radicalized ignorance, something that changes his conventional experience fundamentally, that is transporting in all sorts of unexpected ways, allowing new forms of experience or activity that reconfigure his apprehension of ordinary obstacles and of finitude itself, so much so as to render moot the most pressing existential problems of the human condition, like the fear of death. Unlike the skeptic, he experiences more, not less, as a result of his non-knowing. I will here call this kind of a person an "apophatic mystic."

But there are at least two starkly different forms this attitude can take, depending on what other beliefs are held by the apophatic mystic in question. One of these forms is to renounce one's own knowing, purpose, and will, because of a belief that there is *another,* much greater knowing, purpose, and will to which one would be wise to surrender: the mind of God, who controls and, perhaps, even created the universe. I call such a person a "Theistic Apophatic Mystic," or a "Compensatory Theist," that is, one who renounces his own knowledge and purposes in deference to a *higher* knowledge and purpose, which, though inaccessible to himself, "compensates" for his own renunciation of knowledge and purposes. His renunciation of his own purpose is in the service of obeying a higher purpose. That there is some higher purpose and higher will and higher knowledge is one piece of information that remains unrenounced in his non-knowing, either as belief rather than knowledge, or in a paradoxical mode of being "known" through non-knowing. But as long as some room is made for this esteem for knowledge and purpose as what *would be* most valuable if it were possessed by someone—in this case, by someone other than the mystic himself, that is, by God—we have a Theistic Apophatic Mystic. I call this mode "compensatory" because of its commitment to being the missing piece, of opposite character, that compensates for what God is not: because God is X, this mystic is the opposite of X. Because God knows everything and God's will controls all, the apophatic mystic knows and wills nothing. Knowing and willing as such, far from being denigrated, are here regarded as the highest possible attributes. The watchword here would be, "Let Thy Will, not mine, be done." He abandons his willing and purpose and knowing to a higher willing and purpose and knowing.

In contrast to this is what I will call the "Atheist Apophatic Mystic." Here knowing and willing *as such* are seen as the obstacles to the wonderful state—ecstatic, finitude-transcending, transformative, fear-dispelling, whatever—and this pertains to all beings without exception. One tries to be as like the most non-knowing, non-willing entity of all: for example, the Dao, which unlike God is distinguished from finite beings not by itself knowing and willing more, but by knowing and willing *less.* Rather than compensating for its knowledge by assuming the role of non-knowing, one emulates its non-knowing as much as possible—or, in a further step along the way of the paradox, one does not emulate it, for one cannot know it, or that it exists—and thereby becomes even more like it. To emulate it would be to take it as an ideal; but it is what has no ideals (realized or unrealized), since it is Dao, not God. It also *is* not an ideal, since it is Dao, not God, and thus we are more accurate in saying "isomorphic" rather than "emulative." So, the less he emulates it, or any other entity, the more he becomes like it. He abandons his willing and purpose and knowing, not to another higher version of willing and purpose and knowing, but to purposelessness and non-knowing as such, which are the highest source of all value, including those that operate through local, finite, purposes and knowledges and volitions. The watchword here would be, to borrow a punning slogan attributed to the Chan Buddhist figure Dongshan Liangjie, "Dao has no intention to unite with man; thus man, when having no intention, unites with Dao" (道無心合人，人無心合道).

The "Inner Chapters" (1–7) of the *Zhuangzi,* considered for the sake of argument as if constituting a reasonably coherent single text, will be read in what follows as unfolding a radical form of this Atheist Apophatic Mysticism (Yearly 2010).[1] I believe Zhuangzi's chapter six gives the most comprehensive view of this atheistic mysticism, and it does so precisely when it most seems to flirt with theistic ideas, taking them up, actually inventing them, then scrambling them around, and tossing them into the miscellaneous bin with everything else, ready to make use of them as needed. This chapter disturbs Zhuangzi enthusiasts of a certain stripe, that is, those who are impressed and enlivened by the rigorous, skeptical perspectivism of chapter two but less delighted by other parts of the *Zhuangzi* text that seem to be little more than mystical ramblings about a metaphysical Dao at the beginning of all things—one that seems to come out of nowhere and ignore the skeptical underminings of any such possible knowledge that have been so powerfully advanced back in chapter two. The skepticism seems to these readers to be incompatible with the mystical effusions. For this reason some good Zhuangzi scholars are eager to dismiss chapter six as something that could not possibly be written by the same person as chapter two, or at least not when he was being responsible or serious. Though I think the linguistic similarities strongly suggest a single author for these two chapters, or at least for the key passages of these two chapters,[2] I share the concerns of these scholars. In this article I hope to show that the worries they have about a compromised crypto-theist Zhuangzi in chapter six are unwarranted.

Close readers of the *Zhuangzi* might indeed be surprised to find him trotted out as the ultimate atheist-hero, and understandably so. After all, the *Inner Chapters* of the *Zhuangzi* are not only exceptionally obsessed with "Heaven" (*tian* 天)—so much so that Xunzi criticizes Zhuangzi as someone who is "obsessed with Heaven but does not understand Man" (*biyu tian er buzhi ren* 蔽於天而不知人); they also actually provide the *locus classicus* for what is really the closest term in all classical Chinese literature for something like an anthropomorphic creator deity: *zaowuzhe* 造物者, the creator of things. This is not a term associated with ancient religion, and is unattested until that same chapter six of the *Zhuangzi*, where—some readers might object—it is most emphatically presented as anthropomorphized and intentional creator of all things, to whose intentions one would be wise to submit: a pitch-perfect example of what I have here called Compensatory Theism. Here is the beautiful story where the term first pops up:

> Ziji, Ziyu, Zili and Zilai were talking. One of them said, "Who can see nothingness as his own head, life as his own spine, and death as his own ass? Who knows the single body formed by life and death, existence and non-existence? I will be his friend!" The four looked at one another and laughed, feeling complete concord, and became friends. Suddenly, Ziyu took ill. Ziji went to see him. Ziyu said, "How great is the Creator of Things (*zaowuzhe* 造物者), making me all tangled up like this!" For his chin was tucked into his navel, his shoulders towered over the crown of his head, his ponytail pointed toward the sky, his five internal organs at the top of him, his thigh bones taking the place of his ribs, and his Yin and Yang energies in chaos. But his mind was relaxed and unbothered. He hobbled over to the well to get a look at his reflection. "Wow!" he said, "The Creator of Things has really gone and tangled me up!"

Ziji said, "Do you dislike it?"

Ziyu said, "Not at all. What is there to dislike? Perhaps he will transform my left arm into a rooster; thereby I'll be announcing the dawn. Perhaps he will transform my right arm into a crossbow pellet; thereby I'll be seeking an owl to roast. Perhaps he will transform my ass into wheels and my spirit into a horse; thereby I'll be riding along —will I need any other vehicle? Anyway, getting it is a matter of the time coming and losing it is just something else to follow along with. Content in the time and finding one's place in the process of following along, joy and sorrow are unable to seep in. This is what the ancients called 'the Dangle and Release.' We cannot release ourselves—being beings, we are always tied up by something. But it has long been the case that mere beings cannot overpower Heaven. What is there for me to dislike about it?"

Suddenly Zilai fell ill. Gasping and wheezing, on the verge of keeling over, he was surrounded by his weeping wife and children. Zili, coming to visit him, said to them, "Ach! Away with you! Do not disturb his transformation!" Leaning across the windowsill, he said to the invalid, "How great is the Process of Creation-Transformation (zaohua 造化)! What will it make you become, where will it send you? Will it make you into a mouse's liver? Or perhaps an insect's arm?"

Zilai said, "A child obeys its parents wherever they may send him—north, south, east, or west. Now Yin and Yang are much more to a man than his parents. If they send me to my death and I disobey them, that would make me a traitor—what fault would it be of theirs? For the Great Clump burdens me with a physical form, labors me with life, eases me with old age and rests me with death. Hence it is precisely because I regard my life as good that I regard my death as good. Now suppose a great master smith were casting metal. If the metal jumped up and said, 'I insist on being nothing but an Excalibur!' the smith would surely consider it to be an inauspicious chunk of metal. Now if I, having happened to stumble into a human form, should insist, 'Only a human! Only a human!' Creation-Transformation would certainly consider me an inauspicious chunk of person.

So now I look upon all Heaven and Earth as a great furnace, and Creation-Transformation as a great blacksmith—where could I go that would not be all right? All at once I fall asleep. With a start I awaken." (Ziporyn 2009: 45-6)

The story starts with a shared affirmation of what sounds like a classic Daoist motif: for any given thing, it is first not there, then it's there for awhile, then it's not there again. Any given thing begins as nothing, becomes something for some length of time, and then return to being nothing when it dies. The source from which these things emerge and into which they vanish is simply identified as "nothing," or perhaps simply "the absence of this thing," but certainly not God or Heaven or Dao or the universe or the Good or The One. The three phases—absence, presence, absence—are inseparable, so we are invited to look at them as one body: nothingnesslifedeath. Our consciousness and all its purposes, our love of life and preference for it over death, belong only to the middle section: "life." Our preference for life is itself a part of life, a function of life. Chapter two of the *Zhuangzi* had suggested that the preference common to living beings for life over death is just an example of how each thing affirms whatever its own position is: they are biased in life's favor because they are presently living, just as one roots for one's hometown team just because it's one's hometown. It doesn't mean life is actually of greater value than death: it just looks that way to the living, the way a size-ten shirt might look to be more worth having than other-sized shirts to someone who wears a size-ten shirt. The universe does not prefer life to death. This consorts well with the atheist view that the universe does not produce life on purpose, that the universe has no purposes. And you yourself don't actually prefer life to death, considering you as the inseparable totality of all the phases of existence you have been and are and will be, like the head and spine and tail of a single body: it's just a special case of you "preferring" whatever phase you happen to be in at the time. The spine is pro-spine, but the body is not pro-spine as opposed to pro-head or pro-tail. This consorts well with the isomorphic atheistic mystical view.

But then we find one of the characters becoming ill, and instantly he translates this idea into strongly anthropomorphic language: the Creator is *doing* these things to me. The final *zhe* 者 even stresses the idea of a nominalized agent: whatever is happening to me is happening because someone is doing it: the Creator of Things. This is a strong example of the idea of God the Creator as an intentional doer of whatever happens. There is a controller of things, and if something happens that contravenes our willing and doing, our purposes, it has to be the result not of the breakdown of purpose itself, as perhaps the initial "nothing-life-death" body metaphor would suggest, but precisely because of the doing and willing, the purpose, of *someone else*: the Creator. This is the kernel of theism: the idea that whatever happens, happens because some intentional agent causes it to happen. Even if the Creator is not exactly claimed to be especially intelligent or good here, the call is for the total renunciation of one's own preferences in favor of the putative designs of this Creator. Just as a child should obey his parents and go wherever they send him, we should obey the Creator and become whatever he makes us. This is pitch-perfect Compensatory Theism.

But in the course of making that point, a subtle shift occurs in the narrative. Ziyu speaks of the Creator of Things. When their other friend Zilai get sick, Zili picks up Ziyu's metaphor and uses it to comfort him. But in so doing, he makes one big change: he no longer uses the term *zaowuzhe*, the Creator of Things, but substitutes instead *zaohua* 造化, Creation-Transformation, without the final nominalizing *zhe* (which turns a verb into "the one who does" the verb). The term suggests not an agent who creates, but the process of creation and transformation itself, leaving out the doer and hence also whatever intentions the doer might have. Might we read this as a deliberate modification, suggesting an increasing accuracy and refinement of the basic trope, moving it further away from anthropomorphism? Several factors urge a strongly affirmative answer.

First, we see this morphing of the term for the creative process continuing two more times in the same story, in Zilai's version of the same idea. For there, when making the point about obeying transformation as a child obeys his parents, he actually refers neither to the Creator of Things nor to Creation-Transformation, but simply to "Yin and Yang"—an even more depersonalized non-agent, not even a single entity (in Zhuangzi's time the terms did not yet have their technical meaning, and really just refer to the balance of forces necessary for health in the physical body, as attested both in Zhuangzi's chapter Four (Ziporyn 2009: 28) and in roughly contemporaneous medical texts; or, more generically, to "light and dark," i.e., the diurnal and yearly cycle, which is to say, natural processes). Then a few lines later even this term is replaced by a term with connotations as far away from Personhood as imaginable: The Great Clump *dakuai* 大塊, which in chapter Two is used to mean something like "the whole earth," as that from which the wind comes (2009: 9). In spite of all these name changes, and this clear progression from anthropomorphic to non-anthropomorphic, the lesson remains: whatever it is that makes us sicken and die, and also makes us be born and live, is regarded as a smith forging metal implements: we have our rigid form like a sword (the "life" or spine part of the one body), but this will again be melted down to make other things. The Creator—or rather, now, "Creation-Transformation"—is the smith who makes us and melts us back down to nothingness, and then into something else. The anthropomorphism is really not much diminished in Zilai's version, for his final trope is of not wanting to displease the master smith with his impudent insistence on having only the form of a human.

Thus, if that were the end of the matter, we would have to consider Zhuangzi an admittedly peculiar and slippery but nonetheless undeniable member of the Compensatory Theist club, a Theistic Apophatic Mystic, albeit one who insists with unusual thoroughness on the unknowability and unnameability of this Creator—so much so that we can apply any name we like to it, from the most to the least anthropomorphic. This would make him a maximally agnostic theist, perhaps. Or, a little more charitably and profoundly, we could read this story, if it existed in isolation, as suggesting that it makes no difference whether we think of the one agent as God or as the Universe or as a Great Clump, minded or unminded—we can't know that anyway, one way or the other. But from our point of view, that non-knowing is enough: we have no choice but to do what it has us do, to "obey" it—so, we may say, whether God exists or not, it's all God to me. Whatever-It-Is gives and Whatever-It-Is taketh away. Since I was only alive because Whatever had made me alive, and being alive is what made me think being alive is good, when Whatever makes me dead, transforming me into whatever comes next, is also just as good.

Taken in isolation, then, this story can be interpreted either as the Emulative Theistic—"I should desire it because the Creator desires it, and it is therefore good" or as a more apophatically Compensatory Theistic—"the desires and indeed identity of the Creator are unknowable, but in any case my own desires and identity are not to be taken as ultimate and are best renounced in obedience to what Whatever-Makes-It-So seems to be insisting upon." Focusing instead on the opening trope of "one body of nothingnesslifedeath," we could arrive at the deeply atheistic structure of "it is good to die for the same reason that it was good to live, that is, because *I considered it* good, because it was a function of the exact state I was in at the time: the good-for-me is a consequence of what I am at any given time, and thus what I desire." The latter reading is indeed more consistent with Zhuangzi's chapter Two, so if we consider these texts to be products of the same author, we should perhaps already favor the latter, atheistic meaning. But taking this entire story in isolation, it is outweighed by the theistically flavored tropes that follow it. Either way, it hardly makes Zhuangzi an outspoken atheist-hero.

But that is far from the end of the matter here in chapter Six. In fact, as traditional commentary has pointed out,[3] this story is part of a sequence of three stories about death, and the progression we have seen already beginning within this tale continues into high gear in the following two stories. The first of them begins with a modified version of the trope that began the previous story:

Zisanghu, Mengzifan and Ziqinzhang came together in friendship, saying, "Who are able to be together in their very not being together, to do things for one another by not doing things for one another? Who can climb up upon the Heavens, roaming on the mists, twisting and turning round and round without limit, living their lives in mutual forgetfulness, never coming to an end?" The three of them looked at each other and burst out laughing, feeling complete concord, and thus did they become friends.

After a short silence, without warning, Zisang fell down dead. Before his burial Confucius got the news and sent Zigong to pay his respects. There he found them, one of them composing music, the other plucking the zither, and finally both of them singing together in harmony:

"Hey Sanghu, hey Sanghu!
Come on back, why don't you?
Hey Sanghu, hey Sanghu!
Come on back, why don't you?
You've returned to what we are really,
While we're still humans—wow, yippee!"

Zigong rushed forward and said, "May I venture to ask, is it ritually proper to sing at a corpse like that?"

The two of them looked at each other and laughed, saying, "What does this fellow understand about the real point of ritual?"

Zigong returned and reported this to Confucius, asking, "What kind of people are these? They do not cultivate their characters in the least, and they treat their bodies as external to themselves, singing at a corpse without the least change of expression. I don't know what to call them. What sort of people are they?"

Confucius said, "These are men who roam outside the lines. I, on the other hand, do my roaming inside the lines. The twain can never meet. It was vulgar of me to send you to mourn for such a person. For the previous while he had been chumming around as a human with the Creator of Things, and now he roams in the single vital energy of Heaven and Earth.

"Men such as these look upon life as a dangling wart or swollen pimple, and on death as its dropping off, its bursting and draining. Being such, what would they understand about which is life and which is death, what comes before and what comes after? Depending on all their diverse borrowings, they yet lodge securely in the one and only self-same body. They forget all about their livers and gall bladders, cast away their eyes and ears, reversing and returning, ending and beginning, knowing no start or finish. Oblivious, they drift uncommitted beyond the dust and grime, far-flung and unfettered in the great work of doing nothing in particular. Why would they do something as stupid as practicing conventional rituals to impress the eyes and ears of the common crowd?"

Zigong said, "Since you know this, Master, of which zone do you consider yourself a citizen?"

Confucius said, "As for myself, I am a casualty of Heaven. But that is something you and I may share."

Zigong said, "Please tell me more."

Confucius said, "Fish come together in water, and human beings come together in Dao. Those who meet each other in the water do so by darting through the ponds, thus finding their nourishment and support. Those who meet each other in Dao do so by not being bothered to serve any one particular goal, thereby allowing the flow of their lives to settle into stability. Thus it is said, fish forget one another in the rivers and lakes, and human beings forget one another in the arts of Dao."

Zigong said, "But please explain to me about these freakish people."

Confucius said, "They are freakish to man but normal to Heaven. So it is said, He who to Heaven is a petty man is to the people an exemplary man, while he who to Heaven is an exemplary man is to the people a petty man." (Ziporyn 2009: 46–7)

Things have changed here. We notice that all reference to the personal Creator has dropped out. Indeed, in the opening trope this time we have not the three phases forming a single substantial body, equal parts of a whole, nor a subsequent (though temporary) tracing back to a personal or purposeful agent as in the first story, but a reduction of even the personal (knowing, purposive) dimension of themselves, in the sense of interpersonal social relations and intentional purposive activity, to an epiphenomenon of the nonpersonal, the asocial, the unintentional, the purposeless. Here they are coming together, but only through not coming together; here they are acting for a purpose, but only by virtue of not acting for a purpose. What is being undermined here is precisely the ultimacy of the personal and the ultimacy of purpose—the two key underminings of ultimacy that we may identify as characterizing atheistic mysticism. In the previous story, we had the impersonal and the personal as parts of a whole, with the impersonal (nothingness) still at the basis, but with the various parts distributed and distinguishable as the head, spine, and tail of a single body, though each phase was alone prevailing in its time. Now, in contrast, the two aspects are simultaneous and inseparable at all times: even while alive and interpersonal and purposive, they are simultaneously grounded in the impersonal ("without associating with each other") and the purposeless ("without doing anything for each other"). Where this explicitly leads is not to the intention of the Creator to be obeyed, but to *infinity*, another identifying mark of truly atheistic mysticism: transformation without end, without *telos*. When death comes, we are not told how the still alive but dying man looks at it, but how his friends, who share his views, look on the matter now that he is dead. We may read this as the view of the matter from the side of death as seen from life. Just as the living are more at home in life, the dead are more at home in death. Feeling complete accord, the friends sing of the feelings of the dead man: he has comfortably returned to what we all really were all along, the purposeless and noninterpersonal;

but they also make ironic reference to their own aliveness: again, the two are now simultaneous for them.

In the conversation that follows, Confucius then very clearly reveals the relation of the two stories, and their relation to the anthropomorphized Creator. First, he reiterates the trope about the fish in water that appeared in the uninflected authorial voice earlier in the same chapter.[4] The interpersonal and the purposive are like fish spitting on each other when stranded on the shore. They are ways of using a bit of the water, to be sure, and are derived from it, but full immersion in that same water would eliminate the interpersonal and purposive, like fish forgetting each other in the water. The personal is a pinched, emergency usage of the impersonal. Purpose is a straitened, last-ditch survival application of the purposeless, which would eliminate it if fully embraced. Purpose is a narrow, somewhat pathetic application of the purposeless, which both sustains it and dissolves it. But this view thus gives a place to both the life side and the death side, the personal side and the nonpersonal side: "For the previous while he had been chumming around as a human with the Creator of Things, and now he roams in the single vital energy of Heaven and Earth." The previous story related the way living humans related to the Whatever which is the source of all things. That is, as human. The human see things in human terms, so they relate to the Whatever humanly, as a human. So while alive, the dying men felt an intimate chumminess with the Whatever from which they come: they related to it as human, spitting on the Whatever with the spit of the personal, and feeling the waters of the Whatever only as the Whatever's spit on them, that is, his personal regard, intention, purposes. Being still intentional beings, they took the Whatever up as a companion in having intentions.

Again, for Zhuangzi, it is the perspective that determines the values. So a living, personal being relates to the Whatever as a living, personal being, values in terms of living and life and intention: it is natural for a purposive, personal being, a living human, to project personality and purpose on the Whatever, and relate to it as the Creator of Things, and to chum around in that sort of a relationship with it. In contrast, in the second story we see *also* (not exclusively, but additionally) how it is after one ceases to be a human, "roaming in the single vital energy (qi) of Heaven and Earth." The image is starkly anti-personal: no separate being, no solid thing, no consciousness, no goal, just qi, constantly transforming energy conceived as a fluid formless flowing medium, a continuum that sometimes congeals into concrete entities, like ice in water, and then disperses again. My ultimate life-and-death-on-one-string spells a parallel life-and-death-on-one-string for the Creator: that Creator too is only human and purposive as long as I am, and to the extent that I am, and in the specific, temporary, ironic modality that I am. Both the personal and the impersonal sides of the equation are now in view, connected by Zhuangzi's central perspectivism, which is precisely his deep atheism.

Hence, in this and the previous story, we see a certain willingness to talk theistically when talking to people who are talking theistically. Theistic language is even used as a wedge to move past itself: Heaven or the Creator can be used to undermine accepted distinctions, overturn them, reverse them, to unsettle things and dissolve them into the process of transformation. And then the same is done to the concept of Heaven or Creator itself. Each thing is affirmed, but this affirmation is also the way in which it moves beyond itself. This is an example of "responding with unlimited rights and wrongs" explored in depth in chapter Two: going by the rightness of the present This (*yinshi* 因是) (Brook 2009: 12–14)—in this case, This living human speaker, with his invocation of the Creator. Zhuangzi is being consistent here, and thoroughgoingly atheistic: so atheistic that he can even lightheartedly use Creator-talk, and then flip it over. Zhuangzi is more tolerant of theism than the typical militant atheist, but this should be viewed as a consequence of a more, not less, thoroughgoing and consistent atheism.

But that is not yet the end of the sequence. Following this tale, we have a third consecutive story about death:

> Yan Hui went to question Confucius. "When his mother died, Mengsun Cai wailed but shed no tears, unsaddened in the depths of his heart, observing the mourning but without real sorrow. Lacking tears, inner sadness and real grief, he nonetheless gained a reputation throughout Lu as an exemplary mourner. Is it really possible to have a reputation that is utterly at odds with reality? I have always found it very strange."
>
> Confucius said, "Mengsun Cai has gone to the very end of this matter, beyond merely understanding it. For when you try to simplify things for yourself but find it impossible to do so, things have already been simplified for you.
>
> This Mr. Mengsun understands nothing about why he lives or why he dies. His ignorance applies equally to what went before and what is yet to come. Having already transformed into some particular being, he takes it as no more than a waiting for the next transformation into the unknown, nothing more. And if he's in the process of transforming, what could he know about not transforming? If he's no longer transforming, what could he know about whatever transformations he's already been through? You and I, conversely, are dreamers who have not yet begun to awaken. As for him, his physical form may meet with shocks but this does not harm his mind. His life is to him but a morning's lodging, so he does no real dying. This Mr. Mengsun alone has awakened. Others cry, so he cries too. And that is the only reason he does so.
>
> "We temporarily get involved in something or other and proceed to call it 'myself'—but how can we know if what we call 'self' has any 'self' to it?
>
> You dream you are a bird and find yourself soaring in the heavens, you dream you are a fish and find yourself submerged in the depths. I cannot even know if what I'm saying now is a dream or not. An upsurge of pleasure does not reach the smile it inspires; a burst of laughter does not reach the jest that evoked it.[5] But when you rest securely in your place in the sequence, however things are arranged, and yet separate each passing transformation from the rest, then you enter into the clear oneness of Heaven." (Ziporyn 2009: 47–8)

Here we have the real culmination of the matter. Now there is neither the Creator nor *qi*. There is only forgetting and transformation. Non-knowing trumps everything, as it does in the more theoretical parts of Zhuangzi's writing in chapter Two, where he develops his skeptical, relativist perspectivism. The ultimacy of non-knowing is of course the atheistic trope par excellence. For here the non-knowing is so thoroughgoing that it is not mere agnosticism, that is, the human subject's lack of knowledge, which eliminates all reference to a creator, a doer, a substrate, a prior state, a later state. It recognizes that we cannot even know, as negative theologians claim to know, that there is something out there that we don't know: we can't even say there is something called Heaven or the Creator or *qi* which we don't understand. At the source of everything is not even a something or a nothing: it is just the unknown, so unknown that the idea of a *source* as such now drops out entirely. The ultimate source is not here claimed to be mind, person, purpose, or *nous*, that much is obvious; but more than that, even to call it "the source," as if we knew that, is already much too *nous*-ey, too much a concession to intelligibility. There is only the taking up of each transformation, being whatever you are for awhile, with all the concomitant values and purposes and cognitive commitments that are internal to it, and then dropping it all and becoming something else with other commitments. The claim to know in a stable, perspective-independent way that there is or is not some Creator, even a completely unknowable one, or that we are all made of a formless Qi, would get in the way of this forgetting and this transformation. We no longer even need "the one body" that connects and enfolds nothingness, life, and death. There's just being some "this" and then letting go of being this. Even in being this, non-knowledge is the ultimate: it's not just that I am alive and human now, but that I ecstatically accept that I don't know what I was before or what I will become or where any of these changes come from or what they mean: I don't even know if I'm alive now, if I'm a human now, if I'm myself, "if there's any self to myself." The knowing and the non-knowing are not arranged as parts of a whole, strung together: they are simultaneous at all times. Even when I know, even in knowing, I don't know. Not-knowing, the impersonal, the non-purposive, pervades everything, thoroughly saturates even any and all knowing, purpose, person that might or might not exist. That is the real apex of atheistic mysticism.

All of these stories come from the middle of chapter Six of the *Zhuangzi*. Right afterward there are three more short dialogues which bring the chapter to an end. These three final dialogues may be seen as roughly recapitulating the steps of this progressively structured, perspectival atheism in another form. In the first, Yierzi asks Xu You for instruction about Dao, but is rebuked as incapable of receiving it because his mind has already been ruined by moral ideas and prejudices, by ideas of "right and wrong." Yierzi says, Okay, but maybe you can tell me a little about it, "just the outskirts"? Xu You says no, you're already mutilated, crippled, blinded by your prior instruction. Then Yierzi invokes the Creator of Things as the source of all sorts of unpredictable change: "How do you know the Creator of Things will not wipe away my tattoo and restore my nose, making me intact to follow you?" Xu You responds:

> Ah! It is indeed unknowable. I will speak for you of the broad outlines then. My teacher! My teacher! He destroys all things, but he is not administering responsible justice. His bounty reaches all things, but he is not being humanely kind. He is an elder to the remotest antiquity, but without being old. He covers and supports Heaven and Earth and carves out all forms, but without being skillful. It is all the play of his wandering, nothing more. (Ziporyn 2009: 48–9)

So here, as in the first of the three death and mourning stories, the theistic-sounding term Creator of Things is invoked, in this case by someone already identified as brainwashed and ruined by prior moral instruction. The Creator is invoked even by this speaker, however, only as a support for *non-knowledge*: how can you or anyone know that I can't be restored to mental health in spite of my prior moral instruction, or for that matter that someone might magically grow back his nose after it has been cut off? Anything can happen, who knows! As with Confucius's remark about the freaks and normals to Man and to Heaven above, only the sense in which the Creator overturns and subverts any positive knowledge is invoked. In this sense, the idea of Heaven serves temporarily as a first way of aiding and abetting the sense of transformation and forgetting. Xu You agrees with the "I don't know" thrust, and thus yields and consents to give him "the broad outlines"—and here he speaks in Creator-of-Things argot, the conceptual system of his interlocutor, but inserting key modifications to eliminate the moral prejudices implied in the idea of a conscious Creator.

Chumming about with the Creator while one is oneself a human, he deploys the anthropomorphism only to assert that the Creator is his teacher—that is, his role model. In what way? Precisely in his lack of intention, his lack of justice, his lack of humaneness, his lack of oldness, his lack of skill—which yet destroys and creates and carves out all forms and encompasses Heaven and Earth. Xu You wants to emulate "his" play (note that there is no personalized and gendered possessive pronoun in Chinese, where "its" is identical to "his" or "her"—this is added in English only to accord with the anthropomorphizing trope of "teacher"), his wandering, his non-intentionality, his *wuwei* as the real source of all emergent values, even conscious and consciously sought values. Here we have Zhuangzi showing how what I call his "wild card" works, going by the rightness of the present This as a way to allow it to transform endlessly, speaking in terms of Compensatory Theism and tweaking it directly into Emulative Atheism.

In the next dialogue, as in the second death and mourning story, forgetting and non-knowing are now moved to center stage. Yan Hui says he is progressing in that he has forgotten precisely those ideas of right and wrong that distorted the mind of Yierzi: Humaneness, Righteousness, Ritual, Music. Then he says he reaches a state of "sitting and forgetting":

"It's a dropping away of my limbs and torso, a chasing off of my sensory acuity, which disperses my physical form and ousts my understanding until I am the same as the Transforming Openness.[6] This is what I call just sitting and forgetting."

Confucius then says, "The same as it? But then you are free of all preference! Transforming? But then you are free of all constancy! You truly are a worthy man! I beg to be accepted as your disciple." (Ziporyn 2009: 49)

Preference would imply intention (echoing the creator of things); constancy would imply a single substrate (echoing the one body of nothingnesslifedeath); together they would give us an agent, a doer behind changing actions and events. Free of preference, free of constancy, endless transformation, and openness: the opposite of the intentional anthropomorphic Creator of Things, who has been forgotten along with the rest: precisely freeing oneself of these preconceptions, of the idea of the Creator as intentional and as a genuine agent, are what make him one with the "Transforming Openness," the real source of things, the opposite of God.

In the final story, ending the chapter, Ziyu finds his friend Zisang in undeserved and unbearable distress, asking who did this to him. This may remind some readers of the *Book of Job* in the Old Testament: terrible things happen to an innocent man, seemingly for no reason, and he wants to find out why. But unlike Job, who questions the justice of his suffering and the comprehensibility of its source but not the existence or even the identity of that source, Zisang dispels precisely the claim to know where this all comes from, or even that there is some source from which it comes. Here it is again *non-knowing* that is the final word. Zisang asks who did it? Father? Mother? Heaven? Man? "I have been thinking about what could have caused me to reach this extreme state, and I could find no answer. My mother and father would surely never wish to impoverish me like this. Heaven covers all equally, Earth supports all equally, so how could Heaven and Earth be so partial as to single me out for impoverishment? I search for some doer of it all but cannot find anything—and yet here I am in this extreme state all the same. This must be what is called Fate, eh?" (Ziporyn 2009: 49). Note well: *not Heaven*. Heaven has been explicitly mentioned as one of the possible agents, and rejected. It is now not Heaven, not the Creator of Things, that does it. Acceptance of Fate is *not* accepting the will of Heaven. On the contrary, it is reached only when one has dispelled progressively, as in the preceding steps, the very idea of Heaven as some particular entity. No doer is found anywhere, for anything that happens. *That's* about all the word "Fate" can mean, its actual content: "I don't know"— as indeed even Mencius is willing to say when pressed (see *Mencius* 5A6). The appeal is not to God or Heaven as the unknown knower of the unknown plan, but to Fate as the unknown but also unknowing planlessness.

We can now begin to see how poorly Xunzi's characterization of Zhuangzi, that he so obsessed by Heaven that he does not know man, applies to the Inner Chapters.[7] For the same chapter that ends this way, and that includes these stories of the Creator of Things, chapter six, *begins* with a discussion reiterating the perspectival skepticism concerning *all* knowledge that played so key a role in chapter two, aimed here specifically *against* the privileging of Heaven over man, which would require precisely the kind of knowledge that Zhuangzi critiques. The passage starts with the traditional clear-cut division between Heaven and Man, which it then savagely deconstructs in favor of non-knowledge, exemplified by the Genuine Persons of antiquity, in a typical Zhuangzian three-step we have already seen in this sequence of stories: (1) a perspectivist-skeptical overcoming of apparent distinctions through a provisional oneness of agent (e.g., the Creator), and then moving on to (2) totality (the One Body of life and death), and then (3) *rejecting both (1) and (2)* through the continued application of the perspectival skepticism, in favor of transformation and forgetting, the ultimacy of purposelessness and non-knowing, which are ever-present and unobstructed even in all acts of purpose and knowing, and thus in all putative goods willed and all putative truths known:

"To know what Heaven is doing and also what is to be done by Man, that is the utmost."

"To know what Heaven is doing": Heaven, as Heaven, is the generation of whatever happens.

"To know what is to be done by the Human": that would be to use what your knowing knows to nurture what your knowing does not know. You could then live out all your natural years without being cut down halfway. And that would indeed be the richest sort of knowing.

However, there is a problem here. For our knowing can be in the right only by virtue of a relation of dependence on something, and what it depends on is always peculiarly unfixed. So how could I know whether what I call the Heavenly is not really the Human? How could I know whether what I call the Human is not really the Heavenly? Tentatively, then, [let us instead say that] there can be "Genuine Knowing" only when there is such a thing as "a Genuine Person." (Ziporyn 2009: 39–40, modified).

The term "Heaven" is used by Zhuangzi to provisionally indicate the source or process of generation of whatever happens, including all experiences, all knowings. As a source, this is not only unknown but also unknowable, "what knowing does not know." Earlier in his text, back in chapter two again, he had asked where our moods come from, where our thoughts come from, where our values come from, where our perspectives come from, where events come from (Ziporyn 2009: 10, modified). He noticed that he did not know. He noticed that he could not identify any particular source or doer of what happens. He noticed also that there seemed to be no way for him ever to know, since all his knowing occurred within one of these happenings, one of these experiences, one of these perspectives. No awareness, no act of knowing, can directly witness the event of its own emergence, its transition from not-occurring to occurring, since this requires an act of awareness to be aware also of the time before it was aware. Since its knowledge is confined to the post-emergence awareness, it can only speculate and make inferences about the state prior to its existence and about the transition from that state to its present state of occurring. But speculations and inferences also occur only as existing states of consciousness, and they are themselves observed to vary according to the mood, commitments, and canons of reasoning implicitly embraced at different times and places and by different agents—that is, in different knowledge-events. Each particular act of knowing thus seems to affect and color all that is within its purview, and its extrapolations about an origin for itself, an otherness from which it emerged to be what it is now, cannot be trusted to be applicable to the mood, commitments, and canons of other acts of knowing. Any state's act of determining where it came from is also deeply and hopelessly internal to its own present state. Its "before" is a "before as seen from now"; its "cause" is "cause as what remains of the impact of the cause already internalized into the effect." Even its knowledge of its contrast to other states is knowledge internal to the state that it is, as is any sense it might have of the consistency of canons of reason or facts that remain constant across states.

Zhuangzi here uses a traditional word for default agent that makes things happen, which is Heaven, the more usual term standing in the position of Creator-of-Things, but again, he uses it purely in a negative sense. As mentioned above, the Confucian thinker Mencius, Zhuangzi's contemporary, offered this shorthand functional definition of heaven when pressed: "What happens although no one makes it happen; what is done although no one does it" (*Mencius* 5A6). Mencius possibly meant this in a less-than-radical sense, that is, "Heaven is the doer of whatever happens for which we can find no other cause." Heaven means whatever is beyond human control—a way, traditionally, of passing the ball. In this more traditional view, what is beyond human control must be under the control of someone or something else: an anthropomorphic deity, or the ancestors, or a loose collection of spiritual forces, or simply an impersonal set of natural processes. In that view, some definite something was the real cause that, if known, would give a full account of what happens and why. Even, however, in Mencius's scaled-down definition of heaven we find a hint of Zhuangzi's more radical understanding of the term, which takes the Mencian definition quite literally: heaven is not merely what is beyond human control; it is that to which the notions of definitive "control" and "cause" and "determiner" do not apply at all. As we have seen for Zisang above, if we seek for a doer, we end up only with a term like "Fate," which also means specifically *not Heaven,* or any other agent.

Zhuangzi's opening passage to chapter six thus begins by offering us a commonplace regarding the proper division of labor for human knowledge: know Heaven and the difference between Heaven and man, what is in your control and what is not in your control—that is, know the natural world and whatever moral or religious obligations that may entail, and what you can do in relation to that unfathomable source which lies beyond human control, for that would be true knowledge, true wisdom. But then Zhuangzi twists this platitude, as is his wont: if heaven, or the heavenish aspect of things, is the unknowable, then this division of labor could only mean, at best, that we should take the knowing part of ourselves (knowledge, purposiveness, personality, *youwei*) and use it to nourish, rather than to know, the unknowable part of ourselves and of the world. The relation of "nourishing" is in itself the highest possible knowledge, of a kind that folds the relation to nonknowing into itself, sustaining a definite relation between knowing and nonknowing: this Daoist position is perhaps close to the one sketched in parts of the *Daodejing*: the unnamable and formless, and thus unknowable background of all names and forms and knowledge is the unhewn (*pu* 樸), the true source of life and growth and being, and we can devote our knowing minds not to getting information about it, which is impossible, but to making sure that it continues to flourish into the known by maintaining the intimate connection between the unseen "root and soil"—the unhewn—and the valued blossom (see *Daodejing* 1, 28, 52, and throughout).

But how can we nourish something we do not know or understand? We must have some knowledge at least about its proper care and feeding! The nutriments we offer may prove poisonous to it, or to ourselves when they return to us—in the waste products, as it were, of the unknowable. Changing the terms of the relation from attempts to "know" the unknowable to merely trying to "nourish" the unknowable does not solve the problem of nonknowledge, which overrides all possible solutions. More radically still, Zhuangzi extends a second-order application of nonknowledge even to the question of knowledge and nonknowledge: "So how could I know whether what I call the Heavenly is not really the Human? How could I know whether what

I call the Human is not really the Heavenly?" (Ziporyn 2009: 39–40). These questions echo the still more pointed formulation found earlier in Zhuangzi's work (chapter two again): "How could I know whether what I call knowing is not really not-knowing? How could I know whether what I call not-knowing is not really knowing?" (2009: 17). This progression might seem like a reductio ad absurdum of a radically agnostic position—and, indeed, similar arguments in Western philosophy since Plato's time have been taken in that way: if knowledge is impossible, we cannot know that knowledge is impossible, and thus the claim that knowledge is impossible cannot fail to contradict itself, and *therefore it must be abandoned*. Zhuangzi, however, does not accept the italicized upshot of this argument.

Instead, he sees the radicalization of the problem of nonknowing as bringing with it its own kind of solution. The conclusion he reaches after asking his series of "How-could-I-know?" questions is a left turn: "Tentatively, then, [let us instead say that] there can be 'Genuine Knowing' only when there is such a thing as 'a Genuine Person'— an odd and easily misleading way of saying that the term "Genuine Knowing" shall henceforth, in his writings, be employed only as an honorific title for a kind of mental state and existential attitude. For we cannot take Zhuangzi to simply be ignoring his own question of the previous sentence and asserting some kind of genuine knowledge by fiat. Having dismissed all possible knowledge in the literal sense, he is free to redefine what *would* count as the highest knowledge in another sense: not true justified belief about how the things are, but rather a particular state of mind. We might prefer to translate *zhi* here simply as "wisdom": since there is no other true knowledge, the only thing worth talking about as knowledge is the wisdom of the Genuine Person. What then is this wisdom? Just the non-knowing, the state of "drift and doubt," he has just landed us in, and which applies also to these stipulations about the Genuine Person. This entails neither that he *knows* this state of mind is the best or truest, nor that this state of mind involves any knowledge of how things are. Now that knowledge has been ruled out, however, there is nothing to prevent us from freely stipulating an attitude of mind and looking at what it might do, what might happen for one who has that attitude. This attitude of total non-knowing, it turns out, unexpectedly does the most important work we may have wanted from the other kind of knowledge, and thus is worthy of the name, ironically. We have here a repurposing of the term "Genuine Knowledge" so that it no longer means accurate information or objective truth about the world, or about Dao, or things, or Heaven, or of the line between what Heaven does and what Man can do, but is offered purely as an honorific for whatever the state of mind of the Genuine Person is. The passage that follows describes that kind of person, as imagined by Zhuangzi. What is Genuine Knowledge like, that is, what is the state of mind of the Genuine Person? Far from being knowledge of Dao or Heaven or world or things or self, it is described precisely as a thoroughgoing embrace of *nonknowing*: not taking apparent want as real want and therefore not taking the action that would follow from that knowledge, that is, rebelling against it; not taking apparent success as real success and thus not having the response that would follow from that knowledge, that is, rejoicing in it. Since such people really *do not know* whether life is better than death, they *do not know* to delight in life and abhor death. This is not because of having secured knowledge that there is no reason to do so, that life and death are one, or are equally valuable, or knowledge of anything else for that matter. It is just a consistent application of nonknowing. The by-product of simply not knowing is thus presented as a state of flowing along, swooping in and out of each situation, forgetting it and moving on, without trying to know or take an attitude toward what precedes or succeeds it—precisely what we saw Mengsun Cai doing when his mother died in the third of the death and mourning stories cited above.

The climax at which the passage finally arrives is this: "In their oneness, they were followers of the Heavenly. In their non-oneness, they were followers of the Human. This is what it is for neither the Heavenly nor the Human to win out over the other" (Ziporyn 2009: 42). This is the final twist of the screw in Zhuangzi's complex isomorphic apophatic atheism. Definite knowing excludes non-knowing, but the drift and doubt of nonknowing does not exclude the temporary emergence and submergence of all sorts of acts of knowing in its redefined sense, all sorts of ideas and views about the world. Knowing is, we are told, a "temporary expedient" (42). Nonknowing is just the allowing of diverse acts of "knowing"—that is, ways of viewing the world—to come and go, without needing to sort them out to arrive at a final univocal consistency. Non-knowing turns out to be a kind of second-order union of knowings and not-knowing, of the "human" and the "heavenly," the purposive and the purposeless—or, more strictly, not a union, which might suggest an achieved synthesis, but rather an openness to the free flow of knowing and non-knowing, of seeing and forgetting, so that "neither wins out" once and for all, neither is at any given time the definitive answer to the questions, "What is this? Is it knowing or is it non-knowing? Do I know or not-know?" Every moment is the emergence of a perspective that has its own way of knowing, its own values, its own purposes. But, as Zhuangzi had shown in his second chapter, the very identity of this perspective is defined by contrast to the alternate perspectives, a contrastive relation that is thus essential to and inseparable from it, so that the original perspective now appears also as the contrasted and negated other; in this way the very positing of the first perspective entails the positing of the alternate perspectives that necessarily undermine it. This process of self-overturning of knowing is depicted there as the found or "obvious" (*ming* 明) structure of all acts of knowing, which are thus always both knowing and non-knowing. We can call it Heaven, the unknown, the upsurgings of perspectives and their relation to alternate perspectives, the grounding but undermining overflow of otherness into whatever is known and valued intrinsic to each knowing. But we can also call it the human, the particular perspective with particular purposes, whatever perspective has surged up, for there is always a liking and a disliking, a This versus a That, a non-oneness, at any given time. It is always both, but only in the specific modality of neither ever being able to definitively win out over the other. Their oneness is one, and their non-oneness is also one.

It is here that we encounter Zhuangzi's way of resolving the self-contradiction of radical agnosticism that has often excluded it from serious philosophical consideration. For Zhuangzi, to accept the human means to take one's position of the moment as one's position of the moment, rather than trying to attain a pristine state of skeptical hygiene that rejects all positions all of the time. To embrace the heavenly means to not-know whether one's position of the moment, the content of one's present knowing, is or is not true knowledge, though it is never a blank, always necessarily involving some kind of determinate content, an awareness that posits some affirmations of some particular states of affairs. The convergence of knowing and not-knowing in the constant transformation of knowings might be understood, not as a fuzzy sort-of knowing, but rather as a bracketed but precise knowing, which is always coextensive with its own undermining: "walking two roads" (*liangxing* 兩行) (Ziporyn 2009: 14).

Obscure impulses, upsurges of perspective, animate "Genuine Persons": they forget what they are doing while they are doing it, they follow no one consistent course, they do not know why they do what they do (in the formulation of *Zhuangzi*, Chapter 20, "now a dragon, now a snake, changing with the times, unwilling to keep to any one exclusive course of action" (Ziporyn 2009: 84)). Like the infant of the *Daodejing*, Chapter 55 who "doesn't yet know the union of the male and female, and yet his penis is erect—the ultimate virility!"—these Genuine Persons who are always both knowing and non-knowing, transforming and forgetting, do not yet have any unified knowledge of the "good" toward which their impulses are aiming them, they have no "mental picture" of their goal. What is present for them is an imageless, knowledgeless impulsion-in-situation; which is to say, they know no definite purpose. This is *wuwei*, action without any prior conscious knowledge of what one is trying to do. But this means the constant transformation of small shifting purposes: like the ancients described in *Daodejing* Chapter 15, they are seemingly hesitant, like men walking on the ice of a frozen river: not walking confidently in a straight line toward their preestablished goal, but gingerly taking one step after another, shifting weight and direction in accordance with what the shifting support under their feet discloses, waiting for the next situation to settle and reveal a direction.

In chapter seven, Zhuangzi introduces his metaphor of mind-as-mirror, destined to have a long career in subsequent Chinese thought:

> In this way, wholeheartedly embody the endlessness, and roam where there is no sign, fully realizing whatever is received from Heaven, but without thinking anything has been gained. It is just being empty, nothing more.
>
> The Utmost Man uses his mind like a mirror, rejecting nothing, welcoming nothing: responding but not storing. Thus he can overcome all things without harm. (Ziporyn 2009: 54)

Given all that has gone before, we should not misunderstand "the mind like a mirror" as calling for the mind objectively to reflect "the way things really are," the way they appear to a privileged Heaven's-eye perspective. The salient features of the mirror adduced here are not its accuracy or reflection without distortion, but its responsiveness and its incapacity for "storing" images. Knowledge and purpose are not to be accumulated from moment to moment; they are not to be made definite or consistent, not to be forced to cohere into an increasingly large system of facts and overall purpose. Knowledge and purpose are a chaos that cannot be compelled to assume definitive shape—hence the striking final parable of Zhuangzi's Inner Chapters, a veritable anti-*Genesis*, which follows directly on the passage just quoted about the Utmost Man:

> The emperor of the southern sea was called Swoosh. The emperor of the northern sea was called Oblivion. The emperor of the middle was called Chaos. Swoosh and Oblivion would sometimes meet in the territory of Chaos, who always attended to them quite well. They decided to repay Chaos for his virtue. "All men have seven holes in them, by means of which they see, hear, eat and breathe," they said. "But this one alone has none. Let's drill him some."
> So every day they drilled another hole.
> Seven days later, Chaos was dead. (Ziporyn 2009: 54)

Primal chaos, the unhewn, cannot be made either an object of knowledge or a subject with a single particular purpose. The mirror, like chaos, is neither a definitely full or empty object nor a definitely full or empty subject: hence its peculiar modality of emptiness that is never blank. Its emptiness—of fixed identity, consistent knowledge, univocal values, unchanging purposes, known agendas—is what allows it to respond to whatever comes to it, to treat both Swoosh and Oblivion so well. It is both knowing and non-knowing, purposive and purposeless, the oneness of the oneness and the non-oneness, the non-winning-out of both Heaven and the human. Zhuangzi's famous story of the monkeys and the monkey trainer can help clarify what he means by mirroring:

> But to labor your spirit trying to make all things one, without realizing that it is all the same [whether you do so or not], is called "Three in the Morning."
> What is this Three in the Morning? Once a monkey trainer was distributing chestnuts. He said, "I'll give you three in the morning and four in the evening." The monkeys were furious. "Well then," he said, "I'll give you four in the morning and three in the evening." The monkeys were delighted. This change of description and arrangement caused no loss, but in one case it brought anger and in another delight. He just went by the rightness of their present "this." Thus the Sage uses various rights and wrongs to harmonize with others, and yet remains at rest in the middle of Heaven the Potter's Wheel. This is called Walking Two Roads. (Ziporyn 2009: 14)

The trainer's going "by the rightness" of the monkeys' "present 'This'" is parallel to the mirror's "responding but not storing." Responsiveness is not mimesis or accurate representation; the mirror contributes something new in its response, doubling and continuing the emergent value-trajectories of the situation from a position outside it. For the mirror does have its own position, its own perspective, enabling it to "overcome," rather than reflect, whatever stands before it, and to do so without harming either itself or what it responds to. By being the way it is, empty, the mirror responds to every monkey bias or purpose that appears, yet stores none of them. The mirror furthers and enhances any and every project it finds appearing to itself, bringing successes as defined by the values posited by that temporary alien project itself; but doing so is an expression of its ownmost emptiness of knowledge, which also enables a passing-beyond of any and every project, a destabilizing negation of all of them. The walking-two-roads structure of the mirror or the trainer exemplifies the non-knowing of Heaven and its undissolvable entanglement with human knowings.

But because Heaven itself is non-knowing, the Heavenlike aspect of the trainer is far from being a "*view* from nowhere," even though we may indeed say that the mirror, too, has a second-order position and embodies its own second-order mirrorlike Heavenly thisness-qua-rightness. The human and the Heavenly have here become indistinguishable, each constantly flipping into the other like any "this/that" pair, precisely because each is both a constant stream of new knowings and a foreclosure of any ultimate knowledge of either itself or the world. The world and the self are in the same boat: both are always positing new transformations of perspective and both never know what's ultimately going on, for both are equally unable to totalize them into any single stable and consistent system of knowledge. The self is unknowing in its every knowing in just the way that Dao is unknowing in its ceaseless generation of unstable, inconsistent knowings, just as the mirror is empty as its own filling and filled as its own emptiness. This is the ultimate reach of the isomorphism between the unknowing knowings of Heaven and unknowing knowings of man--the distinctive Zhuangzian form of apophatic mystical atheism.

Notes

1 In distinguishing several forms of mysticism and attempting to pin a special one on the *Zhuangzi*, I am following a line of thought opened up by Lee Yearley's idea of "intraworldly mysticism," although my conclusions about the content of that distinctive form of mysticism differ considerably (see Yearley 2010).

2 Above all, see the extremely distinctive locutions 庸詎知吾所謂知之非不知邪？庸詎知吾所謂不知之非知邪 ("How do I know that what I call knowing is not non-knowing? How do I know that what I call non-knowing is not knowing?" in chapter two) and 庸詎知吾所謂天之非人乎？所謂人之非天乎 ("How do I know that what I call the heavenly is not the human, or what I call the human is not the heavenly?" in chapter six), and 其所言者特未定也 ("what it speaks of is peculiarly unfixed," in chapter two) and 其所待者特未定也 ("what it depends on is peculiarly unfixed," in Chapter Six). It is to be noted that the two linguistic markers shared in these cases are extremely distinctive fingerprints: 庸詎 appears, in all of Pre-Qin and Han literature, only in these two places, once more in Chapter Four of the *Zhuangzi*, once in the *Huainanzi* within a clear quotation of the *Zhuangzi*, and once in the *Chuci*, while 特未定 appears *only* in these two places, chapter two and chapter six of the *Zhuangzi*. Perhaps most impressive is the use of the character *qi* 蘄 not as the name of a plant or as a place name but as a full verb meaning "to seek": this occurs *eight* times in the Inner Chapters, three times in the rest of the *Zhuangzi*, but only three times in all the rest of extant pre-Qin literature (once in the *Xunzi* and twice in the *Guanzi*).

3 See, for example, Lu Huiqing's comments, translated in Ziporyn (2009: 203).

4 This comes from earlier in this same chapter of Zhuangzi: "When the springs dry up, the fish have to cluster together on the shore, blowing on each other to keep damp and spitting on each other to stay wet. But that is no match for forgetting all about one another in the rivers and lakes. Rather than praising Yao and condemning Jie, we'd be better off forgetting them both and transforming along our own courses" (Brook 2009: 41). We'll talk a bit more about this image later.

5 Reading *pai* 俳 for *pai* 排, the latter being perhaps mistakenly transposed from the following line. Leaving the character unsubstituted would yield, "When you stumble into a pleasant situation there is no time even to smile, and when a smile bursts forth there is no time to arrange it in some particular way," adopting Chen Shouchang's reading (see Cui 2012: 262). Others take the *buji* 不及 in the sense of "not as good as," which yields something like, "Just going wherever you please is not as good as laughing, and offering a laugh is not as good as just taking your place in the sequence of things."
6 Reading *huatong* 化通 for *datong* 大通 ("Great Openness"), as in the parallel passage in *Huananzi* 淮南子, "Daoyingxun" 道應訓.
7 This could mean (1) that Xunzi misunderstood Zhuangzi, or (2) that by "Zhuangzi" Xunzi did not mean the author of the Inner Chapters, which would perhaps support the claim of some recent scholars that Zhuangzi is not the author of the Inner Chapters, or (3) that by "Zhuangzi" Xunzi did not mean the author of *only* the Inner Chapters, but of some larger body of texts, which included many or all of the texts now included in the 33-chapter *Zhuangzi*—which, considered as a single unified work, could be read more easily as justifying the judgment of "so obsessed Heaven that he did not know man"—though even there the judgment seems to ignore more than it notices.

References

Cui Dahua (2012), *Zhuangqijie*, 崔大华，庄子歧解. Beijing: Zhonghua shuju.
Yearly, Lee (2010), "The Perfected Person in the Radical Zhuangzi." In *Experimental Essays on Zhuangzi*, edited by Victor Mair, 126–36. Dunedin, FL: Three Pines Press.
Ziporyn, Brook, trans. (2009), *Zhuangzi: The Essential Writings with Selections from Traditional Commentaries*. Indianapolis: Hackett.

5

Confucius's Irony: Silent Subversion and Critique in the *Analects*

Dimitra Amarantidou

For a philosophical tradition that lacks the equivalent of *philosophy* (*zhexue* 哲學 is only a recent term), the absence of any word corresponding to *irony* is hardly surprising. Though never dubbed an *eirōn*, however, Confucius, a prominent figure in that philosophical tradition, is often portrayed as ironically critical toward the attitudes and deeds of others, as well as his own. In this chapter I will argue that humorous or bitter irony in the *Analects* is more than the charming character trait of a "living Confucius," a linguistic trope of indirectness, or a pedagogical tool encouraging creativity and discouraging arrogance. Looking into its far-reaching philosophical implications, I will argue that Confucius's irony is a Confucian experience and a hermeneutic for Confucius's thought. Responding to a paradoxical reality of change, the Master cannot but change and assume an ironic attitude himself: between *quan* 權 ("weighing things" through constantly adapting to change) and *jing* 經 (embodying patterns of behavior and the stability of moral reference for others). His irony will be read as the only possible linguistic expression of paradoxicality—"taking a standing" (*li* 立) in the midst of change—but also as subtle critique and silent subversion of non-change: the ossification and dogmatization of his teaching. The ironic Confucius remains critical and self-critical to attune with constantly changing circumstances, while at the same time he silently invites us to do the same—to allow his reflections to transform us as we critically engage with and transform them.

Ironic and Humorous Portrayals of Confucius

In his 1971 study on Socrates, William K. C. Guthrie alludes to the predicament and creative potential of any approach to this "altogether unusual character": "in spite of the application of the most scientific methods, in the end we must all have to some extent our own Socrates, who will not be precisely like anyone else's" (Guthrie 1971: 171, 174). As has often been pointed out by today's scholars, whether nostalgically or not, the predecessor of our modern-day professionalized philosophy was no less than "philosophy as a way of life"; this is the philosophy of a time when Socrates was neither

Socratic nor Platonic, when Confucius was not Confucian, and when both were less teachers of some*thing* than embodiments of their own teaching—a teaching "to be felt, experienced, practiced, and lived" (Ames and Rosemont 1999: 5). It seems that what Guthrie presents as our freedom and its limitations is not only that we need to have our own "personal Socrates" and our own "personal Confucius," but also that, in fact, we are left with no choice but to create one, if we are to make anything of their reflections on the good life. Limited to a text compiled and transmitted by many hands though our experience may be, to offer any consistent reading of Confucius's collected sayings (*The Analects*), it seems imperative that we, like so many others before us, decide ourselves on how to portray the founding figure of the Confucian tradition.

In the 1920s, Lin Yutang 林語堂 invited resentment when he offered his own portrayal of the Master. Lin dared not only to proclaim that Confucius had a great sense of humor, but also, and more importantly, to challenge the authority of Neo-Confucian interpreters, as well as "the Confucian scholars and the Western Sinologues" of his own time, who had failed to grasp Confucius's humor, and intense humanity. For Lin, humor was more than a charming feature of the Master's personality—it was an interpretative key. Many of the Confucian sayings could "*only* be understood in the nature of light humorous remarks between him and his intimate disciples" (Lin 1941: 140–1, emphasis added). In his column "The Little Critic," Lin would present a self-critical Confucius and would even go so far as to say that the "true Confucius" was not "an immaculate saint of irreproachable character," but someone who could afford a joke, even under the most dire circumstances, and who was "able to laugh at a joke at his own expense" (1941: 141). Lin is convincing in bringing forth the living and breathing, the erring, inconsistent, and self-deprecating Confucius who did not have all the answers and who, in his mellow middle age, could not but admit his utter failure. Lin does, however, prefer to speak about "humor" rather than "irony." If we accept, as we will in this chapter, that irony, according to Quintillian's definition, is "saying the opposite of what one means," then most of the passages Lin quotes can easily be read as instances of irony,[1] but we might conjecture that a humorous Confucius fitted better with Lin's "human," warm, and smiling Master. Since Lin's time, while many modern scholars still see Confucius as a model of sagely perfection, and read the *Analects* as a set of straightforward dictums providing fixed moral prescriptions and unquestionable guidance, a minority have also appreciated Confucius as the imperfect man and lifetime learner who resorts to humor and irony when faced with the difficulties and frustrations of life. Some scholars have also, at least to a certain extent, explored the philosophical implications of his irony. If there is no *one*, "true Confucius," as Lin Yutang would have it, and if we find more sense in Guthrie's suggestion to construct our own personal figure of the Master, we are justified to create an "ironic Confucius," focusing on his subtle, jocular or bitter irony as an expression of critique and self-critique.

In 1990, Christoph Harbsmeier would somehow follow in Lin Yutang's steps and create his own "human" portrait of Confucius, viewing the Master as "an impulsive, emotional, and informal man, a man of wit and humor, a man capable of subtle irony" (1990: 131), as well as self-irony and even self-satire. Harbsmeier provides substantial linguistic evidence to prove his claim that the text has an overall informal and unceremonious tone, unlike what traditional commentators have seen in it. At the same time, he reads many of the passages as open to both earnest and jocular interpretations, since Confucius's "subtle words" (*wei yan* 微言) were difficult to understand and easy to misunderstand, "like subtle little jokes" (1990: 137). In a thoroughgoing analysis that challenged traditional interpretations of "Orthodox Confucians," for whom a joking Master was simply unimaginable, Harbsmeier refreshingly noted:

> The more un-Confucian and unsagely the humorous passages we discover in the *Analects* are, the more likely they are to be faithful to the man and his personal history, and the more likely we are to hear the Master's Voice, the Master's *ipsissima vox*. (1990: 160)

Once again, as with Lin Yutang, we have here an attempt and a promise: to see the *true* face of Confucius through the lens of humor and irony. The qualification and limitation that Harbsmeier seems to point out is that of the "mirror effect": we tend to see in these figures what we are looking for. But that is hardly regrettable—it is part and parcel of any interpretative endeavor.

Almost a decade later, in 1999, Roger Ames and Henry Rosemont would venture to take "the Confucian way on its own terms," namely, free from familiar Western experiences and vocabularies, offering a groundbreaking philosophical translation of the *Analects*. In their extensive introduction, they devote a few lines to the "human" side of Confucius and note, *apropos*, that the Master evidenced "a wonderful sense of humor," while also being "a harshly exacting mentor with his students," dedicated to cultivating their "moral character" and to reanimating his rich cultural Chinese past. Some years earlier, in their 1987 work *Thinking through Confucius*, David Hall and Roger Ames focused on Confucius the sage and "master communicator," explaining sageliness in terms of the ability to employ a "language of deference" (1987: 295, 296). Confucius's ironic remarks in the *Analects* can thus be explained as instances of indirectness—an important aspect of the Master's allusive, evocative language not of reference, but of deference;[2] it is a language that "postpones" meaning (since it is not referential) and "yields," because "meaning is disclosed and/or created by virtue of a recognition of mutual resonances [tradition] among instances of communicative activity." In other words, Confucius "appeals to present praxis and to the repository of significances realized in the traditional past" (Hall and Ames 1987: 294–5).

More recently, expanding on the philosophical implications of Confucius's humor and irony, Katrin Froese portrayed her own, very convincing, "comic character of Confucius" (2014: 295–312). She uses "humor" and "irony" interchangeably, based on a commonsensical understanding of the two terms, without clarifying how they overlap without being identical. Froese does not merely recognize irony and humor as aspects of Confucius's mellow and charming character, but actually sees them as instruments of self-deprecation and mocking critique, especially "directed at ritualistic behavior [*li* 禮] which has become mechanistic" (2014: 295). Moreover, she seems to point to a reading that allows for a questioning of strict boundaries between Confucianism and Daoism, since the Confucius we find in the *Zhuangzi* is both a ridiculed moral pedant and "someone who has understood the message of the *Dao*" (2014: 311).

Drawing on the insights of the abovementioned scholars, I intend to look deeper into the philosophical significance of Confucius's irony as critique and indirect subversion and, moreover, into its ontological premise: a paradoxical reality of constant change that necessitates and is necessitated by critique. This analysis will be premised on two basic assumptions: first, that a portrayal of the man is not supplementary but decisive for an interpretation of his sayings, his philosophy, and, by extension, of the tradition he is credited with inaugurating; second, that Confucius's irony is more than a personal trait, a form of indirectness, a linguistic strategy in the service of persuasion, a pedagogical tool meant to prompt his interlocutors to think for themselves, or even a silent, embodied lesson (*wu yan zhi jiao* 無言之教). More than celebrating the living, imperfect, and humorously ironic Confucius or the extraordinary teacher, this chapter aims at exploring the far-reaching philosophical significance of Confucian irony as indirect critique against ossification and as silent subversion of dogma. Irony will be taken to be Confucius's only way of linguistically responding and attuning to an ever-changing reality, which demands that he maintains a paradoxical attitude of standing (*li* 立) in the midst of incessant flux—inescapably caught in the paradoxical reality of interdependence between the flexibility of *quan* 權 ("weighing things," transformation) and the stability of *jing* 經 (patterns, points of moral reference, principles). In a world where he experiences the paradoxical constancy of change, Confucius cannot but change himself and thus encourage others to change through ironic critique and self-critique: he does so by resisting fixed linguistic formulations of morality and by, indirectly, at times even silently, subverting the fixity of mechanized, uncritical behaviors, and dogmatism.

Silent Subversion: Responding to the Paradoxicality of Change

子在川上，曰："逝者如斯夫！不舍晝夜。

Standing on the riverbank, the Master said, "Passing just like this, never ceasing day or night!"[3]

While not containing an ironic statement, this passage concretizes in the archetypal image of the flowing river (change) and the standing man (constancy), what I would like to call a paradoxical reality. When we look closely into the relation of Confucius to the river and to his remark about it, that remark evokes and reveals the inherent awareness of the paradox Confucius finds himself in and embodies: the constancy of change. In the midst of change, the Master cannot but change himself, as he critically assesses circumstances and adapts to them, taking a standing (*li* 立). Change necessitates critical and self-critical reflection, which are the conditions of making sound, but not copiable judgments, and offering wise but not reiteratable answers. At the same time, critique and self-critique create the preconditions for change, since any decision based on them has to be reevaluated, adapted to ever-new realities. In this way, constancy and change define and generate one another. The river's flow (change) makes the river what it is; an expanse of unchanging water would not be a river any more, but a pool. The river is also, however, defined by its banks (constancy). Similarly, Confucian patterns of behavior need to change through personalization to remain "alive" and nurturing: intelligible and relevant. They also, however, need to be understood and personalized *as* patterns—as general reference points which, like the river banks, give the river flow a general direction, but do not determine its speed and can be, at any given moment, transformed by a flood.

Confucius himself, more than observing the river, becomes the river: he embodies the paradoxical coexistence and interdependence of the constancy of *jing* 經 (patterns, "river banks") and the flexibility of *quan* 權 ("weighing things," "river flow"). Or, more radically, by becoming the river he is becoming himself. Becoming the river entails standing (by the river) and flowing (like water). Is it possible to stand and flow at the same time? Standing by the river, responding to the going and coming of change, Confucius is also inevitably "taking a standing." In these terms, we can understand how the Master is someone who does not have "presuppositions as to what may or may not be done" (*wu ke wu bu ke* 無可無不可).[4] In his commentary to this passage, Fu Peirong 傅佩榮 explains how Confucius acts by adapting to circumstances and following a flexible course of action, but only after he determines his desired goal (Fu 2012: 295). He is like a river, flowing toward a definitive direction, but flowing in unpredictable and unrepeatable ways. This is perhaps why his teaching remains obscure even for his best student. At 9.11 we read:

顏淵喟然歎曰：「仰之彌高，鑽之彌堅；瞻之在前，忽焉在後。夫子循循然善誘人，博我以文，約我以禮。欲罷不能，既竭吾才，如有所立卓爾。雖欲從之，末由也已。」

Yan Hui, with a deep sigh, said, "The more I look up at it, the higher it soars; the more I penetrate into it, the harder it becomes. I am looking at it in front of me, and suddenly it is behind me. The Master is good at drawing me forward a step at a time; he broadens me with culture (*wen* 文) and disciplines my behavior through the observance of ritual propriety (*li* 禮). Even if I wanted to quit, I could not. And when I have exhausted my abilities, it is as though something rises up right in front of me, and even though I want to follow it, there is no road to take."[5]

In his commentary to this passage, Li Zehou views Yan Hui's 顏回 remarks as the highest possible praise to a teacher, and argues that this perception of Confucius earned him his religious and mystical portrayals, while Yan Hui's difficulty is only the indispensable component of learning (Li 2017: 124). Fu Peirong's commentary emphasizes a "lively," "vibrant" wisdom, which involves reaching an impasse before moving to the state of "no bewilderment" (*wuhuo* 無惑) and the ability to weigh things and make decisions (Fu 2012: 139). Rather than assessing them as mystical or wisely adaptable, we could read Confucius's teaching, often contained in ironic statements, as thoroughly self-critical and thus changeable and always relevant. Yan Hui found "no road to take" (*wei you ye yi* 末由也已), because the Master has to readjust his steps on the way. He in fact seems to praise Yan Hui's state of feeling at a loss as the mark of the true lover of learning (*haoxue* 好學).[6]

To those who are conscious of having no road to take, Confucius offers the road of no road: insights that point to possible paths. His remark at the river could be read as a reminder that the exemplary person is not a vessel (*qi* 器)[7] and he himself is not one filled with ready-made itineraries and life proposals. In that case, there would be no need for critique or self-critique. All possible problems and dilemmas would have been addressed once and for all, and the Master's collected sayings would be no more and no less than a Decalogue. The river does not possess water, necessary for our survival; the river *is* water. In a similar way, Confucius does not possess the answer to every question that is necessary for our emotional and social survival, but *is* the answer to every question; an answer that, like water, one can only drink for oneself, and drink every day, throughout one's lifetime. Undeniably, Confucius has very clear and strong ideas about appropriate conduct and ritual performance. He himself is described as adhering to a set of rules that extended from how he dressed to how he addressed his superiors. Nowhere, however, in his recorded sayings do we find a clear, unambiguous injunction to his disciples to behave the same way. He himself does not copy himself and does not behave or respond in the same way to different people. The "river passage" is an indirect thwarting of his students' expectation: to extract reiteratable lessons from their Master. In a changing world, each has to experience, to *become*, his own change, and respond in his own way, realizing and concretizing patterns through personalization. One has to drink their own water.

Confucius's remark in the "river passage" is a silent subversion of dogmatism and of his own image as an unquestionable authority. His statement can serve as an indirect warning against surrendering oneself to the comfort of generalization, fixed prescriptions of moral conduct, or copiable behaviors. In broader terms, the "river passage" is also a silent subversion of conventional opinions regarding the important things in life: fame, beauty, wealth. In a world that changes as the river flows, all desired states or goods are bound to disappear, and any attachment to them is not only futile but also harmful. Just as the river does what rivers do without expecting artists to paint it or poets to celebrate it, but also without fearing that it might go unnoticed, so Confucius stresses how not caring about others' opinions is the sign of the *junzi* 君子, the exemplary person; and it is a sign of the Master himself. We can sense his "indifference" in this specific passage, where he spontaneously utters a phrase that is not addressed to anyone. He almost seems like he is talking to himself; as if something had been bothering him all the way to the river and he offered an answer to his own self without caring about whether there was an audience or whether someone was taking down notes. In this way, Confucius also silently subverts the conventions of communication and descriptive or referential language. He is not describing the river—what is there to describe?—nor is he referring to the transitoriness of life using an allegory. In a sense, Confucius's remark could be seen as purposeless; his words do not stand for some hidden truth that underlies deceptive reality. Confucius *is* that reality and thus unintentionally invites others to experience themselves *as* that reality, as well. Paradoxically, being that changing reality himself, and thus subverting his own image and his students' expectations for a stable source of authority, Confucius creates his own unique, but also shared and intelligible, terms of a new normativity—a standing by the river of change.

Ironic Critique and Self-Critique

季文子三思而後行。子聞之，曰：「再，斯可矣。」

> Ji Wenzi only took action after thinking about it three times.
> On hearing of this, the Master said, "Twice would suffice."[8]

For He Yan 何晏 (d. 249), Confucius's remark is a praise to Ji Wenzi's efficaciousness (*de* 德) (He 2016: 47), while Zhu Xi 朱熹 (d. 1200), along similar lines, also interprets it as praise for thinking things over and not acting in a rash way. Thinking about something three times can puzzle you; this is why the Master mocks this behavior (*ji* 譏), as Zhu Xi notes. Thinking twice is being cautious, but one shouldn't overdo it. The *junzi* 君子 should "cherish decisiveness" (*gui guo duan* 貴果斷) (Zhu 2013: 65). Lin Yutang seems justified to observe that "the characterization of Confucius completely changed at the hands of Neo-Confucian interpreters, who refused to recognize the pranks and light-heartedness that abound in his texts" (Lin 1967). Fu Peirong 傅佩榮 also seems to miss out on the irony and takes Confucius's words literally; for Fu, *san si* 三思 ("thinking over three times") means cautiousness, but thinking too much might mean too much hesitance and missing out on an opportunity. *Zai* 再 ("twice") here could mean that one has to think: Do I need to do this? How should I go about it? Commenting on Confucius's remark in terms of adherence to ritual behavior (*li* 禮), Katrin Froese does not fail to recognize it as ironic:

> Since *li* constitutes a particularly human way of integrating ourselves into the cosmos, there are ample opportunities for blunders to occur. Human beings often are not as flexible as is warranted, and Confucius interjects humour to remind us of this. In fact, the ritualistic behaviour that he appears to hold in high esteem is sometimes deflated through irony, particularly when he believes that *li* is part of a self-righteous social display or represents exaggerated punctiliousness. Confucius mocks Ji Wenzi, known for his earnestness in ritual manners, for only taking action "after thinking about it three times." (2014: 298)

Drawing on Froese's reading, I argue that Confucius's irony in this case is not simply mockery at a specific individual's ignorance, but a broader critique against the ossification and dogmatization of a set of rules of conduct. Unlike the mystical figure of Confucius that Li Zehou saw in Yan Hui's expression of puzzlement, what we have here is a Confucius who, to the contrary, demystifies: he critiques not only past knowledge (Ji Wenzi died thirteen years before Confucius was born), but, generally, blind, conventionalized, and uncritical admiration of moral exemplars. The Master is in a certain way demystifying men and numbers. The number three (thinking over things three times before acting) is not the magic number that guarantees efficaciousness.[9] He is also, however, subtly self-critical. Demystifying exemplars and numbers (moral recipes), he also demystifies himself as a model for his students. This is not to say that he denounces or is not aware of his role as a model for others. This is the man who proclaimed that "strolling in the company of two"[10] he is bound to find a teacher.

Confucius is thus fully aware of his role not only as a teacher in his professional capacity, but mainly perhaps as a teacher for anyone, at any occasion, and at any time, present or future, in a similar way that men of old served, positively or negatively, as timeless examples for Confucius himself and his contemporaries. However, Confucius is reluctant to contain his teaching in repeatable rules that magically effect the desired result. It is in fact from the mouth of Zengzi, not of the Master, that we receive two "rules of three."[11] Confucius's critique of Ji Wenzi's inflexibility is ironic because he is saying the opposite of what he means: he is replacing one number ("three") for another ("two"), because he wants to think and encourage others to think beyond numbers. He is talking in numbers because he does *not* want to talk in numbers. We might also say that this ironic, indirect critique is Confucius's way of picking his audience and mentally "winking" at those who have ears to hear his silently subversive lesson: reflecting (*si* 思) before acting has as many chances to be valuable as it has to be mechanized and useless.

At 9.2 of the *Analects* we find one more instance of Confucius's ironic, subtle critique, and silent lesson in critique and self-critique.

達巷黨人曰：「大哉孔子！博學而無所成名。」
子聞之，謂門弟子曰：「吾何執？執禦乎？執射乎？吾執禦矣。」

A villager from Daxiang said, "How grand is Confucius! He is broad in his learning, and yet he is not renowned in any particular area." The Master on hearing of this, said to his disciples, "What should I specialize in? Perhaps charioteering? Or maybe archery? No, I think I'll take charioteering."[12]

In He Yan's commentary, the passage is explained as an example of Confucius's humility (*qian zhi shen yi* 謙之甚矣) in the way he turns and asks his disciples which art he should take. Among the six arts, he chooses the one that is considered inferior—charioteering. Zhu Xi offers a brief discussion on *bo xue* 博學 (broad learning) which does not acquire a specific name/fame (*ming* 名); it cherishes vastness and thus does not take the name of any one of the arts. Along similar lines with He Yan, Zhu Xi reads Confucius's remark as a humble response to praise. He decides to take up an art that is considered inferior (charioteering), while the villager recognizes the Master's broad learning, but laments the fact that he has not gained fame for himself. Fu Peirong understands "not renowned in any particular area" (*wu suo cheng ming* 無所成名) as an expression of praise, otherwise Kongzi would not be called "grand" (*da* 大). Most people excel in one art, but Confucius has wide-ranging learning and cannot be given any specialty. Choosing charioteering, he reveals his humility and admonishes people to acquire real ability and learning (*zhen cai shi xue* 真才實學). We can agree with Fu's emphasis on a kind of "real learning" that cannot be reduced to the acquisition of a specific skill. But what is the content of that learning?

At 5.20 mentioned earlier, what we found was a critique of formalized morality. Confucius gives an affirmative reply ("Twice would suffice"), when his intention is to negate any equation of "three" or "two" or any number of times of reflecting to efficaciousness. The Master is thus ironic in his confirmation of what he actually wants to negate. At 9.20 he seems to be doing something similar. According to a literal reading, Confucius is affirming the villager's understanding of *bo xue* as a means of making a name for oneself, and making a name for oneself as the expected outcome of *bo xue*. His ironic affirmation, however, is actually a negation of such a formula for the learned man. Confucius expresses fake eagerness to take up charioteering exactly because he is in fact against taking up any art with a specific *li* 利 (benefit or profit) in mind. Through his irony, the Master, once more critiques mechanization of behavior: there is no direct causation between learning broadly and acquiring anything really. There seems to be nothing more important for Confucius than learning. He is a fervent learner himself, he finds great joy in learning, he admonishes others to learn, and he refers to present and past exemplary learners. But nowhere in the *Analects* do we find a formula of the sort "Learn, so that … ." The benefits of learning cannot be sought after. Learning, or the love of learning (*hao xue* 好學), as a kind of love, cannot be rationally explained or understood and pursued for its benefits. We don't love others "because …," nor do we love them "so as to … ." To the contrary; the absence of reasons and reasoning or calculation are necessary conditions for any genuine feeling of affection toward anything or anyone. In this sense, Confucius's ironic response is a critique of those who establish causal relations between their feelings (in this case, love of learning) and some sought-after gain. What he proposes instead is an "irrational" or a-rational understanding of learning as love and devotion to which we would be willing to give our every waking moment without knowing exactly why, and without expecting anything. In the same way we would reach out to grab the child about to fall in the well, without expecting the parents' praise or fearing their hatred. Whatever is to come out of learning—goodness of character, fame, or simply joy—self-emerges spontaneously. *It just happens.*

Confucius's reversal of the villager's conventional perception of learning and achievement can also be read as subtly self-critical. There are many instances in the *Analects* testifying to the fact that, in his middle age, the Master felt he was a complete failure. "He died … almost surely believing his life had been, on the whole, politically and practically worthless" (Ames and Rosemont 1999: 4). Is the villager in the above passage confirming Confucius's failure and, according to a common understanding, confirming the uselessness of learning when it brings no gains in the form of fame and wealth? Probably he is. With his ironic response, however, the Master seems to reverse such an understanding and actually offers another silent and paradoxical lesson for those who can hear it: the only "useful" kind of learning is learning that remains "useless." In this sense, Confucius may have had his moments of utter disappointment, and may have not enjoyed the influence he wished to gain with rulers, but, ultimately, at the end of the day, he always remained the passionate lover of learning who would not mind dying at dusk, having learned and trodden the Way at dawn. The ironic Confucius, subverting his own image as an unquestionable authority and a source of moral prescriptions, paradoxically emerges as the most reliable authority on the most important questions in human life, as much for his contemporaries as for us today. Being critical and self-critical, Confucius remains open to critique himself, depriving us of the security of readymade answers and the comfort of unquestionable dogma.

Conclusion

A minority of scholars have not failed to recognize and appreciate Confucius less as a model of superhuman perfection than as an imperfect, erring, ironically critical, and self-critical man with an acute sense of humor. Drawing on and inspired by the ironic and humorous, they see the "living and breathing" Master who takes hardship with a smile, "singing in the rain" (Lin Yutang); the unsagely, unceremonious, and spontaneous Confucius with an "irony that verges towards the sarcastic" (Harbsmeier); the sage who is also an "entirely human partner on a quest" (Ames and Rosemont); and the man of self-deprecating humor and irony who takes rituals seriously *because* he is ready to take them in jest (Froese). I have tried to explore the philosophical implications of Confucius's irony as the critical response to a paradoxical reality of change. Attuning with constantly changing circumstances, Confucius has to change himself, remaining critical, self-critical, and silently subversive. Irony is his response to paradoxicality—"taking a standing" (*li* 立) in the midst of change—but also subtle critique and silent subversion of non-change: the ossification and dogmatization of his teaching. Moreover, the ironic hermeneutic could be further explored to excitingly raise and sustain a broader question for us today: What does it mean to be Confucian?

Notes

1. For instance, in *Analects* 9.13: Zigong said, "We have an exquisite piece of jade here—should we box it up and put it away for safekeeping, or should we try to get a good price and sell it off? The Master replied, "Sell it! By all means, sell it! I am just waiting for the right price!" (Ames and Rosemont, trans., 1999: 129). (Page numbers refer to the Ames and Rosemont edition of the *Analects*; all passages from the *Analects* are taken from or modified according to this edition.)
2. Roger Ames, Academie du Midi "Critique and Subversion" Conference, May 2018; personal communication.
3. *Analects* 9.17, Ames and Rosemont (1999: 130); translation modified.
4. *Analects* 18.8, Ames and Rosemont (1999: 216); "But I am different from all these people in that I do not have presuppositions as to what may and may not be done" (我則異於是，無可無不可).
5. *Analects* 9.11, Ames and Rosemont (1999: 128–9).
6. *Analects* 15.16, Ames and Rosemont (1999: 188); "There is nothing that I can do for someone who is not constantly asking himself: 'What to do? What to do?'" (不曰'如之何如之何'者，吾末如之何也已矣).
7. *Analects* 2.12, Ames and Rosemont (1999: 78); "Exemplary persons (*junzi* 君子) are not mere vessels" (君子不器).
8. *Analects* 5.20, Ames and Rosemont (1999: 100).
9. It could be argued that Confucius himself seems to insist on "the power of three" when it comes to how many years one should mourn for their dead parents (17.21 and 4.20). This question falls outside the scope of this chapter, but it could be noted in brief that Confucius's objection to Zai Wo in the oft-quoted passage is not explainable in terms of his insistence on strict observance of *li*; in other words, not in terms of

what *is* right, but in terms of what *feels* right (*an* 安) and about assuming the right attitude to learning and observing *li*.
10   *Analects* 7.22, Ames and Rosemont (1999: 116).
11   *Analects* 1.4 and 8.4, Ames and Rosemont (1999: 72, 121); Master Zeng daily examines his person "on three counts"; "there are three things that exemplary persons (*junzi* 君子) consider of utmost importance in making their way (*dao* 道)."
12   *Analects* 9.2, Ames and Rosemont (1999: 126).

References

Ames, Roger T., and Henry Rosemont Jr. (1999), *The Analects of Confucius: A Philosophical Translation*. New York: Random House.
Froese, Katrin (2014), "The Comic Character of Confucius." *Asian Philosophy* 24(4): 295–312.
Fu Peirong 傅佩榮 (2012), *Lunyu Yijie* 論語譯解. Beijing: Dongfang chubanshe.
Guthrie, William K. C. (1971), *Socrates*. Cambridge: Cambridge University Press.
Hall, David L., and Roger T. Ames (1987), *Thinking through Confucius*. Albany: State University of New York Press.
Harbsmeier, Christoph (1990), "Confucius Ridens: Humor in *The Analects*." *Harvard Journal of Asiatic Studies* 50(1): 131–61.
He Yan (2016), *Lunyu Zhushu* 论语注疏. Beijing: Zhongguo zhigong chubanshe.
Li Zehou (2017), *Lunyu jin du* 论语今读. Beijing: Zhonghua shuju.
Lin Yutang (1941), "Confucius Singing in the Rain." In *With Love and Irony*. London: William Heinemann.
Lin Yutang (1967), *Lun Kongzi de youmou* 论孔子的幽默. www.360doc.com/content/13/0510/15/4775778_284401726.shtml, accessed June 1, 2020..
Zhu Xi (2013), *Lunyu Daxue Zhongyong Jizhu* 论语 大学 中庸 集注. Shanghai: Shanghai guji chubanshe.

6

Efficacious Subversion: Argument by Relegation in Chan Buddhism

Andrew K. Whitehead

The following chapter examines the unique strengths of a Chan Buddhist model of critique that is borne out of distinct conceptions of world and of persons as articulated by select thinkers in the Chan Buddhist tradition. My approach is cross-cultural and comparative in nature insofar as I identify a Chan Buddhist model of critique, draw on contemporary problems, and refer back, explicitly as well as implicitly, to particular existential-phenomenological discussions of habituation, embodiment, and experience. This approach is meant to highlight the aptness of Chan Buddhist philosophy as a meaningful paradigm for rethinking possible avenues of critique and subversion in a contemporary context.

In order to appreciate such aptness, I highlight the habituated realization and reification of the illusory or imagined for the sake of, and in the service of, what we might call "conventional intersubjective existence," that is, the habituated constitution of "the conventional world." My aim is to introduce and develop select sociopolitical strengths of Chan Buddhism in order to consider how we might go about critiquing and subverting deficient and defective social institutions in a contemporary setting from a Chan Buddhist perspective. In this sense, the chapter elaborates upon the transitory nature of conventional reality and how its openness, or "emptiness," can be understood as facilitating an efficacious practice by which to initiate critique and undertake subversion. To this end, I attempt a Chan Buddhist account of rehabituation, such that meaning is understood in the light of the givenness of world, as a correlationally constituted validity, and can be fundamentally altered through the critical philosophical attitude, owing to its openness/emptiness.

In both Eastern and Western historical and cultural contexts, philosophy has been a vehicle for critiques of all kinds. Perhaps too often, such critiques have aspired to a degree of certainty and finality, seeking to provide the last word on a given matter through the annihilation of an opposing position. Despite this tendency, critiques and the findings borne from them, no matter how successful they might seem, must not be allowed to develop into dogmatism—that is, to become sedimented and ossified in a way that prohibits or precludes critical self-reflection; to become the established worldview, the conventional world. In those instances in which they do become dogmatic, we are called to subvert once more. There would seem to be a greater degree of honesty, as well as critical flexibility, afforded by a form of philosophical argumentation that leaves room for the necessary partiality of its own position, even if it should take its own unique partiality as superior in describing the state of affairs at hand. For this reason, I find that one of the most enticing aspects of Chan Buddhism is the rather clear articulation of what might be called a Chan model for critique and critical engagement, a distinct model of argumentation that is perpetually self-undermining as always also a showing of its own (in-)accuracy.

It is worth noting at this point why it is that we should care to consider different forms of argumentation at all. Owing to the current landscape of general and perpetual misinformation, there is a pressing need to broaden and extend our repertoire of critical tools and methods, if only to better address specific concrete issues and audiences as these are encountered on a case-by-case basis. In a variety of instances, what is called for in facing these issues is not a critique in the fashion of reasoned arguments—as in criticism for instance—but a critique in the fashion of critical self-reflection, in the sense provided by scholars such as Merleau-Ponty, and in the sense that it is advocated by Chan Buddhism in the form of practice.

As a first measure, it is perhaps best to explain how I am using the term "argument by relegation." I distinguish arguments by *relegation* from arguments by *refutation*. Concerning the latter, we can say that in using arguments by refutation, one aspires to refute the position of one's interlocutor. This form of argumentation has come to be associated with philosophical practice broadly, and it works to establish the superiority of a given position not only on the strength of its own merits but equally so on its successful eradication of alternative positions, counterexamples, and so forth. By contrast, arguments by *relegation* accept opposing positions as true, albeit only partly or partially true. Arguments by relegation often appear irenic and/or conciliatory. In adopting the relegational form, we might say that "there is a way in which" our interlocutor is correct, but the "correctness" of this position depends on another position, namely the position offered in opposition. It is even the case that some instances in which the "correctness" of a given position, in having failed to appreciate how it is correct, is in fact precisely made possible by a counterposition. More often than not, a relegational argument is developed in such a way that it reflexively draws attention to its own partiality, developed in such a way that it undermines the authority garnered in the very demonstration of its superiority.

With this in mind, I have worked to research and discover instances of argument by relegation, and to document in what contexts these forms arise, and how they are practiced. It is perhaps worth noting that in my research to date I have yet to discover examples of argument by relegation in any school of philosophy that does not adopt some form or other of correlationalism. What I mean here by correlationalism is a view whereby relationality is taken as originary, as that out of which discrete existents are thought to *become*, and this in a way that is specific to the relation that gives way to them. Things and persons are believed to be nonessential in nature, that is, to be correlationally constituted. Most recently, I have been documenting different forms of such arguments in the works of Edmund Husserl (especially the later Husserl) and Merleau-Ponty (especially the earlier Merleau-Ponty), both of whom also adopt correlationalism at least to some extent in their phenomenological understandings of self and world. Husserl's presentation of a number of different positions in *The Crisis of the European Sciences and Transcendental Philosophy*, for example, is representative of a most apt practice of argument by relegation. The positions of Galileo and Descartes, in this instance, are shown to be partial, and are engaged with a generous attempt to articulate how these positions have come to be developed and in what ways one can understand them as legitimately entertained. Having accounted for these positions, Husserl then shows precisely how they require a turn to transcendental phenomenology in order to sufficiently found the necessary questions. In this way, Husserl's approach subverts these opposing positions without annihilating them. In highlighting the limits of an interlocutor's position and the superiority of one's own position, there is no need to annihilate it.[1]

The most significant instance of argument by relegation I have discovered, for our purposes here, has been in the cases of Chan Buddhist masters and the historiographical and hagiographic literatures surrounding their teachings. I would go so far as to say that one of the strongest aspects of Chan critique, in my opinion, rests in its practice of argument by relegation. While I readily concede that there are far more obvious and equally more accessible examples of argument by relegation in other schools of Buddhism, for example, in reference to Japanese masters, using either Kūkai's "Ten Mindsets" or Dōgen's understanding of "intertwining," I nonetheless find many reasons for turning to examples from Chinese Chan Buddhism, not least of which is the impressive means adopted for argumentative performances on the part of Chan masters.

While it is true that arguments by relegation are often in linguistic argumentative form, in the case of Chan we find a distinct turn toward *performative showings* of a position and its superiority. Cases of the Chan Buddhist masters can be taken as particular instances of this type of argumentative showing, as performances that arguably are facilitated all the more by the conceptions of self and world entertained in Chan Buddhism, as well as the various "language-games" played by such masters. The modalities of communicating in the context of Chan must be sufficiently understood in order to assess the argumentative forms undertaken as well as their successes in relegating the other's position.

From a Chan standpoint, the means adopted for dispelling the illusions of self and world begin from the premise that these exist, at least in a conventional or illusory or imagined sense. That being said, no Chan position can entertain an understanding of the self (or the conventional world in which it is located) that is not in line with the theories of inter- or codependent origination and correlationalism. The idea of an autonomous, independent, and non-relational existence is incompatible with the Buddhist worldview. This is equally true of all phenomena, including the self. This relational dependence extends in this same fashion to include the partiality and necessary limitation of any given vantage-point or articulation of the state of affairs at hand; and it extends to any given position the self might hold or argue in favor of.

We might therefore consider how the person is contextually reified and objectified out of a specific relation; consider how the self is encountered in conventional reality.

As any given moment, the self is reified and objectified out of a specific relation (i.e., it is discovered in situ as a correlationally constituted person) as a role, in virtue of the conventional truth (the relational discrimination) of the self being precisely this role, a truth that validates and confirms that the self (the roled activity) corresponds to its reference and is therefore, situationally, the person of the role. This is how the self appears in conventional reality: as activity (to greater or lesser degrees) in accordance with the relational context in which it is discovered. In a movement away from the intellectualization of reality, a number of Chan texts offer discussions on the no-self doctrine that are *existential* as opposed to *epistemological* or *psychological*. They demonstrate that the self exists only relationally, in specific situations, and often in seemingly pre-established roles. The human self is therefore a relational being of engagements, and it is understood as existing as a specific *person* occupying a specific position in the context of the relation in which it finds itself. Existentially, no-thing exists independently. This remains the case, not only with regard to the self but also with regard to all things conventionally existent. In other words, engagements in conventional worlds are the relations that occasion the illusory reifications of self and other. The Chan use of the no-self doctrine, as a use of "skillful means," undermines these relations, thereby disrupting the operations by which conventionally distinct entities arise. In this sense, conventional worlds consist of relational being, and all distinct discriminations are determined in and by the relational context. In accordance with Chan, the no-self doctrine, like the doctrine of the emptiness of emptiness, must be read in light of the insistence on practice for the sake of liberation from attachments. It is a soteriological tool with which to disrupt the conventional worlds and their contexts in order to show no-thing. In this sense, it is a methodological tool, but a methodological tool not unlike Husserl's *épochè*, at least insofar as it is a method that reflexively discovers in its findings the validity of its presumptions. In the case of Chan, all selves stand in relation, as relation, to all others in the context of their conventional world.

In the *Recorded Sayings of Huangbo*, we read: "One day Huangbo ascended the pulpit, and as soon as monks were gathered, the master took up his staff and drove them all out" (Suzuki 1949: 301). Huangbo's behavior in this instance is a means of pointing out how individuals act in accordance with their conventionally real position within a relation, and of disrupting these contextual reifications by negating this position. In this sense, the relational being of all parties is thrown into relief, and a new relation is established through active engagement. By coming to be aware of the emptiness of the self, the context is emptied, the relation is emptied; but this emptying, as the double negation, reaffirms itself as a relational reality. In this sense relations, denoting a particular contextual engagement in which conventionally real entities arise, are able to perpetually shift and reaffirm the relational existence of engagements. Conventionally, persons are these engagements. Without a self, the person becomes an expressive discrimination of the relational. According to Thomas Kasulis: "From the [Chan] perspective, the person does not perform action; rather, action performs the person" (Kasulis 1987: 139). Out of relational engagements, as contexts in conventional worlds, distinct individuals appear to stand in relation to one another. In this way, action performs the person, and activity performs the world.

Whether one takes oneself or an object of the world as a starting point, owing to the correlational constitution of both, the undermining of one accomplishes the undermining of the other. We might here think on Bodhidharma, who is said to have directed adepts to search within themselves and nowhere else, lambasting reliance on anything beyond personal experience, rejecting any other authority, even scripture and religious leaders (himself included). He writes:

> Even if you can explain thousands of sutras and shastras, unless you see your own nature yours is the teaching of a mortal, not a buddha. The true Way is sublime. It can't be expressed in language. Of what use are scriptures? But someone who sees his own nature finds the Way, even if he can't read a word. ... A buddha can't be found in words. (Red Pine 1987: 29)

In the same vein, and again, owing to correlationalism, we can say that it is as the Buddha, and nowhere else, that one exists. It is as the world, and nowhere else, that one exists. It is as one's own consciousness, and nowhere else, that the world exists. We find Bodhidharma taking up scriptures and lambasting dependence on them, working toward the radical realization of what the scriptures themselves speak to. There is a point reached in practice where the practice itself becomes an obstacle to overcome. Chan, as the self-proclaimed practice-focused school of Buddhism, can at times be understood to show this paradoxical moment at which practice arrives at the need for not-practice, to highlight the partiality and limitation of the dharma in its linguistic and scriptural form. To know and understand the texts of the Buddhist canon does not replace the experience the canon aspires to describe. Failing to be able to rely on words and letters, Chan masters are depicted as showing rather than saying, depictions which vary from the comical, to the grotesque, to the compassionate.

It is the openness/emptiness undergirding the conventional world, and the practice of showing instead of explaining, that are, I believe, at the heart of the potency of Chan for the sake of critique and subversion.

We can consider Bodhidharma's engagement with his predecessors and contemporaries, in regard to correct practice, relegational. Against adherents to the idea that one must practice in the seclusion of the meditation halls, Bodhidharma says that "not thinking about anything is zen. Once you know this, walking, standing, sitting, or lying down, everything you do is zen" (Red Pine 1987: 49). In light of correlationalism, the practice of Chan, as the practice of emptiness, is not dependent on particular phenomena for the sake of insight—if it were, this would consist in falsely reifying an illusory hierarchy of illusory conventional entities. To the extent that this is true, however, there is a way in which Bodhidharma's interlocutors' position is true, as the insistence on practice, regardless of the phenomena involved, and therefore including those available in meditation hall practices, holds the possibility of insight. But this is the case precisely because *any* phenomenon holds this possibility, and one ought therefore to open up the practice beyond the meditation halls. Each position is left intact, accounted for, and yet there is evidentiary consensus on the superiority of one of the positions.

We can again consider the figure of Mazu:

He [Mazu] was residing in the monastery Dembōin where he sat constantly in meditation. The master, aware that he was a vessel of the Dharma, went to him and asked, "Virtuous one, for what purpose are you sitting in meditation?"

Daoyi answered: "I wish to become a Buddha."

Thereupon the master picked up a tile and started rubbing it on a stone in front of the hermitage.

Daoyi asked: "What is the Master doing?"

The master replied: "I am polishing [this tile] to make a mirror."

"How can you make a mirror by polishing a tile?" exclaimed Daoyi.

"And how can you make a Buddha by practicing zazen?" countered the master. (Dumoulin 2005: 163)

Here too we find a practice of argument by relegation in the performative vein. There is a way in which the position of Daoyi is true: Buddhist practice is the correct path and ought to be pursued with some zeal; but this truth of correctness is itself conventional. We should, as the *Keitoku dentōroku* summarizes Mazu's position, "not cling to good; ... not reject evil! If you cling to neither purity nor defilement you come to know the emptiness of the nature of sin" (Dumoulin 2005: 164). In this way, we can better appreciate the relegational position of certain Chan figures, insofar as they highlight the phenomenal realm—the realm of conventional reality—and its emptiness/openness, so as to better evidence, through a performative showing, that their position can better account for and afford that of their interlocutors, if only owing to greater breadth.

Perhaps more significantly, we can better appreciate the force of argument by relegation as a general form. Side-stepping the typical butting of heads that so often accompanies argumentation, the relegational form invites the interlocutor to entertain both positions as relationally constituted in the first place. In other words, a common ground is indicated by correlationalism, at least insofar as our situation implicates one another in one and the same lifeworld. This lifeworld in common makes possible the recognition of the mutual entanglement of partial positions owing to intrinsic relatedness, and this mutual entanglement, in turn, evidences the extent to which it is necessary for one to appreciate one's relation to the interlocutor, and thereby relate to him or her. This is significant insofar as engaging an interlocutor beyond a knee-jerk reaction of an outright and unquestioned defense of their position is the first step toward a constructive dialogue. In many ways, the relegational form invites (which sounds better than compels) an interlocutor to consider alternative positions, and thereby, through a critical self-awareness, to consider their own prejudicial biases and how these come to inform their position. This is not to say that an interlocutor will abandon their position, but instead that they will, at the very least, be forced to contend with an understanding of their position as afforded only by virtue of another position, which may or may not be diametrically at odds with their own. Gradually, this kind of critical and self-reflexive analysis, as it becomes a habit, comes to inform the very position being considered in the first place.

To the extent that this is the case, we discover in Chan Buddhist performative practices of argument by relegation a demonstration of alternatives that can itself become the impetus and outcome of a radical rehabituation, such that our critiques can bring about the very subversion we aspire to.

Note

1 Husserl's engagement with other philosophers is similarly characterized by the same relegational attitude. See, for example, the treatment of Descartes in the *Cartesian Meditations* or of Kant in the *Crisis*. Husserl's interlocutors are always right about something, albeit not entirely so in the end.

References

Blofeld, J. E. C., trans. (1994), *The Zen Teaching of Huang Po*. New York: Grove/Atlantic.
Dumoulin, Heinrich (2005), *Zen Buddhism: A History*, vol.). Bloomington, IN: World Wisdom.
Husserl, Edmund, and David Carr, trans. (1970), *The Crisis of European Sciences and Transcendental Phenomenology*. Evanston, IL: Northwestern University Press.
Husserl, Edmund, and Dorion Cairns, trans. (1977), *Cartesian Meditations*. Dordrecht, NL: Kluwer Academic.
Kasulis, Thomas P. (1987), *Zen Action Zen Person*. Honolulu: University of Hawai'i Press.
Red Pine, trans. (1987), *The Zen Teaching of Bodhidharma*. New York: North Point Press.
Suzuki, D. T. (1949), *Essays in Zen Buddhism*. New York: Grove Press.

7

Scolding the Buddhas, Abusing the Patriarchs: An Outlook on the Subversive Hermeneutics of Chan, through Case Four of the *Blue Cliff Record*

Rudi Capra

The pedagogy of Chan Buddhism relies on a binary trend: on the one hand, it requires careful study and active participation in formalized rituals and ceremonies; on the other hand, it requires the simultaneous emancipation from such means and practices, since the transmission of the truth has the character of suddenness and immediacy. In other words, the subversion of standard doctrinal interpretations and ordinary pedagogical strategies is itself an essential part of Chan training.

This chapter analyzes the fourth Case of the *Blue Cliff Record*, which exemplifies in a bright fashion the self-negating dialectics of Chan pedagogy. First, the analysis focuses on the narrated event; second, it moves at the level of meta-narrative, focusing on glosses and commentary. The purpose is to show that the subversive hermeneutics of Chan take place at both levels, narrative and meta-narrative, demanding (and favoring) a proactive and critical progression toward understanding.

Chan Buddhism and the Praxis of Subversion

The earliest texts of Chinese philosophy already display a peculiar fondness for the apophatic stance. We are told, for instance, that "if it can be specified as a Dao, it is not a permanent Dao" and that the Dao is "constantly without name" (Moeller 2007: §1, §32). The tradition of Chan (together with Japanese Zen) pursues this negative rhetoric to the extent that its teachings are often enclosed within an endlessly circling dialectics, in which whatever is asserted must be immediately disowned, negated, canceled out, performing in a certain sense a "perpetual iconoclasm" (Arntzen 1979: 10).

The fact is that the pedagogy of Chan is characterized by a self-undermining trend: if, on the one hand, Chan students are required to pursue a zealous study and comply with strict regulations, on the other hand, they are encouraged to maintain (and train) a flexible, intuitive mindset. In fact, Chan does not involve the abjuration of sacred scriptures—as some interpretations have suggested in the past (Wang 2003). Rather, Chan emphasizes that studying is not a *sufficient* condition for seeing one's true nature, as the transmission of truth occurs directly, from mind to mind. Like any other religious tradition that has developed within the context of monastic institutions, the history of Chan includes codes, rules and regulations, formalized rituals and practices, recognized hierarchical structures, and a wide range of codified pedagogical means and strategies (Foulk 1999: 220).[1] In this light, the notorious advice "Do not rely on words and letters" does not imply a rejection of pedagogic mediations, but rather warns of the futility of relying on them for the purpose of awakening.[2]

Likewise, this formative process of learning represents, in relation to Chan practice, both a necessary condition and a likely hindrance, because the cultivation of speculative thinking implies a serious risk to fostering the action of "karmic consciousness" (*yeshi* 業識).[3] Karmic consciousness is naturally "discriminating" (*jianze* 揀擇), since it keeps the student distant from the opportunity for experiencing "insight" (*jianxing* 見性).[4] For this reason, Chan masters developed a broad array of pedagogical means that aim at deconstructing the degree of certainty acquired throughout the learning process. As erudition and emulation do not ensure emancipation, students need to compensate for the natural action of karmic consciousness by "cutting off" (*duan* 斷) the stream of consciousness. Hence, the pioneering use of the controversial "shock techniques" that became a paradigmatic feature of Chan lore: shouting, hitting, recourse to paradox and negation, and even joking and playing.

In other words, Chan teachings imply a relentless self-subversion, because the theoretical side of training is backed up by a wide range of deconstructive pedagogical means, the purpose of which is preventing recourse to rational thought, thus bringing the mind to a psychological impasse in which no logic can be applied. Then, the student has the opportunity to demonstrate understanding, and the master has the opportunity to evaluate the degree and the authenticity of that understanding within the agonistic field of "dharma-battles" (*fazhan* 法戰).

Indeed, as the violation of the ritual is gradually integrated into the praxis, the anti-ritualistic side of Chan training becomes in its turn ritualized, subsumed into a wider dialectic of education and subversion that, once it has reached a certain degree of stability, necessitates novel shocks and disruptions, to which the pedagogical trend will gradually adapt, reigniting the whole process. Curiously, the overall pattern is displayed in a short parable by Franz Kafka:

> Leopards break into the temple and drink to the dregs what is in the sacrificial pitchers; this is repeated over and over again; finally, it can be calculated in advance, and it becomes a part of the ceremony. (1969, 93)

Case Four: Main Case

In particular, Case Four of the *Blue Cliff Record* offers a brilliant exemplification of such ritual praxis of anti-ritualistic subversion. Still today, the *Blue Cliff Record* (*biyan lu* 碧巖錄) stands among the most influential and significant texts in the history of

Chan Buddhism. It is, as several collections of gongans, an original product of Chinese Buddhism, an unprecedented evolution of the *yulu* ("recorded sayings") genre. In particular, the text gained rapid and wide diffusion after its first edition, to the extent that it was emulated in China, Korea, and Japan, and became a standard scripture for Japanese Zen (Sekida 1996). The hundred gongans of the collection, selected and commented on at first by the monk and poet Xuedou Chongxian 雪竇重顯 (980–1052) and later by Chan master Yuanwu Keqin 圜悟克勤 (1063–1135), inspired and instructed countless generations of students, to the extent that it earned the label of "premier Chan scripture" 禪門第一書 or 宗門第一書 (Heine 2016: 1).

Like several other gongans, Case Four narrates the encounter between two revered figures of the Chan tradition, which quickly degenerates.

> When Deshan arrived at Guishan, he carried his bundle with him into the teaching hall, where he crossed from east to west and from west to east. He looked around and said, "There's nothing, no one." Then he went out.
>
> But when Deshan got to the monastery gate, he said, "Still, I shouldn't be so coarse." So he re-entered (the hall) with full ceremony to meet (Guishan).
>
> As Guishan sat there, Deshan held up his sitting mat and said, "Teacher!"
>
> Guishan reached for his whisk, whereupon Deshan shouted, shook out his sleeves, and left. Deshan turned his back on the teaching hall, put on his straw sandals, and departed.
>
> That evening Guishan asked the head monk, "Where is that newcomer who just came?"
>
> The head monk answered, "At that time he turned his back on the teaching hall, put on his straw sandals, and departed."
>
> Guishan said, "Hereafter that lad will go to the summit of a solitary peak, build himself a grass hut, and go on scolding the Buddhas and reviling the Patriarchs." (Cleary and Cleary 2005: 22)[5]

The two contenders are a young Deshan (Deshan Xuanjian 德山宣鑑, 780–865) and a more experienced Guishan (Guishan Lingyou 潙山靈祐, 771–853). According to the records, Deshan was an insightful student and became a great and influential master, and in his prime, he expressed his understanding with a great deal of vigor and self-confidence (Sekida 1996: 156). In the present case, Deshan shows open disregard for the strict regulations that governed the entirety of monastic life. In this case, he intrudes into the lecture hall carrying a bundle, which was forbidden. Deshan's conduct is only apparently due to negligence; actually, his violations of the monastic code are meant to express the unrestrained freedom and carefreeness that mark the awakened mind. He intends to prove the authenticity of his awakening, although his provocative exhibition is unrequested and ultimately unjustified.[6] Yet, Guishan has the last word on this exchange: "Hereafter that lad will go to the summit of a solitary peak, build himself a grass hut, and go on scolding the Buddhas and reviling the Patriarchs."

Although Deshan appears to be merely negligent, his attitude conceals a specific purpose: proving his own awakening to his fellow monks. Nonetheless, he proves himself psychologically weak, since the attachment to the idea of awakening leads him to act unnaturally. Guishan sees through Deshan's impudence, suggesting with admiration that the lively fellow could one day "scold the Buddhas and revile the Patriarchs." Although Deshan's training is still unripe, Guishan sympathizes with Deshan's purposeful lack of discipline. On a metaphorical plane, the self-negating dialectics which undermines Chan practice is carried forward by both characters: Deshan strikes the mandatory adherence to the ritual protocol that governs every facet of Chan monastic institutions; Guishan aims at the most revered figures of Chan hagiography, Buddhas and Patriarchs. Leaving the agonistic field of the Dharma battle between Deshan and Guishan in the background, the gongan employs the subversive potential of irony to desecrate the sacred, discouraging mystical and intellectual speculations, preserving thus the authenticity of its transmission.

Case Four: Commentary, Capping Phrases

As noted by Steven Heine (2016), the *Blue Cliff Record* is at once a conservative and an innovative work in the context of Chan literature. Conservative, because it discusses a wide range of renowned themes and authors, contributing to their diffusion and relevance. Innovative, because it employs a multifaceted rhetoric composed by mutually reinforcing and contrasting verses (*songgu* 頌古) and capping phrases (*zhuoyu* 著語), along with evaluative commentaries (*pingchang* 評唱) that, according to Heine, always represent the most distinctive feature of the collection and, from a historical point of view, are its most durable and valuable legacy.

In his commentary on Case Four, Yuanwu tunes with the irreverent style of the gongan, recounting a famous anecdote on the life of Deshan. While he was a traveling monk, he asked an old woman for some fried cake to refresh his mind. The woman answered, "I will give you the cake if you answer my question. The *Diamond Sutra* says, 'Past mind cannot be grasped, present mind cannot be grasped, future mind cannot be grasped.' Which mind do you need to refresh?" Then, Deshan burned all the commentaries on the *Diamond Sutra* (Cleary and Cleary 2005: 24).

This kind of anecdote, featuring commoners who outwit and at times humiliate illustrious figures of the tradition, has the clear purpose of subverting the naïve depiction of a "sacred Chan" that would directly imply an ethical or metaphysical distinction with respect to the "mundane world." Complying with this rhetoric of self-desecration, Chan texts frequently offer puzzling advice such as "wash your bowl," which remind the listener (or the reader) that the experience of realizing one's true nature must not be pursued in an abstract world of concepts, but within the earthly core of everyday life.[7]

With the same advice in mind, Yuanwu writes in commenting on the case:

> Look at how the old adept Guishan meets him; he just sits there and observes the outcome. ... Even if someone overthrew his meditation seat and scattered his congregation with shouts, he wouldn't give it any notice. It is as high as heaven, broad as earth. ... Someone who can fulfil Buddhahood right where he stands

naturally kills people without blinking an eye; thus he has his share of freedom and independence. (Cleary and Cleary 2005: 26–9)

The image of killing without blinking an eye, like scolding Buddhas, reviling Patriarchs, burning commentaries, and so forth, responds to the necessity of overturning the natural sense of awe and admiration that marks the mental disposition of a Chan adept. It is easy to see, beyond these lines, an echo of the (in)famous advice given by Linji, "If you meet the Buddha, kill the Buddha" (*fengfo shafo* 逢佛殺佛), which exhorts Chan practitioners to get rid of all conceptions of "Patriarch," "Daruma," "Buddhahood," "holiness," and so forth.[8] In fact, the involuntary reification of such constructs may constitute a further hindrance on the way to awakening, as pointed out (once more) by Yuanwu in the commentary to Case Four: "In the Buddha Dharma there are not so many complications, where can you bring intellectual views to bear?" (Cleary and Cleary 2005: 25).

In the same commentary, attuning with the typical fondness of Chan writings for military jargon, Yuanwu proposes the "Flying General" Li Guang 飛將軍李廣 as a functional model for Chan training (Cleary and Cleary 2005: 29). Captured alive by the Huns, tied between two horses, he played half-dead until he found the right moment to spring up, overthrow the Hun rider, seize horse and weapons, and escape. Precisely this capacity to "shift and turn" (*zhuanshen* 轉身) adapting to circumstances, allowing one to "wrest life in the midst of death" (29), reflects the virtue of "genuine pretending" that Chan masters seek to transmit by means of their unconventional methods and metaphors.[9]

Hermeneutics as a Subversive Tool

Then, it should be clear that the practice of Chan, as envisaged by the *Blue Cliff Record*, includes hermeneutics as an essential task. Each person must engage the way with a challenging spirit, taking advantage of all means capable of bringing about the replication of the original experience of the Buddha. On this path, confrontation and interpretation are not contingent detours, but integral components of the practice. Thus, the quest for the retrieval of the "original meaning" of the Buddha's words acquires a soteriological dimension, as Buddha himself suggested:

> Like gold that is melted, cut, and polished,
> So should monks and scholars
> Analyze my words before accepting them,
> They should not do so out of respect.[10]

The relentless deconstruction of extemporaneous configurations of sense and meaning, as well as canonical symbols, sacred texts and figures, constitutes an integral part of the Buddhist path. The structural subversiveness envisioned by the hermeneutic quest is not opposed to, but ideally consonant with Chan training. The interpretation of a gongan case has no abstract value in itself, since the value has to be found in the process of interpretation, through which the interpreter, already unable to sit at the feet of the Buddha, is trying instead to find her/his own place within the hermeneutic circle through an interpretive effort.

In this regard, it is worth recalling Derrida's notion of *supplément*. In *Of Grammatology*, he writes:

> The supplement adds itself, it is a surplus, a plenitude enriching another plenitude, the fullest measure of presence. It cumulates and accumulates presence. ... But the supplement supplements. It adds only to replace. It intervenes or insinuates itself in-the-place-of; if it fills, it is as if one fills a void. If it represents and makes an image, it is by the anterior default of a presence. Compensatory and vicarious, the supplement is an adjunct, a subaltern instance which takes-(the)-place. (1967: 144–5)[11]

In other words, the *supplément* is at the same time an addition and a compensation for something that is no longer present. Therefore, what is absent and in need of compensation is the live word of the Buddha, his presence. What is added, and supplies this absence, is the infinite variety of interpretations and skillful means designed to help the students on their way to liberation, with the aim of replicating the Buddha's experience, which is the only criterion capable of confirming or denying the validity of such an interpretation.[12] Thus, as the *supplément* tends to reactualize the unsupplemented matrix, the Buddhist practice tends to replicate the original experience of the Buddha, supplementing his absence by favoring a creative, hermeneutic approach.

"Dead words" (*siju* 死句) must be turned back to life, and hermeneutics is the subversive tool that not only encourages but also subtends and allows this operation. Then, the subversion of the ritual becomes a *supplément* that adds to and replaces the ritual, a sort of *supplément*-ritual that is fundamentally formless, since the violation of conventional ritual forms can only be performed by resorting to an intuitive flair for creative expression. In this sense, gongan texts may be regarded as akin to movie scripts, as their inherent openness and their "playability" allow for creative detours from the textual trace and prepare the student for the delivery of a functional improvisation (Capra 2019: 39–44). In relation to this point, McRae proposed the definition of "liturgical skeletons" for gongan cases, since they provide a realistic scenario for the execution of an imaginative performance (McRae 2000: 71).

Indeed, as in music and acting, successful improvisation also depends on training, given the required knowledge of countless intratextual and intertextual references, doctrinal principles, monastic regulations, and so forth. After all, the *Blue Cliff Record* is purposely structured to evoke a polyphony of divergent voices, preventing the reduction to a univocal interpretation. Both the structure and the content of the collection converge toward this end: these several elements discourage recourse to mnemonic learning and literal reading, calling instead for an authentic hermeneutic effort capable of actualizing the meaning in relation to the interpreter.

Furthermore, it is important to note that even if a hypothetical listener would have been able to listen directly to the Buddha's words, we cannot be certain that the "original meaning" would have been perfectly transmitted, because there is no such thing as an original meaning or an original experience. A renowned quote of Gautama Buddha seems to discourage a similar quest, claiming "In my forty-nine years of teaching I did not preach even one word" (Sekida 1996: 384).[13] The Buddha's teaching is thus comparable to Wittgenstein's ladder, which must be put aside once climbed up.

Concluding Remarks: Subverting the Straight Teaching

An analysis of Case Four of the *Blue Cliff Record*, conducted on the edict (*benze* 本則) as well as on the commentary (*pingchang* 評唱), illustrates that the typical rhetoric of self-desecration that characterizes Chan literature on a narrative and meta-narrative level is an integral part of a process of subversive hermeneutics that is ultimately functional in progression on the way of Buddhism.

In fact, the creative reinterpretation, combined with the ironic demotion of apparently incontrovertible firm points, is one among several strategies of performative deconstruction of the theoretical apparatus to which Chan students are necessarily subject. In this perspective, the gesture of scolding the Buddhas and abusing the Patriarchs represents the unavoidable tendency of self-erasure within a tradition that predicates that all forms and manifestations are ultimately empty.

Nonetheless, since emptiness is precisely to be found within form (as stated in the *Heart Sutra*), it is obvious that the playful upheaval of provisional configurations of meaning must come through an act of mindful critique. In this respect the recourse to hermeneutics and its subversive action allows for an intuitive reappropriation of the complementary sides of Chan practice—or rather a relinquishing of all one-sided forms of discriminatory views. Chan master Yunmen Wenyan 雲門文偃 (864–949), in an additional couplet of puzzling Cases (Fourteen and Fifteen), addresses this complementarity through the predication of "a straight teaching" (*dui yishuo* 對一說), and "a subverted teaching" (*dao yishuo* 倒一說).[14]

Notes

1 Foulk writes: "It has often been asserted that the Chan school in medieval China eschewed reliance on Buddhist teachings handed down in sutras and commentarial literature, stressing instead an immediate, personal realization of awakening based on meditation practice and interaction with an accomplished spiritual guide—a Chan master. This characterization is not entirely groundless, but is more accurate as a description of Chan mythology and ideology than as an account of any actual state of affairs" (1999: 220).

2 The legendary quote ascribed to Bodhidharma is 不立文字 (*buli wenzi*). Lai (1985) translates this as "No postulation of any thesis in words" and Welter (2000) as: "Do not establish words and letters."

3 The Sanskrit term *karma* means "action." The Chinese character 業 (*ye*) implies that consciousness (*shi* 識) is already "active," "busy," and works as the source of all dualistic discriminations, often indicated in the *Blue Cliff Record* with the compound *jianze* 揀擇, which occurs thirty-eight times in the text. Cleary (2005) translates it as

"picking and choosing," Sekida (1996) as "choice and attachment." Another solution suggested by Sekida is "preference." Another possible solution is precisely the term "discrimination," which includes both the meanings of "ranking something over something else" and of "growing preferences and thus cultivating partiality."

4 For *jianxing* 見性, literally "seeing-essential nature," I mostly use the term "insight," because it preserves the impression of "seeing-within." Another possible translation is "realization."

5 Unless specified otherwise, all translated passages from the *Blue Cliff Record* are taken from the translation by Cleary and Cleary (2005); however, the names are transliterated throughout according to the most recent *pinyin* rendition.

6 A note by Yuanwu commenting on Deshan's attitude: "He has a lot of Chan, but what for?" (Cleary and Cleary 2005: 23).

7 Steven Heine (1999) describes this aspect using the more neutral term "demythological approach." The *Letters of Chan Master Dahui Pujue* (*Dahui Pujue chanshi shu* 大慧普覺禪師書) are far more explicit in stressing the necessity of cultivating Chan in everyday life and mundane occupations.

8 The motto is found in several sources. Of particular interest is *The Zen Teachings of Master Linji* by Burton Watson (1999: 52). A more integral passage from this source, which is relevant to the present topic, reads: "If you meet a Buddha, kill the Buddha. If you meet a patriarch, kill the patriarch. If you meet an arhat, kill the arhat. If you meet your parents, kill your parents. If you meet your kinfolk, kill your kinfolk. Then for the first time you will gain emancipation, will not be entangled with things, will pass freely anywhere you wish to go."

9 The philosophical significance of "genuine pretending," as well as its inherence in Daoist philosophy, is very well argued and illustrated in H. G. Moeller and P. D'Ambrosio (2017), *Genuine Pretending: On the Philosophy of the Zhuangzi*.

10 Robert Thurman has located the passage in Santaraksita's *Tattvasamgraha*, k. 3587. See Thurman (1984:190). Although there is no evidence that the quotation comes directly from a sutra ascribed to the Buddha, the Tengyur considers it to be canonical. Nagarjuna reiterates the concept in *Ratnavali* (IV 94–6):

> Just as grammarians
> Begin with reading the alphabet,
>
> The Buddha teaches doctrines
>
> That students can bear
>
> To some he teaches doctrines
>
> For the reversal of sin,
>
> To some, in order to win merit,
>
> To some, doctrines based on duality
>
> To some [he teaches doctrines] based on nonduality
>
> To some, the profound, frightening to the fearful,
>
> Having an essence of emptiness and compassion,
>
> The means of achieving highest enlightenment.

11 In the original passage (208): "Le concept de supplément … abrite en lui deux significations dont la cohabitation est aussi étrange que nécessaire. Le supplément s'ajoute, il est un surplus, une plénitude enrichissant une autre plénitude, le comble de la présence. … Mais le supplément supplée. Il ne s'ajoute que pour remplacer. Il intervient ou s'insinue à-la-place-de; s'il comble, c'est comme on comble un vide. S'il représente et fait image, c'est par le défaut antérieur d'une présence. Suppléant et vicaire, le supplément est un adjoint, une instance."
12 This thesis is very well-argued in Lamotte's (1993) "Assessment of Textual Interpretation in Buddhism."
13 Sekida (1996), *Blue Cliff Record*, commentary on Case 92.
14 My translation. The monk's question is "What is the Buddha's whole life teaching?" Yunmen's reply sounds like "A straight teaching" (舉僧問云門：「如何是一代時教？」雲門云：「對一說。」). The koan is one of the most complicated to translate and interpret, and pairs with Case Fifteen, in which Yunmen delivers a complementary and opposed reply, "A reverted (or, subverted; or, upside down) teaching" (倒一說).

References

Arntzen, Sonja (1979), *The Poetry of the Kyōunshū of Ikkyū Sōjun*. Vancouver: University of British Columbia.
Blue Cliff Record 碧巖錄 *biyan lu*. Chinese Buddhist Text Association. cbeta.org. BETA T.48.2003.
Blue Cliff Record 碧巖錄 *biyan lu* (2012), Zhengzhou: 中州古籍出版社有限公司.
Capra, Rudi (2019), "Raising Questions, Cutting Fingers: Chan Buddhism and the Cultivation of Creativity through Ritual Dialogues." *Culture and Dialogue* 7(1): 31–45.
Cleary, T., and J. C. Cleary, trans. (2005), *The Blue Cliff Record*. Boston, MA: Shambhala.
Derrida, Jacques (1967), *De la Grammatologie*. Paris: Minuit.
Foulk, Griffith (1999), "Sung Controversies Concerning the 'Separate Transmission' of Chan." In *Buddhism in the Sung*, edited by Peter Gregory and Daniel Getz. Honolulu: University of Hawaii Press.
Heine, Steven (1999), *Shifting Shape, Shaping Text: Philosophy and Folklore in the Fox Koan*. Honolulu: University of Hawaii Press.
Heine, Steven (2016), *Chan Rhetoric of Uncertainty in the* Blue Cliff Record: *Sharpening a Sword at the Dragon Gate*. New York: Oxford University Press.
Kafka, Franz (1969), *Parables and Paradoxes*. New York: Schocken Books.
Lai, Whalen (1985), "Ma-tsu Tao-i and the Unfolding of Southern Zen." *Japanese Journal of Religious Studies* 12(4): 173–92.
Lamotte, Étienne (1993), "The Assessment of Textual Interpretation in Buddhism." In *Buddhist Hermeneutics*, edited by Donald S. Lopez. Delhi: Motilal Banarsidass.
McRae, John (2000), "The Antecedents of Encounter Dialogue in Chinese Chan Buddhism." In *The Koan: Texts and Contexts in Zen Buddhism*, edited by Steven Heine and Dale S. Wright. New York: Oxford University Press.
Moeller, Hans-Georg, trans. (2007), *Daodejing. A Complete Translation and Commentary*. Chicago: Open Court.
Moeller, Hans-Georg, and Paul J. D'Ambrosio (2017), *Genuine Pretending: On the Philosophy of the Zhuangzi*. New York: Columbia University Press.

Sekida Katsuki, trans. (1996), "*The Blue Cliff Record* and Commentary." In *Two Zen Classics: Mumonkan, Hekiganroku*. New York: Weatherhill.
Thurman, Robert (1984), *Tsong-khapa's Speech of Gold in the Essence of True Eloquence*. Princeton, NJ: Princeton University Press.
Wang Youru (2003), *Linguistic Strategies in Daoist Zhuangzi and Chan Buddhism: The Other Way of Speaking*. London: Routledge Curzon.
Watson, Burton (1999), *The Zen Teachings of Master Lin-Chi*. New York: Columbia University Press.
Welter, Albert (2000), "Mahakasyapa's Smile: Silent Transmission and the Kung-an Tradition." In *The Koan: Texts and Contexts in Zen Buddhism*, edited by Steven Heine and Dale S. Wright, 75–109. New York: Oxford University Press.

Part Two

Sociopolitical Subversion

8

To Become the King of All under Heaven: Mengzi as a Strategist of Regime Subversion

Ting-mien Lee

Scholars of classical Chinese philosophy work primarily on texts composed and/or redacted during the Warring States period (480–221 BCE) and early imperial China (c. 221 BCE–8 CE). These texts were produced in a remote past about which little is known to us today, thus we are cognizant of the danger of not knowing the historical, linguistic, and philological facts that may be crucial for understanding the texts, and we are often reminded that the surviving literature does not permit a clear characterization of classical Chinese philosophy.[1] Such "ignorance" might be productive, in that it gives us room for experimenting with various possible readings of the texts. Thus, this is not always a serious danger as long as we are aware of it and are cautious with the limitation of our interpretive enterprise. However, neglect of certain inconspicuous historical or textual information can sometimes prevent us from making sense of a text if it is read within a context to which it does not belong. This chapter offers a case study of the book *Mengzi* 孟子 (Master Meng), arguing that because we often overlook certain historical and philological facts, we fail to notice that the figure Mengzi, as he is presented in the *Mengzi*, could be appropriately described as a strategist and theorist of regime subversion, a man like Duke Tai (Tai Gong 太公), as depicted in the military text *Liutao* 六弢 (Six Bow Cases, also known as *Liutao* 六韜). This chapter will first explore oft-forgotten facts concerning the intimate relationship and salient resonance between today's widely studied classical "philosophical texts" and classical "military texts" (or "strategic manuals"). The second part continues to present the characteristics of Mengzi as a strategist of military subversion, an aspect which is frequently overlooked because the intimacy of the two groups of texts is often neglected.

To Reunify All under Heaven: Masters as Strategists of Subversion

While it is downplayed in the study of the *Mengzi*, many well-known early philosophers and military strategists were both perceived as and called "masters" (*zi* 子) in the classical period. Additionally, texts now read as "philosophical texts" and those read as "military texts" (or strategic texts) were sometimes classified and grouped together as masters' texts. They indeed seem to share a considerable number of topics, concerns, and discursive features.

The *Mengzi* is listed among the most important early masters' texts. The early masters' texts (or their prototypical versions) were purportedly composed in the Warring Sates period, which is marked by constant *interstate* wars. During the period, rulers of small and weak states struggled to survive and avoid annexation, while powerful and ambitious state rulers tried to annihilate and annex other states to increase their territory, population, and power, so they might ultimately seize the utmost throne (i.e., to become the founding father of a new dynasty). This is the context in which early masters thrived. It is thus unlikely that these early masters, such as Mozi 墨子 and Mengzi, who traveled from one state to another attempting to serve as state rulers' counselors, were not versed in interstate diplomatic and military strategies. Or they were at least aware that the rulers with whom they hoped to win an audience expected to learn more about such strategies than political or moral philosophy. We therefore have reason to believe that early masters' speeches share primary concerns with, or at least superficially resemble those of military strategists. In fact, some of these strategists were also known as "masters," such as Wuzi 吳子 (Master Wu) and Sunzi 孫子 (Master Sun).[2] It is also often overlooked that in the bibliographical treatise of the *Hanshu* 漢書 (*Book of Han*) most of the canonical military texts (*bingshu* 兵書) from the period are not classified in the *Hanshu* under "Military School" (*bingjia* 兵家) but under "Masters," along with Confucianism (*Rujia* 儒家), Daoism (*Daojia* 道家), or Miscellaneous school (*Zajia* 雜家). In this regard they were viewed as masters' texts. It is therefore reasonable to assume that the authors of the military texts and the well-known masters' texts share topics and concerns, a belief held by some early Chinese scholars. By taking a glance at the military texts, we will also notice that the content of the military texts is not limited to such issues as the logistics in war and tactics of battle operations, and that a considerable portion resembles the famous masters' discussions about domestic administration, diplomatic policies, and principles of governance. In brief, many military texts and renowned philosophical texts (such as the *Mozi*, the *Mengzi*, and the *Xunzi*) might have formerly been viewed altogether as masters' texts. This leads to another element of these often-overlooked circumstances.

The significance of the warfare that these texts deal with clearly goes beyond interstate wars: they are *subversive* in nature insofar as they are intended for the purpose of unification wars carried out by state rulers (namely, feudal lords), not by the Son of Heaven of the Zhou Dynasty. State rulers as agents of unification warfare in the feudal system should be considered "semi-rebels" or "semi-usurpers," as nominally the highest sovereignty above all state rulers was the Son of Heaven of the Zhou until the year of 256 BCE. The Son of Heaven within the political system was supposed to be the only man who could authorize or commend a state ruler to attack another state. However, the ambitious rulers of powerful states up until 256 BCE still initiated wars to annex other weaker states, trying to expand their territory and increase their interstate influence. Such acts, without the authorization of the Son of Heaven, were "subversive" in themselves already, not to mention the fact that the ambition behind this annexation was not merely to seize other states' lands and natural resources,[3] but to eventually unify "all under Heaven," that is, overthrow the Son of Heaven and establish a new dynasty. The latter enterprise is often called "to obtain all under Heaven" (*qu tian xia* 取天下) in the *Liutao* 六弢 (Six Bow Cases), or "to become the King of all under Heaven" (*wang tian xia* 王天下) in the *Mengzi*. In this regard, the masters, as political advisors for the powerful and ambitious state rulers, and especially Mengzi, could be considered advisors for subversive unification warfare. As I have shown elsewhere, this might have been common knowledge at that time (Lee 2017b). According to the historical records, Mengzi was active sometime between 390 BCE and 300 BCE. If the text of the *Mengzi* represents the thought and behavior of the figure Mengzi faithfully, that is, if he encouraged and advised powerful state rulers to aspire to become the king of all under Heaven through initiating wars to *liberate* the people of other states, this would be considered an act of agitation, of subversion. According to the *Mengzi*, the historical figure Mengzi and the people of his time seem to have acted in such a manner (Lee 2017b).

To summarize the oft-neglected fact this section has tried to indicate, some of the well-known "philosophical texts" and "military texts" were considered as sharing motives and content and thus viewed altogether as masters' texts in the classical period. Their shared discussions concerning interstate warfare is not a mere military issue but also a political issue as the warfare is in essence a subversive power struggle. Due to their strong political significance, many of the masters' statements are about political principles and techniques, giving us the impression that they are moral or political theorists. However, this impression should not prevent us from also considering that most of the masters (philosophers or strategists) depicted in the texts travel between different states trying to provide advice either for weak state rulers who are trying to survive the threat of their powerful neighbors or for powerful rulers to eventually unite other states and become the ultimate sovereign. It is not surprising that ethics play an important role in this historical context, as military campaigns and power struggles are human activities that require convincing moral justifications, or need moral grounds to enhance their chance of success. By keeping this in mind, we can make better sense of many fragments in the *Mengzi* than if we perceived him as a thinker whose primary goal is to promote certain political and moral theories. The following section highlights some aspects of the *Mengzi* that have not been interpreted against the historical background I have described.

Mengzi: A Master of Subversive War of Unification

The *Mengzi* has an intriguing viewpoint. It holds that the Zhou regime should have already collapsed, yet remains. Reading throughout the *Mengzi*, we do not see the figure of Mengzi attempting to become a counselor at the central Zhou court or expressing any opinions regarding how to restore the order from within the existing Zhou political system. According to the *Mengzi*, Mengzi's narratives of the contemporary interstate politics do not give Zhou sovereignty any significant relevance. Moreover, he explicitly complains that a new king should have already been installed. This complaint appears in the following famous paragraph:

孟子去齊。充虞路問曰：「夫子若有不豫色然。前日虞聞諸夫子曰：『君子不怨天，不尤人。』」曰：「彼一時，此一時也。五百年必有王者興，其間必有名世者。由周而來，七百有餘歲矣。[...] 夫天未欲平治天下也；如欲平治天下，當今之世，舍我其誰也？吾何為不豫哉？」

> When Mengzi left Qi, Chong Yu questioned him upon the way, saying, "Master, you seem to have an unhappy countenance. But formerly I heard you say, 'The superior man does not murmur against Heaven, nor grudge against men.'" Mengzi said, "That was one time, and this is another. Every five hundred years, there must arise a new King, and during that time there must be those whose names are known to their generation for their accomplishments. From the founding of the Zhou dynasty till now, it has been more than seven hundred years. ... It may be that Heaven does not yet desire to pacify all under Heaven; if it desires to pacify all under Heaven, who besides me in the present time is there to help do it? Why would I be unhappy?" (Mengzi 2001: 126, 2B13)

It seems that Mengzi is deeply concerned with the order of the world and the well-being of the people and thus laments that no sage-king has arisen. However, one thing that should not be neglected is that he does not think a good Son of Heaven of Zhou Dynasty is a possible candidate as the ideal king.[4] As one can see from the quote above, he is unhappy about the fact that Zhou has not yet collapsed. In addition, Mengzi does not try to serve the Zhou court. He believes that founding a new dynasty is the only way to bring about peace and order. For him, the ideal king should be the founder of a new dynasty and the possible candidates are to be found among state rulers whose military prowess is powerful enough to attack other states while not indulge in slaughtering. "One who has no pleasure in killing people can so unite it [all under Heaven]," as Mengzi says (2001: 1A6).

Judging from the narratives of the *Mengzi*, Mengzi believed that the most feasible (or perhaps even the only) way of ending the Warring States is to reunite all states under a new sovereignty. He was thus frustrated when making the "five hundred years" claim as he left the state of Qi. Qi was one of the most powerful states at the time, so Mengzi was once convinced that it had the potential to unite all other states. He therefore visited Qi with the hope that he could help the king of Qi conquer the other states and become the new ultimate authority. He seized an opportunity, advising Qi to attack another state, Yan, but "unfortunately" the king of Qi did not follow the standard strategic principle: he killed the innocent and destroyed the ancestral temple of Yan. This provided other states with the moral grounds to create allies and rally troops to attack Qi. The Qi ruler once again sought Mengzi, who thus devised a strategy to solve the crisis caused by other states' preparation to launch a punitive war at Qi. Mengzi was thus left disappointed and frustrated. He was mocked by others because he failed to see that the ruler of Qi had no potential to become the founding father of a dynasty.[5] It is in this context that Mengzi "murmur[ed] against Heaven" that Heaven did not wish to bring about peace to the world; otherwise, he was the only capable man to help accomplish this and he was supposed to make his name known as the arch-strategist of the king of the new dynasty in his generation (rather than becoming a target of derision).

As Mengzi's approach to pacifying the world is an appeal to a subversive war of unification, his ambition and career did not differ much from the arch-strategists of the founding father of the Zhou Dynasty, namely the legendary military strategist Duke Tai. It is therefore not surprising that the *Taigong bingfa* (Taigong's strategy), also known as *Liutao*, is classified together with Mengzi under the same category of *Ru jia* 儒家 (Ban Gu 1997: 1725). The subversive nature the *Mengzi* shares with the *Liutao* is salient in this well-known statement: "I have heard of the execution of a mere fellow 'Zhou' [紂], but I have not heard of the killing of one's ruler" (Mengzi 2001: 125, 1B8). This statement is frequently cited by *Mengzi* scholars to show how brave and liberal-minded Mengzi was that he dared to say to a ruler's face that the people could legitimately kill their rulers.[6] It is however often neglected that according to the context of this statement, the agents of killing and banishing the rulers are subjects/officials (*chen* 臣) instead of *the people*. Mengzi made the statement in a conversation with the king of Qi, a subject of the Zhou Dynasty, whom Mengzi tried to convince to overthrow the Zhou. It is in this context the king of Qi mentioned the historical events of the banishing of Jie 桀 and murdering of Zhou 紂, and then asked Mengzi whether it is permissible for a subject to oust and kill his lord (the king of Qi being a subject of the Son of Heaven). This famous conversation therefore does not imply that Mengzi was a fearless hero who challenged the authority of the ruler he was speaking with, and his statement might not be meant to suggest that the people are permitted to eradicate a brutal ruler. It might be more likely intended to encourage the king of Qi to aspire to replace the Son of Heaven on the throne and build a new dynasty. It is also worth noticing that the historical events addressed here are the subversions by king Tang of Shang 商湯王 and king Wu of Zhou 周武王, who overthrew their rulers and became founders of new dynasties, and thus were praised by Mengzi. It seems clear that the "sage-kings" whom Mengzi encouraged his contemporary state rulers to emulate were usurpers whose major accomplishment did not lie in their successful governance but in their conquering of the previous regimes. In other words, most of Mengzi's conversations with other state rulers seem unlikely to be concerned with how to govern all under Heaven, as a state ruler is a territorial ruler, so he cannot govern the Son of Heaven's realm. The conversations that Mengzi had with powerful state rulers primarily revolved around the question of how to subvert all under Heaven.

Because Mengzi's remedy for the chaos and constant warfare is war for unification, it requires a man with strong military force. For this reason, he does not seem to be very interested in rulers of small and weak states and does not genuinely believe in the ideal of the moral sage-king. It may appear that Mengzi is convinced that a benevolent ruler has no enemies because he can win the hearts of the people and thus eventually becomes the King. Mengzi also repeatedly claims, with the examples of King Tang and King Wen, that a benevolent ruler does not need a large territory in order to become the King.[7] It thus appears that Mengzi indeed endorses the approach of a morally superior man uniting the world. Nevertheless, it might be easily overlooked that there are preconditions that seem to be at odds or even contradictory to this morally transformative or soft-power approach, that is, the benevolent ruler should have a minimum of realistic advantages, including a large territory, high population, and sufficient military strength. Not any random ethical man can meet the minimum requirements. This is indirectly suggested in many passages of the *Mengzi*. For example, in a conversation with the king of Qi, Mengzi emphasizes the size of one's territory.

> 曰：「鄒人與楚人戰，則王以為孰勝？」曰：「楚人勝。」曰：「然則小固不可以敵大，寡固不可以敵眾，弱固不可以敵彊。海內之地方千里者九，齊集有其一。以一服八，何以異於鄒敵楚哉？蓋亦反其本矣。今王發政施仁，使天下仕者皆欲立於王之朝，耕者皆欲耕於王之野，商賈皆欲藏於王之市，行旅皆欲出於王之塗，天下之欲疾其君者皆欲赴愬於王。其若是，孰能禦之？」

> Mengzi said, "If the people of Zou and the people of Chu fought, who does your Majesty think would win?" [King Xuan of Qi said,] "The people of Chu would win." [Mengzi replied,] "So the small definitely cannot match the big, the few definitely cannot match the many, the weak definitely cannot match the strong. Within the four seas there are nine divisions of territory that have a thousand *li* square. All Qi together is one of them. To subjugate eight with one, how is it different from Zhou matching Chu? Simply return to the fundamentals. Suppose your Majesty were to bestow benevolence in governing, this will cause all under Heaven who serve others to all want to take their place in Your Majesty's court. ... All under Heaven who are aggrieved by their rulers wish to come and complain to your Majesty. If it were like this, who could stop it." (2001: 122, 1A7)

Mengzi's conclusion is that by bestowing benevolent governance, a ruler of a "small state" such as Qi can still win the hearts of people from other states, and his becoming the utmost king cannot be stopped (*yu* 禦). As stated earlier in the same paragraph, "By caring for the people one becomes the King. This is something no one could stop" (2001: 119). However, it is also clear that Qi is deemed as "small" here only because it is compared to the rest of all under Heaven. If one compares Qi with other states, one would have a judgment similar to Mengzi's: Qi is capable of uniting all under Heaven "with benevolence" because of its large territory and military prowess. This is made rather clear in another paragraph of the *Mengzi*, where Mengzi says to the king of Qi that Qi is a big state with a thousand *li* square, so it should not fear other states, rather other states should feel afraid of it (1B18). This suggests that Mengzi does not consider hard power less necessary than benevolent governance and moral charisma for one to become the new king of all under Heaven. Despite the emphasis on moralistic aspects of a regime or sovereignty, the candidates for the King-to-be he has in mind are always large and powerful territorial rulers.

For this reason, Mengzi would not promote the idea of "becoming the King of all under Heaven" (*wang tian xia*) to rulers of small states that could not even meet the minimum requirements. No matter how benevolent they are, they could not be a match for other states, let alone become the founder of a new dynasty. This is transparent particularly in his exchanges with Duke Wen of Teng 滕文公, the ruler of a small and weak state. When the ruler asks Mengzi about how to survive between the two big states Qi and Chu, Mengzi says he cannot be of much help, as Teng's situation is so difficult that it is undoubtedly beyond Mengzi's strategic expertise. Mengzi continues, saying that the only thing Duke Wen of Teng could do is to strengthen fortifications, guard the state with the people, and be prepared to die with the people alongside him until his death (1B20). Mengzi does not advise the ruler to bestow benevolent governance, nor does he tell him that everyone can become Yao 堯 and Shun 舜, or that a benevolent ruler has no enemies. Instead, he suggests that the ruler prepare to die in his defense. As the reader can see from the same chapter of the *Mengzi*, Duke Wen of Teng, terrified by the state of Qi's campaign, does not give up and pushes Mengzi again. Mengzi gives him a second option: giving up the territory and leaving the state (1B21). Intriguingly, the *Mengzi* has Duke Wen of Teng push Mengzi again with the same question. Mengzi repeats the same advice, suggesting that he either cede the territory to a strong state or die in the war. He says, "I ask you, prince, to choose between these two options." This is how Mengzi ends the conversation with the duke (1B22). Apparently, Mengzi does not think moral cultivation or moral governance is a possible option for the ruler of the Teng state, because it is too weak. He even advises the ruler to yield the territory to Qi, one of the powerful states that Mengzi is hoping to help annex and unite other states.

Conclusion: Beyond the Narrative of Moral Hero

Negligence with regard to relevant historical circumstances and crucial philosophical information can sometimes prevent us from noticing textual details that have significant impact on our interpretation of classical Chinese thought. In the interpretation of the *Mengzi*, neglect of the intimate connection between philosopher-masters and military-masters has long prevented us from noticing its prominent strategic and subversive nature. It is often overlooked that early masters were mostly political strategists during a wartime context, as was Mengzi. The war that the masters were strategizing was subversive insofar as it was an encroachment on the authority of the highest sovereignty, its ultimate goal being to overthrow the current dynasty and establish a new one. Bearing this in mind, we would see that Mengzi, as he is presented in the compilation of the *Mengzi*, is very unlikely to be an exception. According to this interpretation of the *Mengzi*, he is a political advisor who aims to assist a state ruler in becoming the new king of all under Heaven. As Mengzi says, he aspires to become the teacher of the King-to-be, in other words, the chief counselor who creates the founding father of a new dynasty. This interpretation can explain the apparent echoes between the *Mengzi* and the *Liutao*, a military text that narrates how the legendary strategist Duke Tai assisted King Wen and King Wu in undermining the Shang Dynasty, eventually overthrowing it. That is, the major figures of the two texts, Mengzi and Duke Tai, share the enterprise, and both argue that "benevolence" is indispensable in the strategy of regime subversion, and that one cannot overthrow a dynasty with pure force. More importantly, it can make sense of many other facts that a purely moral-philosophy reading of the *Mengzi* cannot. For example, it is believed that

Mengzi is deeply concerned with the chaotic situation of the world and with how much the people suffer from constant wars. Out of this deep concern, he travels near and far to promote the values of benevolence and righteousness to convince state rulers to cultivate their virtue and care for the well-being of the people. Therefore, revered as the Second Sage in Confucian tradition, Mengzi is often depicted as a brave hero and a champion of moral philosophy; he defends morality and the well-being of the people by confronting state rulers at court. However, an interesting situation is often overlooked in that Mengzi never argued that the order of the world could be restored by a virtuous Son of Heaven of the Zhou: the moral quality of the existing political authority is irrelevant in Mengzi's discourses. Instead, Mengzi holds that order will be restored by having the Zhou Dynasty extinguished and by establishing a new regime. For this reason, Mengzi travels between different states, seeking to find state rulers with good opportunities and advising them about how to conquer other states and eventually become the utmost power. Mengzi is in this sense an agitator of usurpation. This is why we have the famous statement by Mengzi, which says that King Wu's military coup against King Zhou of Shang is a punishment of a mere fellow, not a regicide of one's lord. This statement is often understood by interpreters as showing Mengzi's audacity in defying political authority in public and as pointing to his belief in moral governance and to his support for the people to oust a tyrant. Nevertheless, it should be noted that by making this statement, he is justifying King Wu's military coup in a conversation with the ruler of Qi, an ambitious subject of the Zhou. As I have argued above, in this conversation Mengzi attempts to encourage the ruler of Qi, an aspirant to the seat of the Son of Heaven, to carry out his ambition, namely, the ambition of ousting or wiping out the Son of Heaven and becoming the king of all under Heaven. By justifying Zhou's regicide in such a context, Mengzi would by no means defy the ruler of the Qi, nor would he endanger himself by making the statement. Conversely, he would more likely please the ruler by providing "theoretical support" for his "great desire" (*da yu* 大欲), an euphemism used by Mengzi to refer to the subversive desire to seize the ultimate power and establish a new dynasty. As I also argued, this can explain why the *Liutao* and the *Mengzi* belong to the same bibliographical category and why the sage rulers Mengzi reveres are founders of new dynasties rather than rulers who are well-known for good governance. Modern interpreters often read a moralistic political philosophy into Mengzi's statements about King Tang, King Wen, or King Wu and believe that Mengzi venerates these kings for their *ruling the world by virtue*. As founders of new dynasties, the "sage-kings" are successful usurpers instead of good rulers proper: they subverted the previous regimes through military coups and took power. In fact, they could hardly be said to be virtuous true kings of all under Heaven: King Wen of Zhou, throughout his entire life, never became the king of all under Heaven, and his son King Wu died a few years after he subverted the Shang regime. A strategic and subversive reading of the Mengzi can explain also Mengzi's superficial inconsistences. On the one hand, he tells some state rulers that the benevolent man has no match or enemies, and has the chance to become the king of all under Heaven. On the other hand, he advises other territorial rulers to give up their territory and prepare to be killed by strong enemies. A purely moralistic reading of the *Mengzi* could hardly explain this inconsistency without acknowledging that Mengzi is hypocritical or self-contradictory. By contextualizing Mengzi as primarily a strategist rather than a moralist, however, we can dissolve the seeming contradiction. As I have argued in this chapter, as a subversive strategist, the target audience he has in mind is, naturally, state rulers who have sufficient military power. Therefore, to apprehend Mengzi's thought, and to better grasp the subversive and strategic nature of his thought, we need to consider the context of war during this time period and take military texts into serious consideration.

Notes

The first draft of the paper was presented on 22nd Symposium of the Académie du Midi. I am indebted to the participants' useful suggestions. I would also like to express my gratitude to Daniel Sarafinas for his incisive comments. Any errors are my own and should not discredit the expertise of these esteemed scholars.

1 Many sinologists write about related issues, for example, Michael Nylan (2016).
2 Some might argue that it was exactly because of the constant wars that the masters had to strive to promote morality to prevent brutal use of violence. I do not disagree with this explanation. Discourse concerning ethics often proliferates following frequent, abusive use of violence. In one regard, people may emphasize the normative ideal in an attempt to improve the situation. On the other hand, justification for the use of violence often appeals to some common moral norms. What this chapter disagrees with, therefore, is not that ethics plays an essential role in classical Chinese philosophy, but rather the assumption that the masters (Mengzi, in particular) intended to articulate their own moral theories that can be applied universally in human societies or day-to-day human life. I am of course not the first person to reconsider this assumption in the study of Mengzi. For an example, see Chan, Alan Kam-leung (2002).
3 An example is the story narrated in the "Gongshu" 公輸 chapter of the *Mozi,* in which the king of the Chu had Gongshu build cloud-ladders for attacking the state of Song. It is obvious that Chu would not have material gains from invading the Song, and the king was aware of it. For an analysis of the story, see Lee (2017a).
4 I do not suggest that Mengzi is thus not loyal to the Zhou regime. According to the feudal system of the Zhou, he was not an official subject of the Son of Heaven, so he did not need to be loyal to the regime. Nor do I suggest that he is morally flawed. His line of thinking might indicate that he is politically realistic. Whether his judgment is accurate, however, would be another issue.
5 For more details, see Ting-mien Lee (2017b).
6 For example, Angus Charles Graham (2003: 113–17). For an example of portraying Mengzi as a brave hero, see Bryan Van Norden (2007: 302).
7 For example, Mengzi 2001: 2A3.

References

Ban Gu (1997), *Hanshu* 漢書. Beijing: Zhonghua shuju.
Chan, Alan Kam-leung, ed. (2002), *Mencius: Contexts and Interpretations.* Honolulu: University of Hawaii Press.

Graham, Angus Charles (2003), *Disputers of the Tao: Philosophical Argument in Ancient China*. Chicago: Open Court.
Lee, Ting-mien (2017a), "Mozi as a Daoist Sage: An Intertextual Analysis of the "Gongshu" Anecdote." In *Between History and Philosophy: Anecdotes in Early China*, edited by Paul van Els and Sarah Queen, 93–112. New York: SUNY Press.
Lee, Ting-mien (2017b), "'Benevolence-Righteousness' as Strategic Terminology: Reading Mengzi's 'Ren-Yi' through Strategic Manuals." *Dao* 16(1): 15–34.
Mengzi (2001), "*Mengzi*." In *Readings in Classical Chinese Philosophy*, translated and edited by Philip J. Ivanhoe and Bryan W. Van Norden, 115–60. Indianapolis: Hackett.
Nylan, Michael (2016), "Academic Silos, or 'What I Wish Philosophers Knew about Early History in China.'" In *The Bloomsbury Research Handbook of Chinese Philosophy Methodologies*, edited by Sor-hoon Tan, 91–114. London: Bloomsbury.
Van Norden, Bryan (2007), *Virtue Ethics and Consequentialism in Early Chinese Philosophy*. Cambridge: Cambridge University Press.

9

A Daoist Critique of the *Huaxia* Civilization Project

Daniel Sarafinas

Ancient Chinese texts are replete with the semantics of inner-outer (*neiwai* 內外), a motif used in a wide range of descriptions, from virtues as internal feelings that correspond with external duties to the ideal circumstances within a state and its relationships with those abroad. Rather than merely providing a conceptual model for moral and political theory, however, the inner-outer distinction in classical literature also functions in strengthening bonds of identity among the *huaxia*[1] 華夏 by creating a narrative constructed around "we" and "them," in-group and out-group. In this context the *neiwai* distinction was often expressed as a clarion call for the *huaxia* people to maintain loyalty to their in-group against the oppositional out-group, such as in "the *zhuxia* are internal, the *yidi* barbarians are external" (*nei zhuxia er wai yidi*, 內諸夏而外夷狄) (Wangdao, 4). This inner-outer dichotomy regarding sociopolitical boundaries exemplifies the *huaxia* construction of a sociopolitical identity in contradistinction to those whom they perceived to be the barbarian others. In fact, the evolution of the term *huaxia* itself occurred alongside a growing awareness and vocabulary used to refer to the non-*huaxia*. It was particularly during the Spring and Autumn period (771 BCE–476 BCE), a time during which the Zhou state lost much of its power and was constantly attacked by barbarian tribes, that the people of the central states, as Wang Mingke 王明珂 describes,

> united under the "*huaxia* identification," and it was at this point in history when the "*huaxia*" appellation began to be used in documents. In the historical memory of the *huaxia* people, the Spring and Autumn period was a chaotic time of invasions by the *yirong mandi* 夷戎蠻狄 barbarians. In fact, these concepts of alien people's group and one's own group exist in relation to one another, which is to say, this time in which they discovered their "self" as *huaxia* also led to an intense reaction and discovery of the "not-me" in the existence of the *yirong mandi* barbarians. (2013: 129)

I argue, however, that this was not a process in which they "discovered their 'self' as *huaxia*," but one in which the *huaxia* identity was created. I refer to this process as the "*huaxia* civilization project." As I understand this "civilizational project," it is fundamentally a process of formulating a sociopolitical *identity*, creating a sense of "we" in contradistinction to "them," as well as the concomitant perception of a shared history through which this identity persisted and served as a foundation for the establishment and legitimacy of a political body. For the purposes of this discussion, the "*huaxia* civilization project" can thus be defined as an ideology that informs the *huaxia* people's identity—constructed mainly through a geopolitical worldview, a sociopolitical history, and perception of "the barbarians." Just as the enlightenment thinkers predominantly defined civilization in contradistinction to "rudeness" or "barbarism," discourse surrounding the establishment of civilizational identity in ancient China is likewise constructed in large part around *huaxia* identity in contradistinction to the *manyi rongdi* 蠻夷戎狄, or "barbarians."

Despite the dominance of this ideology, there were internal voices that brought the *huaxia* civilization project under critical scrutiny. This chapter will examine the inner chapters of the *Zhuangzi* 莊子 as a critique of the *huaxia* civilization project, focusing on the subversive function of what I refer to as the *Zhuangzi*'s "barbarian-sages." Before moving on to this investigation, a few caveats are in order. First, I will use the often vaguely defined concept "ideology" to refer to the specifically political discourse surrounding the formation of the *huaxia* civilizational identity. As a working definition, ideology will be used to refer to a system of ideas characteristic of a political community that is used to make sense of the world, which employs, as Emile Durkheim writes, "the use of notions to govern the collation of facts, rather than deriving notions from them" (2013: 51). An ideological system thus operates as a model of the world; and ideological enthusiasm, enthusiasm in the sense of being consumed by the spirit, implies treating that mere model of the world as the world itself.

The term "critique" is often similarly vaguely defined, spanning almost as many definitions as there are writers who use it. Many critical interpretations often propose a paradigm in which Daoist texts like the *Zhuangzi* and the *Laozi* 老子 are read as oppositional to other masters or dominant schools of thought, most glaringly Confucianism. Other critical interpretations read these texts as compatible with the dominant philosophical and political discourse, exposing elements of the Confucian worldview that are found lacking or problematic and supplementing it with complimentary concepts. The concept of critique that will be utilized here can be characterized as revealing the conditions for the possibility of certain phenomena, concepts, modes of thinking, and so forth (à la Kant), which bracket off normative claims and value judgments in deferment to an investigation of the conditions under which such normative claims might be considered "natural," "necessary," or "given" (à la Foucault).

Such an investigation ultimately serves as a therapeutic to alleviate some of the pathological tendencies of moral or religious enthusiasm, ideological extremism, nationalism, and so forth (à la Moeller). This framework will read the *Zhuangzi* as a text that is not intended to provide any alternative political or social model (as is characteristic of "primitivist" readings) but rather to problematize elements of the intellectual and cultural foundation of the *huaxia* civilizational identity that often exist in the form of unquestioned assumptions. More specifically, I will address how the *Zhuangzi* portrays characters who would have been considered geographically and/ or sociopolitically "barbarian" subversively, as sages, in order to expose ideological elements of the *huaxia* civilization project as narrow-minded, absurd, or paradoxical.

Zhuangzi's Barbarian-Sages

The development of the *huaxia* identity, as described by Wang Mingke above, was reinforced by a greater consciousness of the "out-group," couched in such terms as *man* (蛮), *yi* (夷), *rong* (戎), *di* (弟), and various combinations thereof, corresponding to the Western notion of "barbarian." These terms should not be understood as ethnonyms, and although they often refer to peoples and tribes beyond the geographic boundaries of the central states, they were not limited to geographic outsiders. Rather, they were used to refer both to people living outside of the geopolitical limits as well as those outside of the *huaxia*'s particular form of civil life who did not exhibit the corresponding set of values, virtues, and social practices. I argue that the *Zhuangzi*'s critique of *huaxia* civilizational identity is provided primarily through the vantage point of barbarian-sages. I use this term to refer to the way in which the figure of the sage, portrayed in classical Chinese literature as a legendary historical figure who represents utmost wisdom and the ideal form of governance, is supplanted by another type of sage in the *Zhuangzi*, by characters who are ironically (and often humorously) depicted as doing and saying the opposite one would expect of a typical Confucian sage like Yao 堯, Shun 舜, or Confucius. Not only are these figures described as having different values or methods of governance than the traditional sages, but they are portrayed as not being *huaxia* at all. Rather, they are depicted as "barbarians" by the way in which the text places them: (1) geographically in distant lands beyond the *huaxia* sphere of influence; (2) outside the civil life and customs characteristic of *huaxia* civilization; and (3) in reference to classical literature portraying barbarians as "birds and beasts" (*qinshou* 禽獸) and "jackals and wolves" (*chailang* 豺狼), by using animals as a metaphor for those whose ways of life are other than that of the *huaxia*.

The *Zhuangzi*'s sagelike and miraculous characters are often viewed as a literary device used to create that sense of unrestricted spiritual freedom so often associated with the *Zhuangzi*. Yet these barbarian-sages and the sense of expansiveness they bring to the text can also be read as an important heuristic device in the service of critiquing the *huaxia* civilizational identity by "critically de-centering" the reader, allowing her to view those dominant *huaxia* values, forms of civil life, modes of thinking, and civilizational identity with which she identifies so intimately through fresh, "foreign" eyes. A critically de-centered perspective constitutes an important function for any critique, as it relocates those elements of society and culture that might be taken as "natural" or "necessary" when a culture is "working," placing them in an unfamiliar context, from the perspective of one for whom that culture does not necessarily "work." In Chapter 11, Robin Wang describes how feminine values in the *Daodejing* 道德經 and the lived experience of *kundao* 坤道 (the way of femininity, female daoists) are used in the service of creating a "critically de-centered" perspective, which:

> compels us to reorient our epistemic, social, cultural, and personal framework related to the identity of the woman. In other words, Kundao experiences provide us a point of departure for a critique of so-called ideal womanhood, which consigns women to modes of desiring self-abnegation rather than their own well-being.[2]

This "point of departure for a critique" offered by shifting from the dominant masculine perspective to a feminine perspective reveals to us "on what kinds of assumptions, what kinds of familiar, unchallenged, unconsidered modes of thought, the practices that we accept rest" (Foucault 1988: 154). Just as the *Daodejing*'s critique does not imply the feminine ought to be valued over and above the masculine, as a form of critique that brackets off normative claims and value judgments, the *Zhuangzi*'s barbarian-sages, unlike the "noble savage," are not meant to depict any specific way of life as more "virtuous" or untarnished by the corrupt influences of *huaxia* civilization. They do not represent any specific political group of people, but can be seen as "general barbarians," an empty space or vantage point from nowhere through which the reader is brought into a critical relationship with her own "civilizational identity," *huaxia* or otherwise, to recognize the contingent conditions of such an ideology as well as its inconsistencies, incongruencies, paradoxes, and absurdities, but not demanding a rejection of it. The *Zhuangzi*'s first endeavor to "critically de-center" the reader shifts us outside the geographic "center," its target being no less than *tianxia* (天下, under heaven) itself.

"Wandering Beyond the Four Seas": Geographic Barbarian-Sages

Spring and Autumn and Warring States period texts often pair the term *tianxia*, or the Zhou cultural-political realm,[3] with concepts such as order 治 or pacify 平. These terms function as an exhortation to and description of the ruler's duty to bring order to the Zhou sphere, indicating an understanding of their sociopolitical position within a geographic worldview as well as a set of moral-political duties that result from that position. The geographic understanding of the world and corresponding set of moral-political duties that undergird the entire civilization project will be referred to as what Yao Dali 姚大力 calls *tianxia zhongguo guan* (天下中國觀, the view of the central states under heaven). We can understand this particular worldview as one (1) in which *Huaxia* political control exists in the very center of the world that is populated by *huaxia* and non-*huaxia* peoples; (2) surrounded by non-*huaxia* barbarians on the margins of the "central states" within the four seas (*sihai* 四海); (3) that is further surrounded by those lands of bizarre and grotesquely shaped creatures with no moral or political order to speak of. Yao describes an attitude inseparable from this geographic conception of the world as follows:

This one [*huaxia*] culture and civilization unifies all others, which is to say China has the duty to "*jiaohua*" [教化, transform through moral education, civilize, cultivate] and the surrounding communities have the desire to "*xianghua*" [向化, move towards becoming transformed, civilized, cultivated]. The ultimate conclusion of the duty to *jiaohua* and the desire to *xianghua* is that ... civilization covers *tianxia*, or under heaven, in a great unity. (2018: 1)

The entire *huaxia* civilization project is ultimately founded on this inner-outer distinction, and along with this geographic conception of the world is combined a moral duty on behalf of the *huaxia*, a kind of ancient Chinese manifest destiny.

As a critique of the dominant ideological and sociopolitical system, the *Zhuangzi* subverts the *huaxia* worldview that serves as a precondition to the civilization project, exposing *tianxia zhongguo guan* as not merely a geographic designation, but one which is strongly shaped by politics, and thus drastically limited by whatever human political projects are being carried out. In fact, the very first story in the text presents to us a much broader geographic view, so broad that the question is posed "Does its distance have any extreme limit?" (Chen 1995: 3). The chapter opens up in the Northern Oblivion with Kun 鯤, a giant fish, transforming into Peng 鵬, a giant bird, flying to the Southern Oblivion, of which the Ming dynasty commentator, She Deqing 釋德清 writes that it "is a land far from what the world of humans have seen" (Chen 1995: 2). At the very outset of the text we are provided a view of the world that includes the realm of the *huaxia*, but is not narrowly limited to it. The first character to whom we are introduced, Peng, is a barbarian-sage who provides us with a birds-eye view of the extremities of earth outside of the *huaxia* geopolitical boundaries, asking the reader to call into question the underlying assumptions of that worldview, or any ideological worldview whatsoever.

Another account of this geographic category of barbarian-sage occurs when Jian Wu asks his teacher about Jieyu's description of the spirit-man living on the distant mythical Mount Guye who "rides upon the air and clouds, as if hitching his chariot to soaring dragons, wandering beyond the four seas" (Ziporyn 2009: 7). The semantics used in the classical texts to describe those places beyond the Zhou cultural-political realm imply that they are not merely different and unknown, but are chaotic (*luan* 亂), rebellious, and oppositional to the *huaxia* geopolitical project of "ordering" (*zhi* 治) *tianxia*. Likewise, those barbarian lands and people in the *Zhuangzi* are often associated with such terms as wild (*ye* 野) and crooked (*qu* 曲) in juxtaposition to order and straightness (*zhi* 直) used to symbolize the Confucian *dao*, while the barbarian-sages, like the spirit-man, "allow[s] the present age to seek out its own chaotic order. How could he be bothered to try to manage the world?" (Ziporyn 2009: 7). The question of how to manage or order *tianxia* is asked in the *Zhuangzi* several times, ironically often posed to barbarian-sages living in "wild" or "chaotic" lands.

Imagery evocative of the distinction between the wild barbarian and ideologically dogmatic Confucian is put in the mouth of the madman Jieyu once again, who is overheard by Confucius singing:

Drawing a straight line upon this earth and then trying to walk along it—danger, peril!

The brambles and thorns, which so bewilder the sunlight, they don't impede my steps.

My [crooked] stride amid them keeps my feet unharmed. (Ziporyn 2009: 32, with minor alterations)

Here we have another barbarian-sage described along with references to walking "crooked 曲" and uncultivated land of brambles and thorns, which Southern Song commentator Wang Yinglin 王應麟 associates with "wild people" (Chen 1995: 141). In contrast to this crooked style of walking, Confucius is described as "drawing a straight line." Paul J. D'Ambrosio writes that this straight line "refers to a preconceived plan that does not allow for as much flexibility when maneuvering through the world. And just like this story of the madman in the *Zhuangzi*, the straight lines that are drawn by an aspiring Confucian are completely imaginary" (2017, 33). Whereas D'Ambrosio interprets this as a reference to forms of cultivation, within a civilizational framework we can read it to mean creating an ideological model of the world and "walking along it" as if it were the world itself, a line that distinguishes the "straight" *huaxia* lands from the "wild" barbarians' lands. Jieyu warns Confucius of the dangers of walking "straight," or rigidly adhering to a strict ideological vision of the world. Unlike Confucius, he is able to cross these arbitrary boundaries by walking crooked, thereby keeping his feet unharmed. This reveals another characteristic of the barbarian-sage shared by the spirit-man, Jieyu, and repeated through the *Zhuangzi*: avoiding harm.[4]

Jieyu's feet are unharmed by the brambles and thorns of the wild lands, and the spirit-man on Mount Guye is "harmed by no thing. A flood may reach the sky without drowning him; a drought may melt the stones and scorch the mountains without scalding him. From his dust and chaff you could mold yourself a Yao or Shun" (Ziporyn 2009: 7). One characteristic of this barbarian-sage that makes him so much greater than the *huaxia* sages Yao and Shun is his ability to avoid harm. However, this harmful ideological rigidity does not only exist in the form of creating geopolitical divisions between wild and ordered land, just as one need not live "beyond the four seas" to be considered a barbarian. The *Zhuangzi* illustrates its critique through social barbarians as well.

"Now I Lack a Foot": Social Barbarian-Sages

Many cultural heroes that were said to have transmitted the Zhou *dao* in classical literature, from Hou Ji 后稷 down to Gong Liu 公劉, are described as having "lived amongst the *rongdi* barbarians" (Zhaoqi 2008: 115). The terms denoting "barbarians" were thus also applied to those living inside the geographic boundaries of the Zhou political/cultural realm, but outside its form of civil life. The second types of barbarian-sages in the *Zhuangzi* are those who are outside of the margins of *huaxia* political and social life, either by choice or by force. This group is most notably represented through the three characters who have had their feet cut off by the state as punishment, all introduced in the fifth chapter, "Markers of Full Virtuosity (德充符)." These figures committed some (unknown) crime against the state and were punished in such a way that made them recognizably "deplorables," marked with a scarlet letter that signaled to *huaxia* society that they are "uncivilized." This punishment is one of the "five punishments" (*wuxing* 五刑), a method of governance contrasted with *li* (禮, ritual, etiquette), the more "civilized" method to govern social conduct (at least for the nobility). The Confucian thinkers had a complicated relationship with corporal punishment, or *xing* (刑), portraying it as a practice that came from non-*huaxia* barbarians,[5] yet it was used by those very sage-emperors Confucians venerated so highly.

Playing on this uncomfortable relationship between *li* and *xing*, the *Zhuangzi* portrays Confucius himself interacting with Toeless Shushan. Confucius looks upon Shushan as unfit to be in civilized society, and says to him "You were careless in your past behavior and thus have ended up in this condition. Isn't it a little late to come to me now?" Shushan rebukes him for his pettiness, "Now I lack a foot, but I come to you with something worth more than a foot still intact" (Ziporyn 2009: 35). Missing the point about external social positions and distinctions not being truly "markers of full virtuosity," Confucius says to his students:

> Learn from this, my disciples! For Toeless is a one-footed ex-convict, but he still endeavors to learn, so as to make up for the ugliness of his past behavior. How much more should you do so, you whose virtuosity is still intact. (Ziporyn 2009: 35)

Having been completely consumed by the moral dogma imbedded in the dominant *huaxia* ideology, Confucius believes that Shushan's severed foot, a punishment inflicted for not acting according to the sociopolitical form of life governed by *li* and impersonal legal statutes, is tantamount to a lack of virtue, those considered civilized having their feet and "virtuosity still intact." Although Shushan's body, and thus social position, was punished by the state, Confucius's punishment is that he seeks, as the text reads, "some bizarre, deceptive, illusory, freakish thing like a good name, not realizing the Consummate Person views such things as handcuffs and leg chains" (Ziporyn 2009: 35). Shushan the Toeless exhibits the characteristics of a barbarian-sage, that is, the ability to cross boundaries into the "wild" (not "handcuffed" to a single ideological model of the world), thereby avoiding harm, in this case harm to one's virtue. Unlike the spirit-man and Jieyu, however, Shushan is not crossing geographic "lines upon this earth" into the lands "beyond the four seas," but is, like Jieyu, walking "crooked" among sociopolitical forms of life, or customs.

Perhaps the most well-known form of *li* in Confucianism is the mourning ritual. Some of the more memorable passages from the *Zhuangzi* involve characters who flaunt the Confucian mourning rites yet are paradoxically praised for their sagacity by typically Confucian characters. One such passage features Mengzifan and Ziqinzhang mourning for their recently deceased friend, Zisanghu. Confucius sends his student Zigong to pay his respects and finds the two friends playfully mourning for their friend, singing together rather than treating it with the rote and contrived solemnity that Confucian funeral rites demand. Upon returning to Confucius, Zigong asks "What kind of people are these? They do not cultivate their characters in the least" (Ziporyn 2009: 46). Chen Guying interprets this as "They do not adorn their virtue with the use of *li* or *wen* 文 (adornment, arts and letters, refinement)" (Chen 1995: 195). Zigong is expressing a sentiment for which the Confucians were often criticized, the deft performance of *li* being treated as virtue itself when it is merely an adornment (文) used for signaling sanctimonious piety, usually for the sake of reputation. Confucius responds to his student "These are men who roam outside the lines (*fang* 方). I, on the other hand, do my roaming inside the lines" (Ziporyn 2009: 46).

Fang has the connotation of place (*difang* 地方), and thereby suggests that these figures are barbarian-sages because they "roam" outside the geopolitical limits of the *huaxia* sphere. Confucius adds that because they are able to exist outside the *huaxia* limits, the barbarian-sages, as opposed to Confucius and by extension those who are limited to within the *huaxia* sociopolitical sphere, would never "do something as stupid as practicing conventional rituals to impress the eyes and ears of the common crowd" (Ziporyn 2009: 47). It becomes evident that they are speaking about more than merely geopolitical areas, and another connotation to the term *fang* is revealed: custom and practices. Chen Yun 陈赟 writes that the relationship between *fang* as geographical place and *fang* as custom is implicit within the term. Just as each place has its unique geography, appearance, and climate,

> In a cultural sense, every place has its own dialect, customs, habits, traditions, history, lifestyle, and system of civilization ... *fang* implies the system of *li* on earth or amongst people. ... The reason *li* is expressed as *fang* lies in the connection between *li* and the *dao* of earth. (Chen 2016: 18)

Each place (*fang*) having its own customs (*fang*) implies that the barbarian-sages are able to practice the different customs outside the *huaxia* geographic *and* sociopolitical realm, unlike the straight-walking Confucius. Whereas Confucian literature differentiates *li* from *fengsu* 風俗 (vulgar customs), the *Zhuangzi*'s usage of the term *fang* presents the Confucian *li* as just another form of the many ways of life. This does not mean that the Confucian *li* is somehow devalued or that the barbarian sages never practice the Confucian *li*. It only becomes harmful when it is steadfastly adhered to or put in a rigid hierarchy over other forms of custom regardless of the circumstances. The barbarian-sages, on the other hand, "come together in [*dao*]" and are "not bothered to serve any one particular goal, thereby allowing the flow of their lives to settle into stability" (Ziporyn 2009: 47). The cause of the Confucian's shortsightedness and the condition for the possibility of destructive ideological enthusiasm involves another important theme found throughout the text, particularly in regard to the third category according to which barbarian-sages are depicted, that is, as animals.

"Which 'Knows' What Is the Right Place to Live": Animalistic Barbarians

One of the most common ways to indirectly refer to barbarians in classical Confucian texts is found in the description of or comparison to animals using terms like "birds and beasts (*qinshou* 禽兽)" or "jackals and wolves (*chailang* 豺狼)." The association of non-*huaxia* with animals surrounds the notion of them being disordered because they were perceived to have (1) no real political order,⁶ (2) no order among the "five relationships,"⁷ and (3) a lack of the proper virtues, which informs *huaxia* political and familial order.⁸ Animals are thus often used in the *Zhuangzi* to represent non-*huaxia* people with different social and political forms of life within the *Zhuangzi*. One example occurs during a conversation between Nie Que and Wang Ni in the second chapter, "Equalizing Assessments of Things (齊物論)."

The story begins with Nie Que asking "Do you know what all things agree in considering right (*shi* 是)," to which Wang Ni responds, "How could I know that?" (Ziporyn 2009: 17). The discussion that follows contributes to an important subject of debate within classical Chinese thought surrounding *shifei* 是非 (right-wrong, this-not this) distinctions. Much of the second chapter is devoted to this subject and points to the absurdity of arguing and contending over such distinctions. From a critical perspective, the text can be read as questioning these *shifei* distinctions, not on epistemologically skeptical or relativistic grounds as this chapter is often interpreted, but on the grounds that *shifei* distinctions are the very conditions that allow for ideological enthusiasm in the first place. It is this ideological attachment, or attachment to one singular *shifei* perspective, that prevents people from being like the "Consummate Person" (Ziporyn 2009: 35) who "wanders beyond the four seas" (Ziporyn 2009: 18). Wang Ni does not "*know*" these distinctions because the sage does not *recognize* them as anything more than the "chirping of baby birds" (Ziporyn 2009: 13) or the basis for one of the many, equally acceptable forms of *fang*. This reading regarding the not-knowing of the sage follows Hans-Georg Moeller's interpretation, insofar as this passage

> points out quite exactly what a Daoist sage is supposed *not* to know. Paradoxically, the Daoist philosopher is not an expert in having knowledge, but an expert in not having any knowledge about things that the most normal people feel they know. (2008: 120)

As is the case with self-imposed demarcations between geographical spaces and virtues of civil society, Moeller describes the way in which "the claims to know what is beneficial and what is harmful are making us blind" (2008: 120). The ideological blindness of the Confucians is paired with Zhuangzian blindness to ideology, to *shifei* distinctions. Wang Ni further explains his not-knowing *shifei* distinctions using a comparison to animals as follows:

> When people sleep in a damp place, they wake up deathly ill and sore about the waist—but what about eels? If people live in trees, they tremble with fear and worry—but how about monkeys? Of these three, which "knows" what is the right place to live? ... From where I see it, the transition of Humanity and Responsibility and the trails of right and wrong are hopelessly tangled and confused. How could I know how to distinguish which is right among them? (Ziporyn 2009: 18)

The use of animals in the *Zhuangzi* portrays the key characteristics of the *Zhuangzi*'s barbarian-sages as characters that subvert the Confucian civilization project. More specifically, they are used to critique the drawing of and "walking along" exclusive ideological boundaries and distinctions because such boundaries are founded on extremely problematic, and even absurd *shifei* distinctions, often causing more harm than they are worth. As opposed to the way in which the barbarian-sage responds to the rightness of each particular thing, these *shifei* distinctions can be regarded as ideological notions that "govern the collation of facts," making one blind to novel sociopolitical circumstances. As a few of the passages used above indicate, this distinction manifests itself in the form of a harmful and obstinate adherence to ideology in the typically Confucian quest to order to world, particularly in regard to their relationship with those barbarians on the margins of the *huaxia* political realm.

The *huaxia*, and more specifically Confucian fixation on ordering the world, was ideally carried out through civilizing or "moral transformation through education (*jiahua* 教化)" with the use of law and proper customs (*fadu* 法度). The *Zhuangzi* portrays this method of "civilizing" as projecting *shifei* distinctions onto others in order to control them. After his encounter with Wang Ni, Nie Que went to Puyizi who gave him further instruction using the example of the Youyu and Tai clans:

> A Youyu still harbors Humanity in his breast, with which he tries to constrain other human beings. He may be able to win people over that way, but in doing so he never gets beyond *criticizing* people, in considering them wrong (*fei* 非). A Tai, on the other hand, lies down to sleep without hurry and wakes without cares. Sometimes he thinks he's a horse, sometimes he thinks he's an ox ... they never involve him criticizing other human beings, in considering them wrong. (Ziporyn 2009: 50)

The description of the Tai man's freedom (or blindness) from the onerous attachment to *shifei* distinctions and the projection onto others that follows such attachment, allows him to freely and without anxiety identify with the forms of life of horses and oxen (barbarians). Directly following this passage is a story that combines this theme with the avoidance of harm. When the madman Jieyu asks Jian Wu what his teacher taught him, he responds with the semantics typical of many schools of thought during the Warring States period, "If a ruler can produce regulations, standards, judgements, and measures derived from the example of his own person, none will dare disobey him and all will be reformed (*hua* 化) by him" (Ziporyn 2009: 50). This is a direct reference to projecting one's *shifei* distinctions onto others, to which Jieyu responds:

> That is sham Virtuosity. To rule the world in this way is like trying to carve a river out of the ocean, or asking a mosquito to carry a mountain on its back. For when a sage rules, does he rule anything outside himself? ... A bird avoids the harm of arrows and nets by flying high, and a mouse burrows in the depths beneath the shrines and graves to avoid poisons and traps. Do you lack the wisdom of these two little creatures? (Ziporyn 2009: 51)

Jeiyu's response refers to both of the Zhuangzian critique of the ideological use of static *shifei* distinctions and the harm it brings to oneself and others.[9] If we take Jian

Wu's teacher's advice to mean that he should govern through the use of the rule of law and moral standards, Jieyu's comment that the sage does not "rule anything outside of himself (*waizhi* 外治)" is a caution against projecting one's *shifei* distinctions on the world. Using the metaphors of the bird and mouse (barbarians) going beyond where arrows and poisons can harm them, he is urging Jian Wu to have the wisdom to "wander" or walk "crooked" along *shifei* distinctions so that the rule of law and moral standards cannot harm him. In other words, do not become attached to or consumed by an ideological model of the world, and just as Jieyu's crooked walking along geographical distinctions left his feet unharmed, and Shushan's crooked walking among customs left his virtue unharmed, walking crooked along *shifei* distinctions leaves one unharmed from the political wrangling and war caused by ideological enthusiasm.

Conclusion

But if purely philosophical critique merely reveals the conditions for the possibility of certain concepts or phenomena and avoids making normative claims, to what benefit, philosophical or otherwise? This critical distance and ironic detachment is often seen as leading to passivity, even nihilism, which weakens our ethical commitments. Despite the perceived dangers of revealing the foundations of those values that provide meaning to one's life as contingent and accidental, be they ideological, metaphysical, or historical, a philosophically critical attitude may actually help contribute to a psychologically healthier, more meaningful life. The distance philosophical critique maintains between oneself and normative attitudes about ethical and political issues serves an important function within critique: that of a therapeutic.

Borrowing Erik Schwitzgebel's description of humor (1996: 68–96), Moeller and D'Ambrosio relate the critical distance that humor provides in the *Zhuangzi* to the therapeutic function this distance plays, or as they write, "The medicinal or therapeutic effect of 'releasement'... is brought about by humor in the Zhuangzi. ... When read humorously, the text distances itself from the doctrines, morals, or isms that one finds in it when looking for straightforward arguments or positions" (2017: 185). As opposed to critique in the service of liberation adopted by thinkers like Habermas, for example, critique as therapeutic recognizes that each of us, even the philosopher in his ivory tower, is always already within an inescapable web of causal conditions that constrain us, whether it be economic, social, or ideological, and rather than attempt to eliminate these constraints, helps us live within them without destroying ourselves. Regarding the constraints of ideology, insofar as any experience whatsoever must be mediated through a mental model of the world, the world being too complex to grasp in its entirety, any interaction with the world is always already ideological. Recognizing the constraints of the ideological models of the world one has inherited or been thrust into, as well as their historical contingency, helps dissolve the psychologically and socially dogmatic, pathological, and sometimes violent attachment that an overly moralistic discourse can produce. Coming to terms with the powerfully operative concepts and ideas that serve as the conditions for ideological enthusiasm could perhaps help alleviate the fervor and zealotry often encountered in political or religious discourse, not with normative correctives, but through a therapeutic releasement. Likewise, reconciling oneself to the constraints of living in the world might allow one to have a healthy relationship with the values and customs that one's ideology informs and is informed by, perhaps even allowing for a renewed commitment to those very values through a process of sublation or critical reappropriation. I would like to leave the reader with a passage that seems peculiarly out of place within the *Zhuangzi*'s aesthetic of limitless spontaneity and freedom, but one which I hope the interpretation of the *Zhuangzi*'s critique provided in this chapter might make appear a little less foreign.

> There are two great constraints in this world. One is fate (*ming* 命), one's mandated limitations, and the other is responsibility (*yi* 義), doing what fits one's position. A child's love for his parents is fate—it cannot be removed from his heart. An underling's service to a boss is responsibility, the response called for by his position; wherever he goes, he is in service to his boss. It cannot be avoided anywhere in this world … seeing that you likewise cannot change the joy and sorrow it sets before you, thus reconciling yourself to these too as part of your fate, knowing them to be something else you can do nothing about—that is the utmost virtuosity. (Ziporyn 2009: 28)

Notes

1. *Huaxia* 華夏 was the self-appellation of those who identify with the cultural-political lineage and tradition of the Zhou 周 dynasty. This identification as one, unified in-group follows an evolution from *zhuxia* (諸夏, the various *xia* people) to *huaxia*, and eventually to *han* 漢 after the Han dynasty. I will use *huaxia* rather than "Chinese" as it is more accurate in the historical context and refers to an identification with a cultural-political tradition rather than an enthnicity or nationality.
2. Robin Wang's chapter from critique volume.
3. Refer to Yuri Pines (2008).
4. Avoidance of harm and living a long life as ultimate goods is of course a normative stance, seemingly the only examples in the inner chapters that are at odds with the description of critique provided earlier as bracketing off normative claims. These goods were perhaps considered absurd to deny by the compilers of the text or overlooked as "natural" or "given," an excusable omission, as it should not be expected in a critique of a particular phenomenon that *all* phenomena be held at critical distance, an impossible task.
5. "Among the people of Miao, they did not use the power of goodness, but the restraint of punishments. They made the five punishments engines of oppression, calling them the laws." *Shangshu* 尚書, *Lü Xing* 呂刑 (Marquis of Lu on Punishments), 2.
6. "They do not have city walls or permanent living areas and do not engage in cultivating fields" (*Shiji* 史記 "Xiongnu liezhuan 匈奴列传": 4315).
7. "The *rongdi* do not have familial relations and are greedy" (Yang 1981: 936).

8 "Having hearts of tigers and wolves, insatiable and greedy, they pursue profit and cannot be trusted, and do not know *liyi* 礼仪 (the rites and responsibility) or *dexing* 德行 (virtue)" (*Shiji*, "Wei shijia魏世家": 2260).
9 While many examples of the barbarian-sages "avoiding harm" are discussed using metaphors such as "brambles and thorns," it should be noted that the *Zhuangzi* discusses in more direct terms the harm that comes from attachment to *shifei* distinctions and the reputation one has for it. Perhaps the most direct example of this is Confucius's warning to Yan Hui that he will "most likely go and get [himself] executed" as did Guanlong Feng and Wangzi Biqian whom "the ruler did away … with because of their impeccable character" (Ziporyn 2009: 25).

References

Chen Guying 陳鼓應 (1995), *Zhuangzi jinzhu jinyi* 莊子今注今譯 (*Contemporary Annotations and Translations of the Zhuangzi*). Hong Kong: zhonghua shuju.

Chen Yun 陳贇 (2016), *Zhuangzi zhexue de jingshen* 莊子哲學的精神 (*The Essence of Zhuangzi's Philosophy*). Shanghai: shanghai renmin chubanshe.

D'Ambrosio (2017), "Imagination in the Zhuangzi: the Madman of Chu's Alternative to Confucian Cultivation." *Asian Philosophy* 27(1): 33.

Durkheim, Emile (2013), *The Rules of Sociological Method: And Selected Texts on Sociology and Its Method*, edited by Steven Lukes. New York: Free Press.

Foucault, Michel (1988), "Practicing Criticism." In *Politics, Philosophy, Culture: Interviews and Other Writings, 1977–1984*, translated by A. Sheridan et al., edited by L. D. Kritzman, 154. New York: Routledge.

Han Zhaoqi 韓兆琦, ed. (2008), *Xinyi shiji* 新譯史記 (*A New Interpretation of the Records of the Grand Historian*). Taibei: sanmin shuju.

Moeller, Hans-Georg (2008), "Idiotic Irony in the 'Zhuangzi.'" *Chinese Literature: Essays, Articles* (30): 120.

Moeller, Hans-Georg, and Paul D'Ambrosio (2017), *Genuine Pretending: On the Philosophy of the Zhuangzi*. New York: Columbia University Press.

Pines, Yuri (2008), "Changing Vews of *tianxia* in Pre-Imperial Discourse." *Oriens Extremus* 43.

Schwitzgebel, Erik (1996), "Zhuangzi's Attitude toward Language and His Skepticism." In *Essays on Skepticism, Relativism, and Ethics in the "Zhuangzi,"* edited by Paul Kjellberg and Philip J. Ivanhoe, 68–96. Albany: State University of New York Press.

Shangshu 尚書. "Lü Xing 呂刑" (Marquis of Lu on Punishments). Translated by James Legge. ctext.org. https://ctext.org/shang-shu/marquis-of-lu-on-punishments?searchu=呂刑&searchmode=showall#n43254, accessed September 3, 2019.

Shiji 史記. "Wei shijia 魏世家." In *Xinyi shiji* (vol. 5), edited by Han Zhaoqi, 2260. Taibei: *sanmin shuju*.

Shiji 史記. "Xiongnu liezhuan 匈奴列传." In *Xinyi shiji* (vol. 7), edited by Han Zhaoqi, 4315. Taibei: *sanmin shuju*.

Wang Mingke 王明珂 (2013), *Huaxia bianyuan: lishi jiyi yu zuqun rentong* 历史记忆与族群认同 (*The Frontiers of the Huaxia: Historical Memory and Ethnic Identity*). Hangzhou: Zhejiang renmin chubanshe.

Wang, Robin, chapter from this volume.

Wangdao 王道. *Chunqiu fanlu* 春秋繁露. https://ctext.org/pre-qin-and-han?searchu=内诸夏而外夷狄#n22903, accessed May 15, 2019.

Yang Boleng 楊伯峻, ed. (1981), *Chunqiu zuozhuan zhu* 春秋左傳注 (*Edited Collection of The Commentary of Zuo on the Spring and Autumn Annals*). Beijing: Zhonghua shuju.

Yao Dali (2018), "'*Huaxia bianyuan*' *shi zenyang bei manyihua de* '华夏边缘'是怎样被蛮夷化的" (*How the 'Frontiers of the Huaxia' Were Barbarized*). *Sixiang Zhanxian* 思想战线 44(1): 1.

Ziporyn, Brook (2009), *Zhuangzi: The Essential Writings with Selections from Traditional Commentaries*. Indianapolis: Hackett.

10

Li Zehou's Critique of Marx through the Lens of Kantian Philosophy, or the Transcendental Illusion of Class Struggle

Jana S. Rošker

Li Zehou belongs to a group of the most well-known and influential Chinese philosophers of the contemporary era. Hence, I do not think he needs a special introduction in the scope of this collection. However, before I begin introducing the relevant aspects of his philosophy, I should answer the question of how Li's thought can be linked to the topic of the present book, namely *Critique, Subversion, and Chinese Philosophy*.

First of all, we can recall the fact that in the 1980s when Li developed his critique of Marx, particularly his critique of the very notion of class struggle, which is central to Marxism as a theory of socialist and communist revolution, any profound theoretical criticism of Marx was necessarily seen as a form of subversion.

Second, due to his huge influence upon Chinese youth, particularly students and other young intellectuals, his works were prohibited for several years after the disastrous ending of the Tiananmen demonstrations in 1989, and as a result of his criticism of the Chinese government's response to the protests, he was branded soon after the massacre as a "thought criminal" and forbidden to leave Beijing. In 1991, following massive international pressures, he was granted permission to leave the country and visit the United States and Germany. In the United States, he was given permanent residency shortly thereafter, and he still lives there. He has often been seen as one of the most well-known Chinese dissidents of the contemporary era. However, his critical attitude toward Marxist theory began much earlier, in the 1970s, during the later period of the Cultural Revolution.

This chapter deals with Li Zehou's contributions to the discussions of Marxism in the second half of the twentieth century. In Li's philosophy, Marx's theories have been reshaped, modified, and upgraded in a theoretical framework that differs from the original. He agreed with Marx's presumption that tools represented the basic means of production. Nevertheless, he saw Marx's further development of this theory as problematic because he considered it one-sided: progress from the means of production to the relations of production, and then on to the superstructure, concerned only the external developments of the relation between the manufacture and use of tools. At this point, Li was more interested in their internal influences, that is, in the ways in which the making and use of tools has reshaped the human mind. He was highly skeptical toward Marxist economic theories and criticized the crucial concepts elaborated by Marx in his *Capital* through the lens of Kantian "transcendental illusions." Proceeding from his combination of Marx and Kant, this chapter will critically analyze some crucial differences between the Marxist idea of class struggle as a driving force of social progress and Li's own version of historical materialism.

Li Zehou doubtless belongs to the most influential and well-known, but also the most controversial, group of contemporary Chinese philosophers. Due to his intellectual brilliance and charisma, he had a great impact on Chinese youth. Li's popularity among Chinese youth was doubtless due to his emphasis on individual autonomy and democracy, and his questioning of formal authority (Li 2002a: 1–19), a "disobedience" that also found expression in his theoretical essays. Therefore, it is not coincidental that the notion of "subjectality" (*zhutixing* 主体性) is at the center of his theory. It is based on the idea of an active subject forming an independent entity as a potential bearer for the realization of ideals (Li 2002b: 174). It is therefore not difficult to understand the seeds of this attraction; Li sincerely and genuinely believed in the Chinese youth—in their intellectual, emotional, and creative potential. As one of the central representatives of the post-Mao Enlightenment movement, he criticized the remains of traditional gerontocracy that suppressed any form of creativity and independent thought. He openly condemned the academic authorities who demanded from young people only blind obedience, memorization of prescribed texts, and uncritical accumulation of factual knowledge; he encouraged them to believe in themselves: "Young people should be confident; they should not allow themselves to be swallowed and overwhelmed by the huge piles of old Chinese papers" (Li 1985a: 4). Just like China itself, young people exploring its culture should also leave the old, outdated things behind them and go toward the future (Li 1985: 5). Li saw the innovative potential possessed by the young people as something Chinese society still did not value enough. For him, the automatic authority of the old was a relic of the remote past:

> I always feel this is the heritage of primitive societies. In primitive societies, it was clear that people who lived the longest and who had gone through the most things also possessed the best "education." But pre-modern and modern societies are not like that; there are many young people among the genuine inventors. Although they are not so experienced and they don't possess so much knowledge, they can discover a lot and generate numerous important inventions. (1985: 5)

> 我总感觉这好像是原始社会的遗风。在原始社会谁的胡子长，谁的权威就最大。因为他活得长，经历的事情多，「学问」当然也最大。但近现代社会并不是这样。真正的创新家经常有青年人。他们并没有那么多的学问、知识、经验，却偏偏能做出非常重要的发现或发明。

Li was convinced that China could not rely exclusively on experts with tons of accumulated data-driven information, but that it also needed thinkers,[1] and since youth is the best time to develop one's ability to reason and to think independently, he believed young people should make the most of it and should not waste their youth living in fear of the authorities.

Hence, it was not so surprising that immediately after the 1989 tragedy, Li found himself on the black list of Chinese intellectuals who were marked as "black hands" (*hei shou* 黑手) and reproached for attempting to manipulate students for their own goals. Li Zehou was mentioned by name in the official report of the "turmoil" as one of the elite scholars causing chaos. As a result of his criticism of the Chinese government's response to the protests, he was branded soon after the massacre as a "thought criminal" and forbidden to leave Beijing. In 1991, following massive international pressures, he was granted permission to leave the country and visit the United States and Germany. In the United States, he was given a permanent residency shortly thereafter.

Li Zehou's contribution to the sinicization of Marxist thought can be found in his attempts to criticize Marx through Kant, and to complement the latter through the former. In this regard, certain elements of classical Confucian thought are also of utmost importance, especially regarding its historicist, dynamic, referential framework (Brusadelli 2017: 119). However, in this chapter, we will primarily focus upon Li's critique of Marxist economic theories through the lens of Kant's notion of transcendental illusion.

Li's Synthesis of Marx and Kant

We cannot understand Li Zehou's criticism of Marxist thought without being at least basically familiar with a broader context of his writings. They can be described as the search for a synthesis between Western and traditional Chinese thought, driven by the determination to elaborate a system of ideas and values capable of resolving the social and political problems of the modern way of life. In most of his works, he attempted to reconcile "Western" (especially Kantian and Marxist) theories with "traditional Chinese" (especially Confucian, but also, to a certain extent, Daoist) ideas, concepts, and values, in order to create a theoretical model of modernization that would not be confused or equated with "Westernization."

It is not coincidental that early Marx and Kant belonged to the central sources of inspiration for Li Zehou's own theory. However, his system cannot be seen as a mere blend of these philosophies; it exceeds a plain "synthesis of Kant and Marx" by combining their thought with Hegel's and, above all, with that of Confucius. Besides, Li's thought comprises several inventive, essential features that cannot be found in the work of previous philosophers.

He became familiar with the work of Marx from his study at the Beijing University and was fascinated by his concept of historical materialism and early Marxist humanism. But later, as he became acquainted with Kant's transcendental philosophy, the young Chinese philosopher was very much impressed by his emphasis on the idea of human subjectivity and the human subject as an independent, free, active, and morally autonomous agent.

Kant's conception of subjectivity, however, was rooted in the existence of the transcendental forms that decidedly influenced and reshaped the (human perception of) objective realty. While for Kant, these forms were a priori, that is, independent of any kind of (individual or social and historical) experience, Li, who also presupposed the existence of similar forms of subjectivity, placed them into a framework of dynamic historical development. He tried to relocate Kant's transcendental forms into a dynamic and historical context, defined by the principles of a materialist development of humankind. In this sense, he complemented Kant with Marx.

He modified the teleological and deterministic Hegelian-Marxist view of social development through the exciting element of the (morally aware, yet unpredictable) human subject, her free will, and his autonomy.

In this sense, the "meeting point" of Marx and Kant was for him particularly relevant (Li 2016: 154).

Li Zehou agreed with Marx's presumption that tools represented the basic means of production. Nevertheless, he saw Marx's further evolvement of this theory as problematic because he considered it one-sided: progress from the means of production to the relations of production and then on to the superstructure only concerned the external developments of the relation between the manufacture and the use of tools.

At this point, Li was more interested in their internal influences, that is, in the ways in which the making and use of tools has reshaped the human mind. In other words, Li was interested in establishing and investigating the phenomenon of the cultural-psychological formations that were shaped in human inwardness through this process. For Li, this was a phenomenon tightly linked to the central questions of humanness (*ren xing* 人性), for it could reveal the actual difference between human beings and animals (Li and Liu 2011: 77).

In order to proceed a step further on this path of reasoning, Li also offered his own, unique, hypothetical definition of this difference outside of the constructs of behavioral norms, ethics, upright posture, language, or the construction and employment of tools. All these features are not uniquely and specifically human, for they are also displayed by some kinds of animals. Li identifies the crucial difference in the fact that, for human beings, tools are a universal necessity (2011: 77). If humans had only their bodily biological conditions to rely on, they could never survive (as human beings). In Li's view, this is also why humans are "supra-biological" beings.

Marxist Aesthetics and Secret Readings of Kant

Following this line of thought, Li has also contributed some fresh and innovative insights to the development and a dynamic upgrading of Marxist ideas.

His main goal was to clarify the relation between Kant and Marx (neither of whom, in his view, was understood very well in China) and provide for a creative development of the synthesis of their philosophical contributions. In this regard he tried to supplement Kant through Marx, and vice versa. Hence, as already mentioned, the "intersection" of these two theories was of utmost importance (Li 2016: 154). However, he went even further: following this path, Li took the elements he valued most from both philosophies. At some point, he disagreed with both, and from then on, he developed his own theory and followed his own way. He created the great majority of his new, self-coined concepts during the period of the Cultural Revolution, in which he systematically connected Kant and Marx, positing their philosophies in a mutually complementary relation.

As already mentioned, he became acquainted with Marx during his regular studies of philosophy at the Beijing University. Soon after graduation, he started to participate in academic discussions regarding various interpretations of certain Marxist notions. In this respect, he gained a lot of attention in intellectual circles as early as 1956 (when he was 26 years old) with the publication of his first mature theoretical essay entitled "On the Aesthetic Feeling, Beauty, and Art" (*Lun meigan, mei he yishu* 论美感，美和艺术). Later on, he developed his own interpretations of Marxist ideas further, especially in the framework of his aesthetics and epistemology.

His relationship with Kant, however, began under completely different circumstances.

From 1970 to 1972, he was sent to a reeducation working camp at the "May 7th Cadre School" in Henan province. He managed to smuggle into this reeducation camp an English volume of Kant's *Critique of Pure Reason*. There he used to read it secretly, under the cover of *Chairman Mao's Quotes*, pretending to be deeply immersed into the study of this universally enforced reading. In some way, his cynical comments on this situation are quite logical: "In a difficult situation it is good to read a difficult book" (Li 2008: 318).

However, the fact that he took precisely this book along to the reeducation camp was mainly the result of a highly pragmatic decision: it was relatively light, which was ideal since the weight of the luggage he was allowed to take with him was very limited. Also, the book was complex and difficult to understand, which meant that, although a small book, he could read it slowly and it would keep his mind busy and give him intellectual satisfaction for the longest possible time (Li 2008: 318).

In this camp, he also began to work on his first major theoretical monograph *Critique of the Critical Philosophy—A New Approach to Kant* (Li 1990). With this work, Li's own way was paved with a solid theoretical frame. He often admits that, while interpreting Kant, he actually wrote his own philosophy (see, for instance, Li 2016: 153). In this philosophy, he aimed to synthesize Kant with Marx, providing the first with a Marxist historical dimension, but also criticizing the latter because of his philosophy's mechanistic nature and its lack of consideration of the important role of the Kantian human subject.

His later version of sinicized Marxism was completed in the twentieth century and published in Hong Kong as late as 2006 in a book entitled *Marxism in China* (*Makesizhuyi zai Zhongguo* 馬克思主義在中國 (Li 2006). Among other issues, Li has tried in this work to incorporate some Kantian elements into the framework of Marxist dialectical materialism. On the other hand, he also criticized the later Marxist works through the lens of Kant's notion of "transcendental illusions."

Problems of Abstraction and Transcendental Illusions

This aspect of criticism was directed toward Marxist economic theories. In creating his philosophical theory, which is widely known under the name anthropo-historical ontology, Li Zehou was mainly following early Marxist theories. He was always highly skeptical toward Marxist economic theories and criticized the crucial concepts elaborated by Marx in his *Capital*, exposing that Marx had summed up the "two-fold character of commodities" in the "two-fold character of labor." Here, the crucial point was that Marx saw "exchange value" as a product of "abstract labor," since for him, the exchange of commodities was an act characterized by a total abstraction from use value.

In chapter 1 of the *Capital*, Marx described this abstraction of human labor in the following way:

> Along with the useful qualities of the products themselves, we put out of sight both the useful character of the various kinds of labor embodied in them, and the concrete forms of that labor; there is nothing left but what is common to them all; all are reduced to one and the same sort of labor, human labor in the abstract.[2] (Marx 2015: 28)

According to Li, ideas such as socially necessary labor time, which were derived from the concept of abstract human labor, do make sense in rational analysis, but since they are completely separated from the actual circumstances of concrete human lives, they are not empirically operational. In Li's view, Marx has thus completely separated the concept of labor from its concrete empirical environment; he has abstracted the "labor-power" from the actual labor and from the concrete historical practice of making and using tools. This has caused him to slip into an abstract Hegelian, idealistic speculation, in which he aimed to prove his concept of surplus value through a unified and homogenized, abstract idea of the "expenditure of human labor-power."

In this abstract construct, class struggle and the proletarian revolution became necessary, since Marx did not consider any of the complex, historically determined elements (as for instance the developmental stage of technologies in different societies and cultures). In Li's view, such elements decidedly influence the development of societies, which was in Marx's view determined by the relations between the class of the owners of the means of production and commodity-possessors on the one hand, and the working class on the other.

According to Li, this idea of class struggle between capital holders and labor has led Marx to the necessity of eliminating the market-guided production of commodities, which he replaced with planned economy, in which social distribution should be organized according to the maxim "From each according to his abilities, to each according to his needs." In Li's view, such a logic is problematic (Li 2006: 141). He pointed out:

> At the same time, I believe that this logic has no necessary relation with the core part of the historical materialism, which I am emphasizing, namely with the using

and making of tools (and the formation of human language, which stems from it). (2006: 141)

同时我也认为这一逻辑与我强调的唯物史观的核心部分,即使用一制造工具的实践(以及由之而产生人类语言)并无必然的关系.

Li considers the abovementioned abstracted concepts of Marx's economic theory as a form of Kantian "transcendental illusion." Kant defined this as a type of illusion

> which influences principles whose use is not ever meant for experience, since in that case we would at least have a touchstone for their correctness, but which instead, contrary to all the warnings of criticism, carries us away beyond the empirical use of the categories, and holds out to us the semblance of extending the pure understanding.[3] (1987: 385 B352)

In Li's view, such illusions represent conceptions of objects that can only be thought of, but not known, because they are shaped through abstract reasoning without any empirical foundation (2006: 148). They are ideal illusions produced by the transcendental reason. Such transcendental illusions are still actively effective in guiding and organizing human thought, for they help us to achieve the greatest possible unity of reason (Kant 1987: 389 B359). In this regard, Li emphasizes, they positively influence the human ability to act and to change the world. Hence, they have a profound philosophical significance.

However, because of their transcendental nature, that is, because they are completely separated from the empirical world, they cannot be directly applied in concrete strategies and policies of actual societies:

> The system of equal distribution that has been implemented in the past in our people's communes was such a case: it seemingly aimed to achieve justice and equality. However, because it has not considered or taken into account the multifarious other aspects and complex empirical factors, it resulted in stagnation and regression of productive forces. The economic wages were overall equal, but the living standard and the quality of life of the people were stagnating or even deteriorating. (Li Zehou 2006: 146)

列入以前我們人民公社所採取的工分制,就因為沒有考慮,計算其他方面的複雜經驗因素,貌似公正,平等,造成的卻是生產力的停滯和倒退;經濟收入大體平等了,人民生活水準和質量卻停滯或下降了.

In Li's view, this was also the reason why Marx's economic studies could not be developed in the framework of a general economic theory and why his theory of labor value was replaced by various concrete price theories. Although his theory of labor value has a great historical, philosophical, and ethical significance, it completely lacks empirical operability.

A Critical Evaluation of Li's Critique

In many aspects, however, Li's critique of Marx seems to be too generalized or simply too harsh. In the following discussion, I will consider three such aspects, which are, in my view, based on a very superficial reading of the *Capital* and the *Communist Manifesto*.

As we have seen, Li claimed that Marxist ideas, such as socially necessary labor time, were derived from the concept of abstract human labor. He reproached Marx with a denial of any of the complex, historically determined elements (as for instance the developmental stage of technologies in different societies and cultures). However, this critique seems to be somehow a pretense; for, in his definition of socially necessary labor time, Marx explicitly writes about the importance of these factors. In his view, they are historically and culturally defined and represent important elements of the category of socially necessary labor time. According to Marx, these elements can vary throughout different societies and they profoundly influence the value of particular individual and social labor. He writes:

> The labor time socially necessary is that required to produce an article under the normal conditions of production, and with the average degree of skill and intensity prevalent at the time. The introduction of power-looms into England probably reduced by one-half the labor required to weave a given quantity of yarn into cloth. The hand-loom weavers, as a matter of fact, continued to require the same time as before; but for all that, the product of one hour of their labor represented after the change only half an hour's social labor, and consequently fell to one-half its former value.[4] (Marx 1876: 43)

Li's critique, which concentrates on his alleged separation of socially necessary labor time from the actual concrete conditions of the production, is therefore simply wrong, for Marx explicitly emphasizes the following:

> The value of a commodity would remain constant, if the labor time required for its production also remained constant. But the latter changes with every variation in the productiveness of labor. This productiveness is determined by various circumstances, amongst others, by the average amount of skill of the workmen, the state of science, and the degree of its practical application, the social organization of production, the extent and capabilities of the means of production, and by physical conditions.[5] (1876: 44)

Furthermore, Marx never wrote about replacing the market-guided production of commodities with planned economy. Planned economy is a concept developed by the theoreticians of the Soviet-type state-socialism. On the contrary, he even criticized the germs of such theories as could be found in the works of several utopian socialists:

> It may therefore be imagined that one can impose the stamp of immediate interchangeability on all commodities at the same time, as one may imagine, one could make all Catholics popes. The coloring of this Philistinopia is Proudhon's

socialism, which, as I have shown elsewhere, does not even have the merit of originality, but was far better developed by Gray, Bray, and others long before him.[6] (1876: 67)

In this context, Marx also emphasized that no school has ever played more tricks with the word "science" than the utopian socialists.

On the other hand, it is also quite rewarding in this context to compare Li's critique of Marx with the ideas of some other, more widely known representatives of the sinicization of Marxism. If we want to evaluate Li's view of Marx's philosophy against the background of the so-called Chinese Marxism, it therefore becomes very clear that his critique of Marx is completely incompatible with the views of all three of the most important Chinese leaders, who have shaped the Marxist ideology as a legitimization of the current system, namely Mao Zedong, Deng Xiaoping, and Xi Jinping.

Mao's agenda of sinicized Marxism represented an attempt to synthesize the Marxist theory with the specific characteristics of the Chinese society, particularly focusing upon the concepts of permanent revolution and the crucial role of peasantry that should, in his view, fill up the gap existing due to the absence of a large urban proletariat and replace it in the class struggle between labor and capital (see Mao 1937).

Deng's "Marxism" was highly pragmatic. He is often said to have saved the Chinese economy after the Cultural Revolution. He typically insisted on practice almost to the exclusion of theory and famously thought it did not matter if a cat is white or black so long as it catches the mice[7] (Deng 1989: 324).

Xi Jinping has directed attention to what he calls the Chinese dream. According to President Xi, the Chinese dream includes the "Four Comprehensive Strategies" (Sige quanmian zhanlüe buzhu 四个全面" 战略布局) (Xi 2015). This theory refers to the conception of a moderately prosperous society, including deepening reform, governing according to law, and the strict governance by the party.

What they all have in common is the ideational heritage of mechanistic, anti-Hegelian, Soviet interpretations of Marxism, which provided the fundamental basis for autocratic state-socialism. Li's understanding of Marx is utterly different.

On the one hand, Li's critique of Marxism is focused upon his emphasis on the importance of class struggle. Especially in his later years, Li was a sharp critic of all violent and sudden social shifts; he utterly negated the importance of the concept of class struggle and permanent revolution. Instead, he proposed gradual, reasonable changes, and social progress based upon an evolution. In this sense, his view could be—at a first glimpse—seen as similar to that of Xi Jinping.

On the other hand, Li Zehou exposed that there is a great gap between Marx's theories and the theories of so-called Marxism, which, as a system, is a product of later interpretations, beginning with Engels and continuing with Lenin, Stalin, and the Soviet types of interpretations that belonged to the crucial pillars of Chinese Marxism. In this context, Li also highlights that the notion of socialism, which stands in the forefront of all three ideologies, is actually absent in the Marxist theory, for Marx was primarily elaborating on the utopia of communism. Here, he exposed the fact that socialism was a product of later interpretations, the ones that provided the fundamental basis of autocratic state-socialism. In this aspect, Li's interpretation can be seen as a profound critique of all three aforementioned representatives of Chinese Marxism.

Conclusion

Instead of revolution, Li advocated social evolution, customized to free and autonomous personalities, and taking into account the integrity of human subjects. He even argued that Marxism should not merely be seen as a doctrine of revolution; in studying Marx, readers should rather focus upon his "constructive" elements. Hence, he emphasizes that Marxism is not only a philosophy of revolution. It is rather, and even more so, a constructive philosophy, a philosophy for constructing material and spiritual civilizations. This is also a core aspect of Li's critique of Marxism through the lens of Kant's philosophy and his attempts to synthesize the theories of these two German philosophers.

For Li Zehou, the synthesis of Kant and Marx is closely connected with the concept of human emancipation and human dignity, an issue that is also of great importance and relevance for the present era.

Notes

1 Li has elaborated on the difference between these two categories of knowledge in greater detail. In his view experts were good in storing, systemizing, and ordering information, while thinkers could also process it in the sense of analyzing and, above all, synthesizing the data—therefore transforming quantitative information into qualitative knowledge. In a later essay, which he also wrote to and for young readers (see Li 1996: 85), he pointed out that in the future, experts could be replaced by computers and artificial brains, while thinkers would always remain nonpareil.
2 The German original reads: "Mit dem nützlichen Charakter der Arbeitsprodukte verschwindet der nützliche Charakter der in ihnen dargestellten Arbeiten, es verschwinden also auch die verschiedenen konkreten Formen dieser Arbeiten, sie unterscheiden sich nicht länger, sondern sind allzusamt reduziert auf gleiche menschliche Arbeit, abstrakt menschliche Arbeit" (Marx 1876: 42).
3 The German original reads: "Wir haben es mit dem *transzendentalen Scheine* allein zu tun, der auf Grundsätze einfließt, deren Gebrauch nicht einmal auf Erfahrung angelegt ist, als in welchem Falle wir doch wenigstens einen Probierstein ihrer Richtigkeit haben würden, sondern der uns selbst, wider alle Warnungen der Kritik, gänzlich über den empirischen Gebrauch der Kategorien wegführt und uns mit dem Blendwerke einer Erweiterung des *reinen Verstandes* hinhält" (Kant 1998: 405).
4 The German original reads: "Gesellschaftlich notwendige Arbeitszeit ist Arbeitszeit, erheischt, um irgendeinen Gebrauchswert mit den vorhandenen gesellschaftlich-normalen Produktionsbedingungen und dem gesellschaftlichen Durchschnittsgrad von Geschick und Intensität der Arbeit darzustellen. Nach der Einführung des Dampfwebstuhls in England z.B. genügte vielleicht halb so viel Arbeit als vorher, um ein gegebenes Quantum Garn in Gewebe zu verwandeln. Der englische Handweber brauchte zu dieser Verwandlung in der Tat nach wie vor dieselbe Arbeitszeit, aber

das Produkt seiner individuellen Arbeitsstunde stellte jetzt nur noch eine halbe gesellschaftliche Arbeitsstunde dar und fiel daher auf die Hälfte seines frühern Werts."

5 The German original reads: "Die Wertgröße einer Ware bliebe daher konstant, wäre die zu ihrer Produktion erheischte Arbeitszeit konstant. Letztere wechselt aber mit jedem Wechsel in der Produktivkraft der Arbeit. Die Produktivkraft der Arbeit ist durch mannigfache Umstände bestimmt, unter anderen durch den Durchschnittsgrad des Geschickes der Arbeiter, die Entwicklungsstufe der Wissenschaft und ihrer technologischen Anwendbarkeit, die gesellschaftliche Kombination des Produktionsprozesses, den Umfang und die Wirkungsfähigkeit der Produktionsmittel, und durch Naturverhältnisse."

6 The German original reads: "Man mag sich daher einbilden, man könne allen Waren zugleich den Stempel unmittelbarer Austauschbarkeit aufdrücken, wie man sich einbilden mag, man könne alle Katholiken zu Päpsten machen. ... Die Ausmalung dieser Philisterutopie bildet Proudhons Sozialismus, der, wie ich anderswo gezeigt, nicht einmal das Verdienst der Originalität besitzt, vielmehr lange vor ihm von Gray, Bray und andern weit besser entwickelt wurde."

7 黄猫、黑猫，只要捉住老鼠就是好猫。"这 是说的打仗.

References

Brusadelli, Federico (2017), "A Tale of Two Utopias: Kang Youwei's Communism, Mao Zedong's Classicism and the 'Accommodating Look' of the Marxist Li Zehou." *Asian Studies* 5(1): 103–22.

Deng Xiaoping (1989), Deng Xiaoping wenxuan, Di yi juan. 邓小平文选。第一卷。 (Selected Works of Deng Xiaoping, vol. 1). Beijing: Renmin chuban she.

Kant, Immanuel (1987), *Critique of Pure Reason*, translated by Paul Guyer and Allen W. Wood. Cambridge: Cambridge University Press.

Kant, Immanuel (1998), *Kritik der reinen Vernunft*. Hamburg: Felix Meiner Verlag.

Li Zehou 李泽厚 (1985), "Xin chun hua zhishi—zhi qingnian pengyoumen 新春话知识——致青年朋友们 (Knowledge in the New Spring—for My Young Friends)." *Wenshi zhishi* 1985 (1): 3-7.

Li Zehou 李泽厚 (1990), *Pipan zhexuede pipan (Kangde shuping)* 批判哲學的批判(康德述評) (Critique of the Critical Philosophy (A New Key to Kant)). Taibei: Fengyun sichao.

Li Zehou 李泽厚 (1996), *Zou wo zijide lu* 走我自己的路 (Following My Own Way). Taibei: Sanmin shudiuan.

Li Zehou 李泽厚 (2002a), *Meixue san shu* 美学三书 (Three Books on Aesthetics). Hefei: Anhui wenyi chuban she.

Li Zehou 李泽厚 (2002b), *Zou wo zijide lu* 走我自己的路 (Going My Own Way). Beijing: Shenghuo dushu xinzhi Sanlian shudian.

Li Zehou 李泽厚 (2006), *Makesizhuyi zai Zhongguo* 馬克思主義在中國 (Marxism in China). Hong Kong: Minbao chuban she.

Li Zehou 李泽厚 (2008), *Renleixue lishi bentilun* 人類學歷史本體論 (Anthropological Historical Ontology). Tianjin: Tianjin shehui kexue yuan chuban she.

Li Zehou 李泽厚 (2016), "Li Zehou duitan lu 李澤厚對談錄 (Recordings of Li Zehou's Conversations)." *Dai yue ting yu zhu jilu.* http://www.doc88.com/p-7030124841.html. Beijing: Dai yue ting yu ge zhuzang shu.

Li Zehou 李澤厚 and Liu Xuyuan 劉緒源 (2011), "Li Zehou tan xueshu sixiang san jieduan 李澤厚談學术思想三階段 (Li Zehou Discusses the Three Phases of His Academic Thought)." *Shanghai wenxue* 2011(1): 72–7.

Mao Zedong. 毛泽东 (1937), *Maodun lun* 矛盾论 (*On Contradiction*). Beijing: Zhonggong zhongyang wenxuan.

Marx, Karl (1876), *Das Kapital. Kritik der politischen Ökonomie.* Hamburg: Verlag Otto Meissner.

Marx, Karl (2015), *Capital: A Critique of Political Economy, Vol. I, Book One: The Process of Production of Capital*, translated by Samuel Moore and Edward Aveling, edited by Frederick Engels. Moscow: Progress Publishers.

Xi Jinping 习近平 (2015), Guanyu xietiao tuijin "sige quanmian" zhanlüe buju—lunxu zhaibian关于协调推进 "四个全面"战略布局—论述摘编 (On Coordination and Promotion of "Four Comprehensive" Strategic Layouts—Excerpts). Beijing: Zhongyang wenxian chuban she.

11

Kundao 坤道, Daring Odyssey: Female Daoists' Discontentment and Challenge to Confucian Womanhood

Robin R. Wang

Hunting for food, building bridges, subduing an ever-encroaching, malicious nature, and creating triumphs of human civilization: these seemed, in a general sense and across many cultures, associated with the masculine attributes of power, control, and dominance, whereas the feminine was associated with yielding, flexibility, and submissiveness. *Daodejing* inverts the value of these attributes, pointing out the power of the feminine. Traditionally, however, that inversion went against mainstream views, particularly those of the Confucians who dominated social and political institutions. While the governing social models of Chinese culture were for the most part cemented by Confucianism, Daoism (and later Buddhism) was a wellspring for theoretical and practical options. Confronted with the realities encapsulated in the dictums that extolled "the virtuous wife and good mother" (*xianqi liangmu* 贤妻良母) in Confucianism, female Daoists, seen as *Kundao* 坤道 (the Way of Femininity), have had to find their own life journey that does not fit the mainstream narrative. They have contested the gendered grammar of womanhood, where grammar means the rules and structure that assign woman to a position within a script. Thus, Kundao has been an invisible resistance to the Confucian ideal womanhood—a commitment to the path of self-realization and a willingness to live with a critical alternative. This chapter will map some conceptual and practical constellations.

Becoming Female: A Critical Reflection and Subversion of Values

Daoism, a Dao-based and Dao-inspired teaching and practice, has been considered the philosophy of yielding in Chinese intellectual history. One important aspect of yielding is being *rou* 柔 soft, gentle, supple—which the *Daodejing* couples with the infant, water, and the feminine. It attempts to awaken human beings from the intellectual slumber into which we have been socialized and shaped.

All phenomena in nature or, in classical Chinese terminology, "all things under heaven" (*tian xia* 天下) can be distinguished according to their characteristics as either *yin* or *yang*, and man/male/masculinity and woman/female/femininity are naturally identified with this yin–yang matrix (Wang 2012). Unlike other interpretations of the *yin-yang* complementarity in Chinese thought, the *Daodejing* suggests the primordiality, indeed the superior power, of *yin* in general and the female and femininity in particular. From the perspective of the *Daodejing*, the female/femininity is not excluded, shunned, frozen out, disadvantaged, rejected, unwanted, abandoned, dislocated, or otherwise marginalized. Its basic identity as a cosmic potentiality and a necessary part of any and every generative process is highly valued and celebrated. Actually, the spontaneous potency of *Dao* is female, or is becoming female. *Dao* is associated with the female body, a common metaphor for *Dao* in the *Daodejing*. This metaphor reveals not just the importance of *yin* and its generative capacity, but also designates a *yin* origin that is hidden, implicit, or empty.

The *Daodejing* begins:

> As to a Dao—
> if it can be specified as a Dao,
> it is not a permanent Dao.
> As to a name—
> if it can be specified as a name,
> it is not a permanent name.
> Having no name
> is the beginning of the ten thousand things.
> Having a name,
> is the mother of the ten thousand things. (Moeller 2007: 3)

Here the mother is designated as the beginning of all things or the name of all things. In chapter 52 we encounter this mother again:

> The world has a beginning:
> it is considered the Mother of the world.
> 天下有始、以爲天下母 (Moeller 2007: 123)

In chapter 25, the *Daodejing* defines *Dao*:

> There is a thing—
> it came to be in the undifferentiated,
> it came alive before heaven and earth.
> What stillness! What emptiness!
> Alone it stands fast and does not change.
> It can be mother to heaven and earth. (Moeller 2007: 123)

The *Daodejing* explains that the first way to describe the *Dao* is *mu* 母, "mother." The word *mu* has a broader range of meanings than merely "biological mother." It is expanded to mean the source of heaven and earth and the myriad things in them. *Dao*/mother is responsible for the origin of all things, is with all things, and provides the patterns that one should follow. This basic philosophical commitment reflects a view that the cosmos and world are generated, not created, through a multiplicative process. The terms used in classical Chinese texts for the origin of the myriad things incorporate a sense of "life" and "birth," both of which are encompassed by the Chinese term *sheng* 生 (generation). This link between generation and the mother naturally leads to the priority of female energy. It is generation or transformation, not a substance or Being, which builds up the Chinese philosophical landscape or horizon.

The source of the variable and changing lies in the intrinsic femininity of *Dao*. Interestingly, there are no "male" images of *Dao*, such as father or son; nor are traditionally male traits, like force, strength, or aggression linked to *Dao*. In addition to the word *mu* (mother), the *Daodejing* incorporates two other sets of terms in relation to femininity, *pin* 牝 appearing three times and *ci* 雌 appearing twice. It is important to highlight the fact that these terms are different from *nu* 女 (woman in contemporary Chinese) or *fu* 婦 (woman in classical Chinese). The notion of *nu* or *fu* refers to woman in a social relationship. This social construction of woman does not appear in the *Daodejing* at all. Both *pin* and *ci* have been translated as "female"; in fact *pin* refers to female animals in general and *ci* refers specifically to hens, as opposed to *xiong*, which refers to roosters (for more discussion of these two pairs, see Ryden 1997: 29–36). *Pin* and *ci* are ways to demonstrate the natural supremacy and potency of the feminine.

We read in *Daodejing* chapter 6:

The spirit of the valley does not die—
This is called mysterious femininity [*pin*].
The gate of mysterious femininity [*pin*]—
This is called the root of heaven and earth. (Moeller 2007: 17)

Here the *pin* is mysterious, the root of heaven and earth, an unlimited resource. This gendered source without beginning or end, persisting in perpetuity, is the realm of becoming. The character for spirit, *gu* 谷, originally meant generation and is equated with *sheng* (part of the character for gender and nature or tendencies), and its shape is often taken to represent the female genitals.

With respect to the "mysterious femininity," one can notice two interesting directions. On the one hand, there is what we might call the horizontal level in which femininity/yin and masculinity/yang are counterparts, both of which are embedded in the myriad of things. On the other hand, there is a vertical level in which masculinity/yang refers to the things before us, while femininity/yin refers to the origin that is hidden, implicit, or empty, yet the most important aspect of all existences.

The *Daodejing* starts a full-fledged campaign to bring greater pressure on the sage's leadership ability, moral character, and actions. This proclamation ripples through the fabric of Chinese culture, and Sages (which were traditionally men) would now be required to maintain a capacity for fostering femininity.

This view also challenges the gender asymmetry in which the masculine poses as a disembodied universality while the feminine is constructed as a disavowed corporeality.

Femininity is not based on the exclusion of the masculine nor is masculinity a rejection of the feminine. *Daodejing*'s femininity is not a normative ideal, but rather a descriptive feature of experience and a lived body. Conceivably, *Daodejing*'s construction of femininity provides a conceptual alternative to masculine ways of thinking about reason and verifies that reason is not a purely masculine concept.

Kundao: An Invisible Resistance and Negotiation

The *Daodejing* privileges the use of philosophical imagery of the feminine and relies on the feminine as a way of thinking, knowing, experiencing, and desiring. However, femininity, as the *Daodejing* conceives it, was situated in a particular cultural and historical context, and as such the text was not intended to change women's social and political position in China. It does not promote the kind of gender equality that Western feminists fight for. Dao does not govern actually existing gender relations— or, at least, the social and political reality of gender relations is not modeled on Dao, because the patriarchy is not Dao.

Interestingly, in the context of Daoist practice, there are no significant constraints on the leadership roles and possibilities of spiritual attainment for women. Although the *Daodejing* has not been used politically, socially, or economically to advance women's interests and benefits, nevertheless, it has carved out an intellectual and physical space for women in practice. Female Daoists have been active in Chinese society through the history of Daoism, particularly in the religious community. They have formed many notable social groups since the Tang dynasty (618–907), as seen in their poetry and other writings, as well as in their practices. However, female Daoists' works and influences, as a silent voice, have been remarkably underrepresented in academic studies in China and abroad. Let's take the case of *kundao* 坤道.

Kundao is a title of respect for female Daoists who have left home (*chujia* 出家) and entered a Daoist monastery. The term *kundao* is the combination of two important terms from the *Yijing* (*Book of Changes*): *Kun* and Dao. *Kun* 坤 refers to Earth as the complement of *qian*, Heaven. It is the highest cosmic concept that denotes the female and all things representing femininity in the *Yijing*. Dao means the Way. *Kundao* refers to female Daoists but it also implies their habituation of a spiritual and physical space for the reconstruction of their existence and identities, along with their cultivation of perfection (*xiuzhen* 修真).

Whereas "good mother and virtuous wife" became a cultural imperative to produce Chinese women as subjects wired to always perform these two specific social roles, Kundao have been a silent and quiet resistance by committing to the Daoist mission and going to the Daoist temple. They have negotiated different social expectations and a way of expressing "otherness." These personal journeys foreground the epistemological and ontological question of what it means to be a woman and to lead a flourishing life.

Let's consider two examples of Kundao from past to present. Cao Wenyi (1039–1115), whose Daoist name is Daochong, was seen as "the master of tranquility and human virtue and the perfection of the Dao." She was born into a wealthy family in Ningjing, Hebei. According to historical record, she could read and cite poetry at the age of 5 and was capable of remembering things after a mere glance at the age of 15. By the age of 21, she defied the conventional path of arranged marriage and escaped it by fleeing to Yu Hua Mountain where she led an extremely harsh and poor life. Despite these challenges she contributed historical commentaries on the Daoist classics *Daodejing, Zhuangzi*, and other texts.

Many of her writings have been lost, with the exception of a text called *The Song of Ultimate Source of Great Dao* 靈源大道歌 (*Lingyuan Dadaoge*). This work consists of 128 sentences written in poetic and elegant stanzas and was intended to inspire women and men throughout the ages to return to the great source and lead a transformative life. This work is the very first undisputable, and hence the oldest known, authentic Daoist text written by a woman.

This is how Cao starts the first sentence of *Dadaoge*:

What I want to truly talk about is the very root of life;
It comes from a genius source;
Reflecting on one's longevity body is not empty;
Spirited mirror (*lingjie*/body) contains myriad things;
Ultimate (*taiji*) spreads mysterious and human being gets the oneness;
Received oneness should be carefully guarded and do not lose it.
我爲諸君說端的，命蒂從來在真息。
照體長生空不空，靈鑒含天容萬物
太極布妙人得一，得一善持謹勿失

(Chen 1988: 5)

The classical Daoist visions of human life were pursued and actualized in Cao's work. According to Cao, the human mind/heart is *lingjie* 靈鑒 (numinous mirror), which contains and reflects all myriad things; the human body is *lingfu* 靈府 (numinous residence), full of chambers and palaces for the universal spirit and various gods to reside. The numinous mirror must be emptied through cultivation, and the numinous residence or lodging place must be clean to allow the spirits to come and stay. This cultivation is called *xiuzhen* 修真 (cultivation of perfection) to become *zhenren* 真人 (a human of perfection).

The mind is not based on the exclusion of body nor is body a rejection of mind. There is no body outside of the mind and there is no mind outside of the body. This prescribes a developmental and dynamic process that defines an original fullness of the ultimate reality and human being.

Cao's *Dadaog*, Stanza 25–8 read:

Shen (spirit) is *xing* 性 (inner nature), *qi* is *ming* 命 (fate,)
The spirit does not gallop away,
qi will be firmly solidified.
Originally they are intimately linked,
If they ever be dispersed—what will be the primordial handle of life?
Integrated to become one yet forget one,
it can be changed with the primordial transformation"

神是性兮氣是命，神不外馳氣自定。
本來二物更誰親，失卻將何爲本柄？
混合爲一復忘一，可與元化同出沒。

Cao addresses two important notions in Daoist self-cultivation. Unlike Western distinctions between spiritual soul and material body or lofty rational mind and lowly emotional body, Cao perceives the human being as the unity of *xing* and *ming*. The concept of *xing* literally means "inherent disposition" or "innate tendency." The word *xing*, however, appears after the word for life 生 (*sheng*) so it has an intrinsic connection with *sheng*. The character for *xing* is composed of two parts: *sheng* (life, generation) and *xin* 心 (heart/mind). This distinction is a key Daoist presupposition.

Another vital aspect of the human being is *ming*. *Ming* refers to one's vital force or circumstantial trajectories. It connects one's physical aspects such as one's biological conditions, life expectancy, or unexpected events that may occur. The notion of *ming* instantiates a recognition of our limitations in life. These limitations are imposed by one's physical capacities, health, temperament, emotional range, talents, society, culture, and historical circumstances. To be wise is to be attentive to these limitations in the construction of one's patterns, as it would be both foolish to be willfully blind to them.

Cao identifies *shen* 神 (spirit) with *xing* 性 (inner nature) and *qi* 氣 (energy flow or life force) with *ming* 命 (bodily form, lifespan). *Ming* is given by heaven[1] and connected with one's *xing* (form) or physical body, while *xing* is related with the one's *xin* 心 (heart/mind). The connection between *xing* and *ming* has become the testing ground for different Daoist schools. Early Chinese texts use the compound *xingming* 性命, defined as "the two overlapping factors that together determine life's course." They are two aspects of the same human life or same principle. Cultivation of life thus refers to a conjoined cultivation of *xing* and *ming*.

This dual cultivation process brings one's mind, body, and spirit into a stage of "clarity and tranquility" 清靜 (*qingjing*). The unification of the concepts in the form of *xingming* has been recognized as Cao's most cherished and unique contribution to Daoist philosophy—a remarkable contribution to Daoist intellectual history.

Now we turn to the life of a real contemporary Kundao, Li. Inspired by stories of immortality and martial arts novels, Li left a poor village in Anhui Province at the age of 19 and went to the Wudang Mountain for Daoist training. However, she became involved with a male Daoist while there and found herself pregnant. Both were forced to leave the mountain and return to his hometown. Due to the hardships of life in the village, the father left Li and her son to return to Wudang shortly after the child's birth. Li and her young boy, with no place to go, started to wander the streets of the city. Finally, they met a kind man who took them in.

After a few years of living a calm yet challenging farming life, Li wanted to try to pursue her Daoist dream once again. She discussed this with her benefactor and asked him to take care of her son. She left her son and returned to Wudang, where she made a request to visit other Daoist mountains. There is an internal policy among these mountain Daoists that they are permitted to rotate every three years among the mountains as long as someone is willing to host them. Presently, Li—a 32-year-old female Daoist—is in her first year at Nanyue, and after two years she will go to Huashan Mountain in Shanxi.

While speaking to Li a few years ago, I asked about life in the temple and discussed her feelings toward her son. Although she receives a stipend of only 20 yuan ($3.00) per month, all of her living expenses are provided for and she is enjoying temple life because it affords her the luxury to read books, play an *erhu* and *pipa* (Chinese musical instruments), and be free of many of the stresses of life. She remains confident that her now 8-year-old son is well cared for and believes there is no reason to worry about his personal well-being.

Li's life is an eventful story of existential crisis to existential odyssey. From the perspective of a specific interpretation of Confucian social roles, however, we can ask: Did Kundao Li initially make a wrong choice in deciding to go to the Wudang Mountain? In getting pregnant? In defying her proper social roles as a wife and a mother? Who is responsible for her falling out of her roles? What is the relationship between the hegemonic power of social structures and female subjective agency? Is there a line between woman-as-victim and woman-as-agent in historical and social transformations? Confronted with the realities encapsulated in the dictums that extoll "the virtuous wife" and "the good mother" (*xianqi liangmu* 贤妻良母) so embraced by Confucianism, should women like Li have other theoretical and practical alternatives? Which way—being a mother in a poor home or going to the temple without her child—enables her to lead a flourishing life?

Claiming Space and Celebrating Difference

Noticeably, a Kundao's life is out of sync with social and cultural expectations, and it subverts ideal womanhood by shifting our attention toward something different. It compels us to reorient our epistemic, social, cultural, and personal framework related to the identity of the woman. In other words, Kundao experiences provide us a point of departure for a critique of so-called ideal womanhood, which consigns women to modes of desiring self-abnegation rather their own well-being.

Is there only one way to be a woman? Does a woman have to be a mother and wife in order to be a good woman? Should we create more social, intellectual, and personal space for those women who want to lead a life differently than others? Should "otherness" be allowed in a healthy and prosperous society?

These questions stipulate that Confucian culture should offer a *space* for all kinds of womanhood and celebrate a *different* lifestyle that goes beyond socially constructed roles and responsibilities. A different mode of problematizing the good life or well-being for all women in the Confucian culture is the first step to this challenge. This contest can be seen as a *restive* orientation, which allows woman to think in two directions simultaneously: to claim the place one is in while moving toward another place. This restiveness involves an inhabitation of unfitting—not fitting neatly into the mainstream's ideal of womanhood. It also entails an examination of one's wish to move away from socially constructed womanhood yet remain a woman.[2]

Striving for a space mentally or physically has been a Daoist inspiration from *Daodejing* in theory and from Kundao Cao Wenyi and Li in practice. Emptiness in mind or a free mental space is strongly encouraged to live out the best of one's life span. With the same spirit, claiming space here refers to a personal construction of one's own life path, a vision of *du* 独 (solitude) in Zhuangzi's teaching. One needs *du* to lead a flourishing life and not be fully programed into a social system. Claiming space will expand our understanding and give voice to a yearning for self that resists conformity to community.

This space-claiming reveals a difference within women's life, which in regard to the mainstream is an unfittingness. This difference is not a tool of division or subordination, but rather is a site of knowledge that can amplify and sharpen our understanding. Accordingly, Kundao's practices open us to engage the differences as a significant normative and humanistic value.

An argument can be made to support this difference, particularly an argument for a social structure that can nourish all human beings under heaven. If Indigenous American women are theorizing about sovereignty, black Americans theorizing about freedom, Chicanx and Latinx Americans theorizing about immigration, and Asian American and Pacific Islanders theorizing about home, conceivably, Daoist women are theorizing about space and differences within Confucian culture.

We can learn much from *Zhuangzi* to celebrate this difference and become a genuine person. The *du*獨, "solitude" or "alone," is a way to live a genuine life. We read in the chapter Under Heaven (天下):

"But now Mo-zi alone, would have no singing during life."
（今墨子獨生不歌）
… and in the solitude of one's individuality to dwell with the spirit-like and intelligent…
（澹然獨與神明居）;
I will receive the offscourings of the world. Men all choose fullness; he alone chooses emptiness. … Men all seek for happiness, but he feels complete in his imperfect condition ….
己獨取後，曰：「受天下之垢。」人皆取實，己獨取虛…
人皆求福，己獨曲全
He chiefly cared to occupy himself with the spirit-like operation of heaven and earth … .
獨與天地精神往來. (Zhuangzi 2009)

In these writings *Zhuangzi* explores the idea that a man or woman can come to an understanding of his or her self that is not limited to social roles. In another example, the story of the *she* 社 (shrine) tree, Zhuangzi describes how a particular tree goes along with social designations, and yet does not limit its own self-identity to them. The tree allows itself to be viewed as a *she* shrine, and it is not bothered by the fact that this is how others view it. Social designations have little significant impact on how the tree views itself, or actually lives. This is in line with the Zhuangzi's general approach of advocating a view of oneself that is not limited to social roles, or even concrete actions. *Du* is one's attitude, which is not necessarily a rejection of social roles, but a critical reflection on them.³ One does not view one's self in terms of social roles, and is thereby able to surpass cultural constraints. It is a useful attitude to lead a genuine life. According to the *Zhuangzi* one does not have to pity herself and is at home knowing that no social roles can perfectly fit her *zhen* 真(genuine) or natural self.

What Zhuangzi's teaching inherently means is the recognition of differences rather than a demand for uniformity. The claiming of space and celebrating of difference amplifies the complexities of women's lives past and present in China. It demands critical questioning of whether women should internalize ideal values of womanhood in being, doing, and desiring.

In other words, we need to view every person's experience in terms of both its dynamic continuities and its manifold multiplicity, as both a ceaseless processual flow and as distinctive, consummatory events. It is a wholeness of particularity and totality, as Roger Ames defines a focus-field person (2011: 163). Any particular phenomenon in our field of experience can be focused in different ways: on the one hand, she is a unique and persistent particular, and on the other, since she is constituted by the full complement of her relationships, she has the entire cosmos and all that is happening implicated within her. What this means for persons is that they are uniquely who they are as distinct from all others, yet in their magnitude, to give a full account of the social, natural, and cultural relationships that constitute any one of them, we must exhaust the cosmic totality.

Let's apply this perspective to the Kundao's lived experience. Kundao's particular experiences consist of running away from standard social roles for women and stepping outside of basic familiar relations while linking up with their inspirations for cultivation, music, temples, and nature. They are strangers to Confucian role orientation. Should a society oriented around Confucian roles accept them or pity them? Or, should the ideas that orient Confucian roles be used to critique the Kundao's social structure? Hopefully, the Confucian social structure can bring a degree of flexibility, adjustment, and innovation as well as acceptance of personal vulnerability.

The Kundao's odyssey offers a dynamic opportunity to all women. It focuses on the way in which the opportunity is available to each of us to optimize the possibilities that dovetail with the relationships between particular persons and their surrounding conditions. This is what the *Yijing* (*Book of Changes*) means when it says "the mysteries of the world have no squareness and change has no shape" (*shenwufang er yiwuti* 神無方而易無體). Although Kundao's practices appear to lie outside of Confucian role orientation, this role ultimately and invariably serves as an intermediate on the grounds of social roles, teaching of specific persons in their particular situations.

The Kundao's odyssey ignites a paradigm shift to a multilevel complexity that extends from human life to the cosmos. This philosophical thesis involves chance and adaptation to a world in which internal and external factors, living and nonliving things, and mechanistic and organic worldviews are blurred and blended. Scholars have made the case for complexity and for shifting the paradigm, such as Mitchell, who states, "We need to expand our conceptual frameworks to accommodate contingency, dynamic robustness, and deep uncertainty" (Mitchell 2009: 121).

In recent years, a group of scholars, scientists, and activists has defined human beings as planetary beings. Planetary humanity is understood in three senses: (1) that humans are woven together with nonhuman animals, events, and processes into the fabric of deep time variously construed in religious, secular, and scientific cosmological orders; (2) that the human awareness of humans' planetary nature provides a context for philosophy to negotiate its diverse historical-cultural-linguistic framings and its claims to universality and truth; (3) that the novel (or newly remembered) awareness of our planetary nature has also been accompanied by the rapid advancement of global communications technologies, which entail new social, ethical, and political questions regarding the distribution of knowledge, access to information, planetary citizenship, and democratic participation.[4] Fei Xiaotong (1910–2005) in his sixteen Chinese words reflects this spirit:

各美其美，美人之美，美美与共，天下大同。
Understanding yourself and discovering your own form of beauty,
Befriend others and appreciate beauty of different people.
If beauty represents itself with all diversity and integrity;
The world will be blessed with a great harmony.[5]

Conclusion

This chapter attempts to bring a Daoist teaching and practice to critique the socially constructed standard for being a woman, and to bring this critique into a scholarly and intellectual dialogue. According to Kant, one of the many meanings of critique is bound up with an open inquiry, even though we understand that which makes an inquiry open is something that circumscribes and binds the inquiry and so determines a limit to its operation.

In this understanding, *Daodejing* is not simply a call for examination of our own perspectives; rather, it provides a critique to deep-seated common values and social structures. It labors to decenter a singular way to be an ideal woman and to claim a diversified space for women. This decentering operates as a living critique. By decentering institutionalized gender roles that are held as "natural," "given," or "traditional" within mainstream Confucian society, the *Daodejing* and indeed the Kundao expose the contingent nature of the conditions on which those social roles or traditions are built. This living critique of Confucian society reveals that things could be otherwise and that there is a space for difference, both for those who feel a sense of restive unfitness and for those who happily take up their social roles. Embracing the tenet of multiplicity for women's lives is at the heart of this living critique.

Kundao's stories register and open the ways in which women are given more choices and options for a well-lived life. Women have an alternative to living up to what it means to be a "woman." Their lived experiences help us to question the dominant cultural norms and critique the cultural script that may alienate human beings from a deep transformative self, or *zhen* (genuineness).

This chapter proposes that space and differences are the primary interlocutors for women's choices and options for leading a good life. We learn that Daoist theory and

Kundao practices remind us to be cautious about a social construction of one's life, especially not to internalize social rules and live through social functions without critical reflection.

A truly fitting way to end this chapter might be with the *Zhuangzi*'s planetary spirit:

各正性命，各得其所，各得其成，各得其乐。

Each rests his/her propensity and limitation; each gets his/her due; each accomplishes his/her success; each rests in his/her joy.

Notes

1 Confucius thinks that "life and death depend on the *ming*." He also perceives the importance of knowing the *ming*. It took him fifty years to know the *ming* of heaven (50 知天命 *zhi tianming*, *Analects* chapter 4).
2 The term "restiveness" is inspired by the work of Tamsin Kimoto (2018).
3 Paul D'Ambrosio (2010) discusses this idea in "The Role of a Pretending Tree: Hermits, Social Constructs and 'Self' in the *Zhuangzi*'" and "Going Along—A Daoist Alternative to Role Ethics."
4 James Miller outlined this idea in a presentation "Planetary Humanities, Cosmopolitan Philosophies and Social Networks: Perspectives from China and the West" at a Symposium at Duke University, March 2018.
5 From a lecture at his 80th birthday party in Beijing, December 1990.

References

Ames, T. Roger (2011), *Confucian Role Ethics: A Vocabulary, Confucian Role Ethics: A Vocabulary*. Hong Kong: Chinese University of Hong Kong Press.
Barbalet, Jack (2014), "Weber's Daoism: A Failure of Orthodoxy." *Journal of Classical Sociology* 14(3): 284–301.
Chen Yingning (1988), *Commentary on Lingyuan Dadaoge*. Beijing: Chinese Daoist Association.
D'Ambrosio, Paul (2015), "Authenticity in the *Zhuangzi*? Contemporary Misreadings of *Zhen* 真 and an Alternative to Existentialism" *Frontiers of Philosophy in China* 10(3): 353–79.
Despeux, Catherine, and Livia Kohn (2004), *Women in Daoism*. Honolulu, HI: Three Pines.
Fujiwara, Lynn, and Shireen Roshanravan (2018), *Asian American Feminism and Women of Color Politics*. Seattle: University of Washington Press.
Held, Virginia (1993), *Feminist Morality: Transforming Culture, Society, and Politics*. Chicago: University of Chicago Press.
Huang, Zhian (1995), *The Record of Nanyue Immortals*. Hunan: Hunan Daoist Association.
Iannello, Kathleen P. (1993), *Decisions without Hierarchy: Feminist Interventions in Organization Theory and Practice*. New York: Routledge.

Kimoto, Tamsin (2018), "Becoming Restive: Orientations in Asian American Feminist Theory and Praxis." In *Asian American Feminism and Women of Color Politics*, edited by Lynn Fujiwara and Shireen Roshanravan, 138–54. Seattle: University of Washington Press.

Laozi and Hans-Georg Moeller (2007), *Daodegjing: A Complete Translation and Commentary*, translated by Hans-Georg Moeller. Chicago: Open Court.

Miller, Jean Baker (1992), "Women and Power." In *Rethinking Power*, edited by Thomas Wartenberg, 240–9. Albany: SUNY Press.

Mitchell, Sandra (2009), *Unsimple Truth: Science, Complexity and Policy*. Chicago: University of Chicago Press.

Ryden, Edmund, trans. (1997), *The Yellow Emperor's Four Canons: A Literary Study and Edition of the Text from Mawangdui*. Taipei: Guangqi Press.

Wang, R. Robin (2012), *Yinyang: The Way of Heaven and Earth in Chinese Thought and Culture*. Cambridge: Cambridge University Press.

Wang, R. Robin (2016), "Dao Becomes Female: A Gendered Reality, Knowledge, and Strategy for Living." In *The Routledge Companion to Feminist Philosophy*, edited by Ann Garry, Serene J. Khader, and Alison Stone. Abingdon on Thames Routledge.

Zhuangzi (2009), *Zhuangzi: The Essential Writings with Selections from Traditional Commentaries*, translated by Brook Ziporyn. Indianapolis: Hackett, 35–48.

Part Three

Critiques of Concepts and Ideas

12

Critique and Subversion: Rethinking Yang Zhu's Conception of "Self"

Ellen Y. Zhang

Yang Zhu 楊朱 (Yang Chu, 440–360 BCE) was a philosopher of the Warring States period (540–360 BCE) and the founder of a school of thinkers called the "Yangist School" (*Yang Zhu xuepai* 楊朱學派), a precursor of Daoism.[1] As a proto-Daoist, Yang Zhu is perhaps the most misunderstood philosopher in the intellectual history of China, largely due to the misrepresentation given by Mengzi's Confucianism.[2] Yang Zhu's defense of self is interpreted in the *Mengzi* as egoism: "If plucking out a single hair from his body would have benefited the whole world, he would not do it" (*Mengzi* 7A26).[3] According to Mengzi, Yang's principle of self indicates a rejection of the authority of the ruler (*Mengzi* 3B9). In fact, Mengzi criticizes Yang Zhu along with Mozi 墨子 (468–376 BCE), whose principle, for Mengzi, represents an opposite side of Yang Zhu's self, that is, "impartial caring," denoting a refusal to acknowledge the particular affection of one's father. Mengzi then concludes, "To not have a father and to not have a ruler is to be an animal" (*Mengzi* 3B9).

Obviously, Mengzi views himself as a vehement defender of the Confucian tradition and thus sees the teachings of Yang and Mo as the two major contemporary threats to that tradition.[4] This viewpoint was reinforced when Confucianism became the state ideology in the Han period (206 BCE–220 CE). For instance, Yang Xiong 揚雄 (53 BCE–18 CE), a Confucian scholar of the Western Han, pairs Yang Zhu with Zhuangzi, remarking that both are "hedonistic with no self-regulations whatsoever."[5] Wang Chong 王充 (27–100 CE), another Confucian scholar of the Eastern Han asserts, "If the writings of Mo and Yang were not threatening to Confucianism, Mencius would not have written his own work."[6] Jiao Xun 焦循 (1763–1820), a Mengzi scholar of the Qing period (1644–1912), also defends Mengzi's critique of Yang Zhu by insisting that the latter's definition of human nature is not consistent with the fundamental doctrine of earlier sages which, according to Jiao, represents the orthodox teachings of Confucianism and the Dao.[7] However, these negative comments on Yang Zhu fail to represent the complexity of Yang's philosophy and his special contribution to the ideas of individualism and individual freedom in ancient China.

In this chapter, I will explicate Yang's conception of self in terms of self-ownership and self-preservation, showing that his individualistic argument functions as a critique and subversion of the mainstream tradition in Pre-Han China, which values the interest of the empire over individual persons. I will submit the argument that Yang Zhu is the first Chinese "libertarian thinker" in that he maintains a form of negative freedom in the face of the higher power of the state authority and calls for the principle of mutual noninterference. Meanwhile, I will point out the limit of Yang's conception of self in light of Zhuangzi's view of a self that is both owned and disowned, possessed and forgotten, through which one can ultimately transcend binary distinctions between self and other, and the loss of self and self-fulfillment, in order to see things as they are.

Yang Zhu's Conception of Self

In Yang Zhu's thought, *wo* 我 and *ji* 己 are two words understood as "self." In Chinese philosophical tradition, Yang Zhu is often viewed as a proponent of "egoism" because his philosophy is centered on the conception of self, or *weiwo* 為我 (each for oneself). Egoism is often identified with "selfishness" in that one is primarily concerned with one's own interests. For instance, in his essay "Egoism in Chinese Ethics," Kim-chong Chong points out that the term "egoism" in Chinese ethics is usually associated with Yang Zhu (Chong 2016: 241).[8] This association is directly linked to Mengzi's critique of Yang's notion of self. Benjamin Schwartz further explains this point by saying that Yang's egoism is based on the need for comfort and safety or on "the moderate satisfaction of one's sensual desires" (Schwartz 1985: 179). Burton Watson, in his translation of the *Zhuangzi*, calls Yang Zhu "a hedonist philosopher" (Watson 1968: 94). Watson's reading resembles the depiction of Yang Zhu in the *Liezi* 列子, where Yang's philosophy is identified with a philosophy of (sensual) pleasure seeking.

However, if we follow interpretations other than those given by Mengzi or in readings from the perspective of egoism and hedonism, we will see that Yang's conception of self is more complex than an egoist or hedonist position. Before analyzing Yang Zhu's conception of self, I will present a few passages about Yang Zhu from earlier classical texts:

> Even for the great profit of the whole world, he (Yang Zhu) would not exchange one hair of his leg. ... He is one who despises material things and values life. (*Hanfeizi* 50: 4) [9]
>
> Preserving life and maintaining what is genuine in it, not allowing things to entangle one's person: this is what Yang Zhu established. (*Huainanzi* 13)[10]
>
> [A conversation between Meng Sunyang and Qinzi on tearing off a piece of one's skin to get ten thousand pieces of gold and cutting off one of the limbs to get a whole kingdom]. Meng says, "That one hair matters less than skin, and skin less than a limb is plain enough. However, go on adding to the one hair and it amounts to as much as skin, go on adding more skin and it amounts to as much as one limb. A single hair is certainly one thing among the myriad parts of the body, how can one treat it lightly?" (*Liezi* 7)[11]
>
> Our life is our own possession, and its benefit to us is very great. Regarding its dignity, even the honor of being emperor could not compare with it. Regarding

its importance, even the wealth of possessing the whole world would not be exchanged for it. (*Lüshi Chunqiu* 1: 3)[12]

If you heed the arguments of a multitude of individuals as a means of ordering the state, it will be endangered in no time. How does one know that this is so? Lao Dan [Laozi] esteemed softness, Confucius [Kongzi] humanness, Mo Di [Mozi] frugality, Guanyin purity, Master Lie Yukou [Liezi] emptiness, Tian Pian equanimity, Yang Zhu selfhood … (*Lüshi Chunqiu* 17: 7)[13]

It is clearly indicated, from the quotations above, that all texts recognize that Yang Zhu's thought gives weight to self, especially to the person as body. Yang's conception of self can be understood from three interrelated arguments: (1) self-ownership and self-governance; (2) preserving one's own genuineness or authentic nature; and (3) seeing self/life is more valuable than material things.

First, Yang Zhu's argument of *weiwo* or "each for oneself" implies the ideas of self-ownership and self-governance, symbolized by the expression of "not plucking out a single hair" (*yimao buba* 一毛不拔). It is the basic premise for self-impairment and self-cultivation. In other words, self is an intrinsic value by itself that should not be entangled with external forces, particularly if those external forces are coercive. It should be noted that in ancient China, the idea of self-ownership and self-governing based on a strong sense of an individual entity was quite unusual. In taking this perspective, Yang Zhu attempts to de-emphasize the social and cultural construction of "self" characterized by China's familial, social, and political relationality.

Second, Yang Zhu's conception of "self" points to the idea of keeping one's self-nature (*xing* 性). Similar to the *Mengzi*, Yang Zhu believes that the heavenly endowed nature is an important resource for universal, objective forms of authority. Yang also connects what he calls "genuine nature" to the idea of "keeping the whole nature intact" (*quanxing* 全性).[14] What is perceived as "genuine" (*zhen* 真) by Yang Zhu is given further explanation in the *Zhuangzi*, where self-nature is identified as "self-so" (*ziran* 自然) in contrast to "other-so." However, the social-political-intellectual milieu of the time makes Yang's thought extremely radical since it is a total subversion of the dominant ideologies of his time, which focus on the state, the empire, and the ruler. Concurrently, Yang Zhu employs another term, *guiji* 貴己 (valuing oneself or prizing oneself), to designate the notion of personal self or self-identity. As indicated in *Lüshi Chunqiu*, the word *ji* or selfhood is singled out to describe the core thought of Yang Zhu's philosophy. Since *ji* or selfhood entails both body (*ti* 體) and nature (*xing* 性), *weiwo* as self-ownership and self-governance means to safeguard one's authentic self-identity. In Yang Zhu's argument, the expressions of *wei* 為 (serving the purpose of) and *gui* 貴 (valuing) associated with *wo* and *ji* highlight the division between self and the rest of the world to indicate self as an individual entity.

Third, it would oversimplify Yang Zhu's idea of self if the meaning of self were reduced to egoism-qua-selfishness, since "valuing oneself" is associated with Yang's idea of inward care through the principle of "not getting entangled with things" (*bu yiwu hanxing* 不以物害形).[15] This principle has nothing to do with being selfish or hedonistic in the sense that satisfaction of one's sensual desires is what one needs to achieve; rather it means that one should attach utmost importance to life, and it despises material things such as fame, honors, and wealth. This argument is specifically touched upon in the *Hanfeizi*, when the author defends Yang's "not plucking out a single hair from his body" by saying that one should not harm oneself in exchange for anything material, even if it is an empire. For Yang Zhu, too much attachment to external things is detrimental to self-nourishment and self-preservation.

In his discussion of Yang Zhu, D. C. Lau identifies *weiwo* with *guiji*, implying that both words indicate egoism, yet he denies that Yang is a "hedonist" (Lau 1992: 85). Nevertheless, Lau still follows Mengzi's egoist argument, lamenting that "Yang opted out of his moral obligations to society, obligations that can only be met by taking part in public life" (Chong 2016: 7). Ranie Villaver has made a good observation in saying that, for Yang Zhu, *guiji* or valuing oneself "seems to mean valuing one's uniqueness as a human individual," which has been ignored by Yang Zhu's contemporary thinkers (Villaver 2015: 221).

Yet the question remains: can we call Yang's self "egoism?" Or, if we have to use the term "egoism," what kind of egoism does Yang Zhu's philosophy suggest? In the West, egoism is divided into psychological egoism and ethical egoism: The former views selfishness as the motive behind one's action, whereas the latter is a normative ethical position which maintains that every action ought to be in agreement with one's self-interest. If psychological egoism implies that people can only act selfishly, it is obvious that Yang Zhu's egoist argument is more ethical than psychological.[16] I will explicate this point by speaking of Yang's self in terms of the modern concept of self-ownership. Meanwhile, I will argue the ethical implications of Yang's Zhu's self through the conception of universalistic egoism.

Self-Ownership as "Universalistic Egoism"

In modern liberal philosophy, self-ownership refers to the concept of property in one's own person, expressed as "the moral or natural right" of a person to have bodily integrity, and to be the exclusive controller of one's own body and life without infringements from external forces. If we use this idea to examine Yang Zhu's position of "not plucking out a single hair" for the sake of benefiting the empire or in exchange for an empire, we will see that his notion of *weiwo* is emphasized in the context of self, versus the empire. That is, the question for Yang is not simply a choice between self and other, but self and the state, as indicated by Mengzi's critique (i.e., Yang Zhu's "each for oneself" does not acknowledge the authority of the ruler). To follow this line of thinking, what is viewed as selfhood or egoism in Yang Zhu's thought is a way to protect one from being infringed by external forces. In Yang's time, the biggest external force was the power of the state or the empire. Following this line of thought, we could argue that Yang Zhu was the first Chinese "libertarian" thinker.

Of course, Yang Zhu's principle of "not getting entangled with things" seems to be at odds with the modern libertarian concept of self-ownership in which the concept of personal property is the basic condition for self-ownership.[17] Nevertheless, given that there was no such thing as "property rights" in Yang Zhu's time, Yang's defense of owning one's body and the idea of "keeping the whole nature intact" would make him a revolutionary thinker, since his self is a total subversion of the view that the state and the ruler are the sole authority that determines the fate of an individual person. Yang Zhu's self, in this view, draws attention to an agent who is capable of using his free will to define what is a kind of happiness to him. We see a similar argument proposed by Zhuangzi and later Neo-Daoists or "Seven Sages of the Bamboo Grove" (*zhulin qixian* 竹林七賢) of the Wei-Jin 魏晉 period (265–420 CE), known as "Daoist hippies."

In his study of earlier Chinese thought, A. C. Graham points out that Yang Zhu's participation in the philosophical debates of fourth century BCE "provoked a metaphysical crisis which had threatened the basic assumptions of Confucianism and Mohism and set them into a new course."[18] The "metaphysical crisis" here refers to the philosophical debate, during the Pre-Qin era, about *xing* or human nature and its connection to self. For Yang Zhu, *xing* as both body and spirit belongs to one's self, whereas for Mengzi *xing* means "the feeling of right and wrong." Thus, the moral development of *xing* is, according to Mengzi, characterized by benefiting one's family and state rather than benefiting oneself. In contrast to the Confucian ethics of social relationality and playing one's role properly, Yang Zhu's principle of self accentuates the individual person, with the self's power to will and desire. Yang Zhu would ask: Is it okay for me not to play a social role? Is it okay to benefit oneself instead of benefiting the world (*tianxia* 天下)? Yang Zhu's self-as-self is thus a gesture to reverse the Confucian ethic of "cultivating oneself" (*xiuji* 修己) so as to "bring security to others" (*anren* 安人), which implies the notion of "governing others" (*zhiren* 治人). Yang prefers self-governing to being governed by others.

I concur with Yanxia Zhao, who has correctly challenged Max Weber's claim that "the traditional Chinese lacks 'inward care' and lived by a process of 'adjustment to the outside,' so in such a society, 'an individual's place and "self"' are not defined by nature but one's social standing or relationships with others" (Zhao 2014: 182). From Yang Zhu's viewpoint, self-interest should not be sacrificed in the name of the interest of the state or the empire. Therefore, a single hair of an individual could not be harmed without the permission of that person. We should bear in mind that "a single hair" is a metaphor, standing for an integral part of *weiwo*, although it sounds so insignificant.

How then do we understand Yang Zhu's individualism? In contemporary context, the term is usually defined as a social theory advocating the liberty, rights, or independent action of the individual. According to this definition, Yang's concept of self does not have a thick notion of individualism in the sense of "autonomy" used in political philosophy. Nonetheless, Yang's self plays a role as actor, or self-conscious agent, in decision-making. This point can be illustrated by a passage about Yang Zhu in the *Xunzi*:

> Yang Zhu lamented at the crossroads, "if I now make a single wrong step, I will sometimes realize that I will miss the way for thousand miles." In this case, too, the crossroad between glory and disgrace, security and danger are at issue, and it is even more deplorable than in the case of Yang Zhu. (*Xunzi*: 11; Knoblock 1994: 142)

Yang Zhu surely cares about right and free decision-making by an individual, especially when the choice is between security and danger rather than between glory and disgrace. After all, from Yang Zhu's viewpoint, what matters most is to live out one's natural life span. Perhaps, the libertarian ideas of the natural law and natural rights find the expression in Yang's notion of "the term of life" that heaven (*tian* 天) has destined for humanity. This kind of "ownership" is not dependent on any moral principle or social institution since individuals possess this simply through virtue of their existence. Robert Nozick, for example, argues that the moral basis of self-ownership denotes that individual agents have full control of themselves both physically and mentally.[19] He sees self-ownership theory as a secondary principle, derived from a richer and more fundamental conception of the libertarian minimal state, which, as Nozick sees it, is a tool for protecting the self from the compulsion of others and the self's right to freedom. From this vantage point, we can argue Yang Zhu's distrust of external authorities of power by emphasizing the spontaneous order represented by individual *xing*. This argument leads to an anarchist tendency in Yang Zhu as well as in the *Zhuangzi*. John Emerson has observed that "Yang Zhu freed the Chinese elite from the public roles and relationships that defined them, making possible new nonpublic, nonritual forms of individual self-awareness and self-cultivation" (Emerson 1996: 533).

It is quite interesting to note that most Chinese intellectuals of the "New Culture Movement" at the beginning of twentieth century held a positive view of Yang Zhu's philosophy of self.[20] For example, Xiao Gongquan 蕭公權, a political philosopher, regards Yang as the most significant person in Chinese intellectual history who promotes individualism and individual freedom. He further argues that self-affirmation and egalitarianism in terms of self-ownership are based on the natural law of the *dao* (*tiandao ziran* 天道自然), which challenges hierarchical social structures such as Confucianism.[21] Cai Yuanpei 蔡元培, a well-known modern educator, points out that Yang's individualism is a direct reaction to Mengzi's moral principles.[22] Gao Heng 高亨, a famous Daoist scholar, insists that Yang Zhu's self is argued from the perspective of the common people who lived in an era of tyrannical rule.[23]

Furthermore, Yang's concept of self-ownership suggests the principle of noninterference. Tang Yue 唐鉞, one of the earlier Chinese psychologists, contends that Yang's *weiwo*-ism is nothing but asking for "taking care of oneself and not interfering with other people's business."[24] The principle of "mutual non-interference" (*hu bujin* 互不侵) is especially significant when it comes to the relationship between an individual person and the state as a sovereign power. This principle is also the principle of nonaggression, defined as initiating or threatening any forcible interference with an individual or an individual's property. In the case of Yang Zhu, the individual's property is one's own body, symbolized by "a single hair." Even though a single hair seems insignificant, if it can be taken arbitrarily by others, then something else can be taken, such as the skin, the toe, the leg … and the whole person. This is why Yang Zhu condemns even very minor infringements like plucking out someone's single hair. From a libertarian perspective, Yang's self-ownership can be identified with the principle that each agent has a right to maximum, equal, empirical negative liberty, which indicates the absence of forcible interference from other agents when one attempts to do things according to one's own will. Yang Zhu's position of no higher sovereignty over "self" is a strong endorsement of the moral importance and the sovereignty of the individual. It expresses the refusal to treat people as interchangeable objects, such as trading an empire for some one's leg.

To an extent, Yang Zhu's concept of self is subject to the harm principle, which holds that the actions of individuals should only interfere with the freedom of others to prevent harm to other individuals.[25] Such an understanding of self-ownership, I think, leads to the form of "universalistic egoism" implied in Yang Zhu's philosophy. For Yang Zhu, it is not only no harm to *my* hair to attain the world but also no harm to *anyone's* hair for the sake of attaining the world. A. C. Graham thus offers an insightful observation when he says,

> the Yangist does not think of himself as Mengzi (Mencius) sees him, as a selfish man who prefers his own comfort. … He can justly claim to be concerned for life in general, not just his own …: if not a principled egoist, the Yangist is at any rate an individual concerned to benefit his own person and leave others to do the same. (Graham 1989: 54–5)

From this perspective, I contend that Yang Zhu's self-ownership is an "ethical egoism" that requires moral agents not to harm the interests and well-being of others when making deliberations. In a sense, it follows the principle of "to live and to let live." Graham explicates the universalist ethics in Yang Zhu by stating that "the Yangist does not think of himself as Mencius [Mengzi] sees him, as a selfish man who prefers his own comfort to taking office and benefiting the people. He can justly claim to be concerned for life in general, not just his own" (Graham 1989: 59). Therefore, it seems fair to call Yang Zhu an individualist rather than an apologist for selfish egoism. After all, as Erica Brindley has observed, "there is no convincing evidence that Yang Zhu promotes selfishness in the sense that he inspires individuals to seek self-profit through the exploitation of public resources or goods. Moreover, there is no clear indication that Yang Zhu tacitly condones harming or destroying society through his ideal."[26]

Freedom: Self as Owned and Disowned

Yang Zhu's freedom can be understood from two perspectives: freedom from one's internal desires and freedom from external obstruction or coercion. The internal aspect is argued from the viewpoint of self-preservation qua "nourishing one's life," while the external is approached from the perspective of self-ownership and self-governance. Yet for Yang Zhu, there is no strong sense of self-realization and deliberation of freedom as we understand them today, since his self is still based on a naturalistic understanding of "keeping one's nature intact" or "completeness of living," which is viewed as one's destiny mandated by heaven. In order to accomplish self-nourishment, Yang Zhu recommends that people protect themselves by avoiding social and political engagement. That is, he advocates a retreat to the inner realm of oneself in order to avoid confronting the danger of the world.

In the chapter entitled "Yang Zhu" in the *Leizi*, Yang Zhu argues for individual freedom in terms of political anarchism, a kind of view that is accepted, to a certain extent, by Zhuangzi and fully embraced by Neo-Daoists such as Ruan Ji 阮籍 and Liu Ling 劉伶 with their insistence on privatism and a radical rejection of Mengzi's political ideal of virtuous governance from self, to family, to state. This is the very reason Mengzi regards Yang as a dangerous person. When A. C. Graham speaks of anarchist elements in the *Leizi*, he says, "The [Leizi] itself reflects this [anarchistic] tendency … , although very cautiously. The hedonist [Yang Zhu] chapter explicitly recommends a society in which each pursues person his or her own happiness without interfering with others, and thus "the Way of ruler and subject is brought to an end" (Graham 1960: 8). Also, in what Graham calls the "Yangist Chapters" of the *Zhuangzi*, such as "Robber Zhi" and "The Old Fisherman," there are criticisms of the rituals of the Confucians who are seen, from a Daoist perspective, as imposing artificial morality, thereby cramping natural, authentic, and spontaneous human nature.[27] For both Yang Zhu and Zhuangzi, pretentiousness through artificial morality would harm one's nature and thus hurt self-nourishment and self-preservation.

In the manner of Yang Zhu, Yangists call for a retreat from political life to private life, known as "leaving the state behind by a reclusive lifestyle." They recommend escape and retirement from society (political life in particular) and nourishment of one's own life. Against the Confucian moral ideal of *qijia* 齐家 (harmonizing the family), *zhiguo* 治国 (managing/regulating the state), and *pingtianxia* 平天下 (bringing peace to the world), Yang Zhu, Yangists, and their followers all maintain that individuals should pay full attention to their own lives and treasure them, not put their lives into potential danger by either entering a besieged city or serving in the army, as indicated in the *Hanfeizi*. We may call it a Yangist version of pacifism.[28] They also claim that by not benefiting the world, one benefits the world, which is called "the benefit of not benefiting" (*buli zhi li* 不利之利). However, for Confucians, "the adherents of Yang Zhu seemed to represent an attack from the left that undermined the state's authority with their individualism, destroying conventional values with their egoism and attacking social constraints with their self-indulgence" (Knoblock 1994: 56).

In fact, Yang Zhu intends to tell us, if everyone does not harm a single hair, and if everyone does not benefit the world, the world will be well governed on its own. In other words, everyone should mind their own business, "neither giving nor taking from others, and be content with what he has, and in that way, one will be happy and also contribute to the welfare of the world" (Liu 1967: 358). As mentioned above, Mengzi uses the word "animal" or "beast" (*qinshou* 禽獸) to describe Yang's anti-Confucian position. The word "beast" reminds us of a parable in the *Zhuangzi* where Zhuangzi mocks the Confucian understanding of the "state of virtue" by denoting a place of "barbarians" (*manyi* 蠻夷) in the south as an ideal state (*Zhuangzi* 20). Similar to Yang Zhu's argument, Zhuangzi also believes that it is better not to control other people's lives in the name of virtues and moral principles that may entail social and political abuses. Gu Shi 顧實, in his work *The Philosophy of Yang Zhu*, explains Mengzi's humans-versus-beasts discourse by saying that Mengzi's beast charge does not mean that Yang Zhu has done something beast-like, but only shows that Yang's denial of the authority of the sovereign has gone too far (Gu 2011: 49).

Yet from the perspectives of Yang Zhu and his followers, "each for oneself" in the face of the power of the sovereign suggests a form of inner freedom, which can also be translated as "negative freedom" in the sense of modern political philosophy. In his essay, "Two Concepts of Liberty," Isaiah Berlin defines negative freedom as "the area within which a man can act unobstructed by others" (Berlin 1969: 122). Yang Zhu's principle of "mutual non-interference" implies the rejection of obstruction or coercion from various external constraints (such as moral and political authority) placed on a person, despite that his *weiwoism* does not offer any normative claims about what the individual agent should or should not do. That is, one attains what one needs to attain and satisfies what one needs to be satisfied. Furthermore, Yang Zhu views self as "to act for one's own sake" and regards any form of altruistic deed as insufficient to achieve the common good perceived by Confucianism or Mohism. For Yang Zhu, "saving oneself" is more primary than "saving the world."

In the *Zhuangzi,* we can also see Zhuangzi's "deep appreciation for personal space and a profound skepticism toward moralistic certainty as well as embracing value-pluralism" (Jiang 2012: 75). Like Yang Zhu, Zhuangzi sees one's nature as something unique, contending that to recognize the uniqueness of one's nature is a matter of "letting things be themselves." The concept of self-so as self-nature (*zixing* 自性) or "authentic nature" (*zenxing* 真性) in the *Zhuangzi* is emphasized in contrast to the "other," the "external" or any "coercive activity." As such, we can also see a form of negative freedom argued by Zhuangzi's Daoism.

It is, however, worth remarking that there is a significant difference in terms of self between Yang Zhu and Zhuangzi. Even though Zhuangzi values self and challenges the relational nature of existence in the world, he also recognizes a dimension of self that transcends *ji* or the "myself" enunciated by Yang Zhu's self-ownership. According to Zhuangzi, this transcendent, or more precisely, dynamic self is internally and externally aligned with the pattern and process of the Dao. We can see this point by looking at Zhuangzi's concept of no-self (*wuji* 無己), self-forgetfulness (*wangwo* 忘我), self-transformation (*zihua* 自化), and self-fulfillment (*zide* 自得), all of which are fundamental to Zhuangzi's freedom, that is, one attunes perfectly to the vicissitudes of the world. The idea of self-transformation, in particular, marks Zhuangzi's departure from Yang Zhu in that the dynamic and the transforming self is both owned and disowned, possessed and forgotten. Zhuangzi's self of no-self allows a kind of "free wandering" as a way of experiencing freedom within the boundaries of the world without being bound by it. For clarifying this point, Zhuangzi speaks of both a "body" person (*ti* 體) and a "heart-mind" person (*xin* 心), and the latter is clearly not fully developed in Yang Zhu's philosophy of self.

In addition, Zhuangzi's freedom is not simply freedom *from* a higher authority of power, but freedom *through* it, as one sees in the chapter of "In the World of Men" (*Renjianshi* 人間世) and elsewhere in the *Zhuangzi*.[29] Thus, confinement to oneself as Yang Zhu suggests is not the solution to dissolving one's entanglement in relationality, but separates one completely from others. Moreover, from the perspective of Zhuangzi's dynamic self, Yang Zhu's "each for oneself" would be somehow dogmatic and close-minded, which would limit one's experience of true self and life satisfaction. P. J. Ivanhoe summarizes Zhuangzi's position on happiness as follows:

> True happiness requires one to recognize, value, and to some extent give oneself over to the patterns, processes, and rhythms of a certain kind of life: a life that hooks one up with the greater and deeper patterns, processes, and rhythms of the Dao. In other words, according with the Dao requires one, to some extent, to lose oneself in a form of life, and at first this seems odd to regard the loss of myself as the way to fulfill and make myself happy. (Ivanhoe 2014: 265)

Zhuangzi insists that to keep an authentic self and lead a good life means to go beyond dogmatic doctrines, including the doctrine of self and happiness, recognizing the transformative nature of things in the world and embracing the idea of responsiveness and spontaneity.

In sum, Yang Zhu touches on issues of self, private space, and self-governance, maintaining that self plays a significant role in life. His conception of self-ownership functions as a challenge to the ethical norms that downplay individualism and personal freedom. Yang Zhu's ideas of selfhood and self-interest are limited but significantly powerful if we take them as a method of critique and subversion. Nevertheless, it remains a question how to look at the possibility of a shared commonality or "the goal of holism and unitary systematization over atomism and fragmentation" as Erica Brindley calls it (Brindley 2013: 1–13). It was a question for Yang Zhu and Chinese philosophers over two thousand years ago, and it is still a question for us today.

Notes

1. Yang Zhu came from the state of Wei 魏 and is known with the epithet Yangzi 楊子, Yinzi Ju 陰子居 or simply Master Yin 陰生. There are no books known to have been written by a representative of the Yangist school. All that is known about its teachings are quotations in texts such as the *Mengzi* 孟子, the *Zhuangzi* 莊子, the *Hanfeizi* 韓非子, the *Lüshi chunqiu* 呂氏春秋, the *Huainanzi* 淮南子, the *Liezi* 列子, as well as the *Fayan* 法言 and the *Lunheng* 论衡. The so-called Yangist philosophy has been ignored in history, partially due to lack of reliable sources.
2. In this sense, Yang Zhu is most famous because of the criticism he suffered, rather than for his actual influence on the intellectual history of China.
3. The citations from the *Mengzi* in this chapter are based on the translation by Bryan W. Van Norden in *Readings in Classical Chinese Philosophy* (2nd edition), edited by P. J. Ivanhoe and Bryan W. Van Norden.
4. In the *Zhuangzi*, Yang Zhu and Mozi are put together as well. Yet Zhuangzi's critiques of them are not based on moral grounds, but on their rhetorical strategies. Historically, the disciples of both Yang and Mo are well known as logicians.
5. Yang Xiong, the *Fayan* (*Model Sayings*). See Yang 1996.
6. Wang Chong's *Lunheng* (*Arguments Weighed*) is one of the most important philosophical writings of the Han dynasty. In the chapter "Replies in Self-Defense," Wang writes: "Mengzi was grieved that the discussions of Yang Zhu and Mo Di did great harm to the cause of Confucianism, therefore he used plain and straightforward language to establish what was right, and to reject what was wrong." See Zhang 2010.

7 Jiao Xun, *Mengzi zhengyi* 孟子正義 (*Orthodox Interpretation of the Mengzi*). See Jiao (1987: 458).
8 Also see Chong (2003: 241–6) and Donald (1985: 73–85).
9 See Chen Qiyou 陳奇猷: *Collected Annotations on the Hanfeizi* (*Hanfeizi jishi* 韓非子集釋). Gaoxiong 高雄: Fuwen Tushu 復文圖書, 1991.
10 See Feng (1976: 61).
11 See A. C. Graham (1960: 60–1). It should be noted that the authenticity of the *Leizi* as a reliable source on Yang Zhu has been questioned throughout history. For the debate, also see Zhou (2011: 19–44).
12 See Knoblock and Riegel (2000). The citations are based on translations by Knoblock and Riegel, with modification.
13 Ibid.
14 Although we see the argument of "following one's nature" in both Yang Zhu and Mengzi, Mengzi argues, against Yang Zhu, that there are incipient moral inclinations in one's nature (*Mengzi* 6A6) and uses the "sprouts" metaphor to speak of those natural inclinations (*Mengzi* 2A2, 2A6).
15 For detailed argument on Yang Zhu and his critique of material culture, see Fox (2008: 358–71).
16 Very often, Yang Zhu's self has been described as "psychological egoism," that is, that humans are motivated only by self-interest. See the chapter on "Yangism" in Ivanhoe and Van Norden (2005), *Readings in Classical Chinese Philosophy*.
17 It is noteworthy that Yang Zhu's self or individualism is different from that in modern Western tradition in that the former is not based on materialism but on something that is internal. See Zhao (2014: 183) for further argument on this point.
18 See Graham (1985: 73–84).
19 It should be noted that Nozick's concept of self-ownership with its inclusion of private property laws implies a skeptical view of "distributive justice" that is basically absent in Yang Zhu's concept of self, since his idea of "not benefiting the world" is more a metaphysical argument than an economic one. Moreover, the notion of rights embedded in Nozick's concept of self-ownership is also absent in Yang Zhu's thought. For more on Nozick's argument, see his 1974 work *Anarchy, State and Utopia*.
20 The era was known for the rise of diversified ideologies such as nationalism, communism, and individualism.
21 Xiao Gongquan 蕭公權, *History of Chinese Political Thought* (*Zhongguo sixiang shi* 中國政治思想史). See Xiao (1982: 178–82).
22 Cai Yuanpei 蔡元培, *History of Chinese Ethics* (*Zhongguo lunlixue shi* 中國倫理學史). See Cai (2004).
23 Gao Heng 高亨, "The Yangists" (*Yangzhu xuepai* 楊朱學派) in *Defending Inauthenticity of the Leizi* 列子偽辯, cited from "Explication of the Yang Zhu Chapter in the Liezi" (列子-楊朱篇析論) by Zhou Dayu 周大興. See Zhou (2011: 19–44).
24 See Tang Yue 唐鉞, "A Supplementary Study of Yang Zhu (*Yang Zhu kao zaibu* 楊朱考再補). See Tang (1971: 225–6).
25 In his discussion of Mengzi, Tang Junyi 唐君毅 makes an observation that Yang Zhu's argument of "not benefiting" is in fact, a critique of those who benefit themselves in the name of benefiting *tianxia*. In other words, Yang's rejection of "benefiting" is a kind of subversion of "moralists" who lack integrity and genuineness. He further explains that Yang Zhu's self has political implications, in that Yang has exposed moral hypocrisy in society (Tang 1986: 262–6). This kind of view was supported by many of

Yang Zhu's defenders during the New Culture Movement, when Confucianism was seen as an obstacle for China's modernization.

26 See Erica Brindley, "Individualism in Classical Chinese Thought." https://www.iep.utm.edu/ind-chin/, with some minor changes for the sake of consistency with the format of the chapter. Also see Brindley (2010).
27 According to Graham, chapters 28–31 in the *Zhuangzi* are writings by the followers of Yang Zhu. See Graham (1989: 55).
28 In his study of Daoist anarchism, John A. Rapp has observed that the Yang Zhu chapter in the *Leizi* shows a shift from pacifist anarchism to passive nihilism when the original Yang Zhu philosophy is substituted for an unrestrained enjoyment of full sensual pleasures in life (Rapp 2012: 41).
29 In many places in the *Zhuangzi*, Zhuangzi speaks of freedom as a way of dealing with societal limitations rather than as an ascetic or escapist way of life.

References

Berlin, Isaiah (1969), "Two Concepts of Liberty." In *Four Essays on Liberty*. New York: Oxford University Press.
Brindley, Erica (2010), *Individualism in Early China: Human Agency and the Self in Thought and Politics*. Honolulu: University of Hawaii Press.
Brindley, Erica (2013), "The Polarization of the Concepts Si (Private Interest) and Gong (Public Interest) in Early Chinese Thought." *Asia Major* 26(2). 1–31.
Cai Yuanpei 蔡元培 (2004), *History of Chinese Ethics* (中國倫理學史). Taipei 臺北：Sanmin Publisher 三民出版.
Chen Qiyou 陳奇猷 (1991), *Collected Annotations on the Hanfeizi* (*Hanfeizi jishi* 韓非子集釋). Gaoxiong 高雄：Fuwen Tushu 復文圖書.
Chong Kim-chong (2003), "Egoism in Chinese Ethics." In *Encyclopedia of Chinese Philosophy*, edited by Antonio Cua, 241–6. New York: Routledge.
Chong Kim-chong (2016), *Zhuangzi's Critique of the Confucians: Blinded by the Human*. Albany: SUNY Press.
Donald, J., ed. (1985), *Individualism and Holism: Studies in Confucian and Taoist Values*, 73–84. Ann Arbor: Center for Chinese Studies, University of Michigan.
Emerson, John. (1996), "Yang Chu's Discovery of the Body." *Philosophy East and West* 46(4): 533–66.
Feng Youlan (1976), *A Short History of Chinese Philosophy*. New York: Free Press.
Forke, Anton, trans. ([1912] 2012), *Yang Chu's Garden of Pleasure*. New York: E.P. Dutton; republished by Forgotten Books.
Fox, Alan (2008), "Guarding What Is Essential: Critiques of Material Culture in Thoreau and Yangzhu." *Philosophy East and West* 58(3): 358–71.
Graham, A. C. (1960), *The Book of Lieh-tzu*. London: Murray.
Graham, A. C. (1985), "The Right to Selfishness: Yangism, Later Mohism, Chuang Tzu." In *Individualism and Holism: Studies in Confucian and Taoist Values*, edited by Donald J. Munro, 73–84. Ann Arbor: Center for Chinese Studies, University of Michigan.
Graham, A. C. (1989), *Disputers of the Tao: Philosophical Argument in Ancient China*. La Salle, IL: Open Court.
Gu Shi 顧實 (1960), *The Book of Lieh Tzu*. Baltimore, MD: Penguin.

Gu, Shi 顧實 (2011), *The Philosophy of Yang Zhu* (楊朱哲學). Changsha 長沙: Yuelu Shushe 岳麓书社.

Ivanhoe, P. J. (2014), "Happiness in Early Chinese Thought." In *Oxford Handbook of Happiness*, edited by Susan A. David, et al., 263–78. Oxford: Oxford University Press.

Ivanhoe, P. J., and Bryan Van Norden (2005), "Yangism." In *Readings in Classical Chinese Philosophy*, edited by Ivanhoe and Van Norden, 369–78. Indianapolis: Hackett.

Jiao Xun (1987), *Orthodox Interpretation of the Mengzi* (孟子正義). Beijing 北京: Zhuhua Shuju 中華書局.

Knoblock, John (1994), *Xunzi: A Translation and Study of the Complete Works*. Stanford, CA: Stanford University Press.

Knoblock, John, and Jeffrey Riegel (2000), *The Annals of Lü Buwe*. Redwood City, CA: Stanford University Press.

Lau, D. C. (1992), "The Doctrine of Kuei Sheng in the Lu-Shih Ch'un-Ch'iu." *Bulletin of the Institute of Chinese Literature and Philosophy* 2, 51–92.

Liu Wu-Chi (1967), *Encyclopedia of Philosophy*, vol. 8. New York: Macmillan.

Nozick, Robert (1974), *Anarchy, State and Utopia*. Oxford: Blackwell.

Rapp, John A. (2012), *Daoism and Anarchism: Critiques of State Autonomy in Ancient and Modern China*. London: Continuum.

Schwartz, Benjamin (1985), *World of Thought in Ancient China*. Cambridge, MA: Harvard University Press.

Tang Junyi 唐君毅 (1986), *Origins of Chinese Philosophy: Origins of the Dao* (中國哲學原論: 原道篇). Taipei 臺北: Taiwai Xuesheng Shuju 臺灣學生書局.

Tang Yue 唐鉞 (1971), "Supplementary Study of Yang Zhu" (楊朱考再補). In *A Collection of Works on the Liezi* (無求備齋列子集成), vol. 12, 47–60. Taipei 臺北: Yiwen Yinshuguan, 藝文印書館.

Tao Jiang (2012), "Isaiah Berlin's Challenge to Zhuangzi's Freedom." *Journal of Chinese Philosophy* 39(2): 69–92.

Van Norden, Bryan, trans. (2005), *Mengzi*. In *Readings in Classical Chinese Philosophy* (2nd ed.), edited by Ivanhoe and Bryan Van Norden, 115–60. Indianapolis: Hackett.

Villaver, Ranie (2015), "Does Guiji Mean Egoism? Yang Zhu's Conception of Self." *Asian Philosophy* 25(2): 216–23.

Watson, Burton, trans. (1968), *The Complete Works of Chuang Tzu*. New York: Columbia University Press.

Xiao Gongquan 蕭公權 (1982), *History of Chinese Political Philosophy* (中國政治思想史). Taipei 臺北: Lianjin Chuban 聯經出版.

Yang Xiong 揚雄 (1996), *Fayan* (法言一卷). In *Complete Book of Hundred Works* (百子全書), vol. 6. Taipei 臺北: Liming Weihuashiyue Chubanshe 黎明文化事業出版社.

Zhang Zongxiang 張宗項 (2010), *Commentaries and Notes on the Lunheng* (論衡校註). Shanghai 上海: Guji Chubanshe 古籍出版社.

Zhao Yanxia (2014), "Yang Zhu's 'Guiji' Yangsheng and Its Modern Relevance." *Philosophy Study* 4(3): 173–88.

Zhou Dayu 周大興 (2011), "Explication of the Yang Zhu Chapter in the *Leizi*" (列子·楊朱篇析論). *Newsletter of the Institute of Chinese Literature and Philosophy* (中國文哲研究通訊), 21(4): 19–44.

13

Subversive Cosmology in the *Zhuangzi*: On the Dispensability of Ritual

Manuel Rivera Espinoza[1]

Early Chinese cosmology is an intricate subject, and Zhuangzian cosmology in specific is particularly elusive. This chapter does not aim to provide a final answer to the subject but simply to adumbrate a new way of addressing it, mainly in reference to one single, but important, passage of the *Qiwulun* 齊物論. In my view, properly understanding Zhuangzian cosmology ultimately comes down to determining the specific philosophical status of the cosmology of spontaneity or self-movement (*ziran*自然)[2] posited in the *Zhuangzi* 莊子: What is the philosophical *specificity* of this cosmology? And how should we evaluate it? Here I will argue that, in order to answer these questions appropriately, we have to read Zhuangzian cosmology vis-à-vis the cosmology that revolves around the practice of ritual, that is, ritual-centered cosmology, as I call it. To the extent that the latter remains elusive, the essentially *subversive* character of the self-moving world of the *Zhuangzi* will remain unrecognized, and thus unexplained. Therefore, it is crucial we first precisely elaborate the specific features of ritual-centered cosmologies.

Li 禮 and *She* 社 in Ancient China: Continued Ritual Action as Guarantor of Cosmic Stability and Cohesion

In this section I will explain that ritual-centered cosmologies are not an instance of *ziran*,[3] to the extent that, in such cosmologies, cosmic movements are not seen as occurring spontaneously.[4] These processes, in fact, take place as a result of the *coercion* effected by a series of ritual activities. The coerciveness of ritual agency, however, does not preclude[5] but permits the articulation of a human-nature (human-divine) continuity[6] and, furthermore, the generation and maintenance of the very structure of the world as a *kosmos* (κόσμος), that is, as an order.[7] More precisely, in early China, ritual activities were thought to guarantee the very preservation of cosmic order, primarily by means of *actively establishing hierarchical distinctions*, which was, in fact, the main function of ritual (*li* 禮), according to a variety of ancient Chinese texts (Boileau 1998: 108–13; Lewis 2006: 25–6). Conversely, the maintenance of the ordered structure of the world was understood as being in perpetual danger of being irremediably lost *if* ritual practices, and the stratified distinctions inherently embedded in them, were ever to be abandoned and/or forgotten.

The association of ritual with hierarchical differentiation is clear in various passages of the *Liji* 禮記 and the *Xunzi* 荀子, among other *ru* 儒 texts. For example, the *Yueji* 禮記 chapter of the former text assures: 禮辨異 "Ritual distinguishes (that which is) different." That is, to engage in *li* is to *bian* 辨 what is *yi* 異, that is, to distinguish or divide that which is disparate. The understanding that the function of ritual is to differentiate and/or separate entities appears in various other passages of the same text. The *Qulishang* 曲禮上 chapter asserts the following:

> Ritual is that which furnishes the means of determining (the observances towards) relatives, as near and remote; of settling points which may cause suspicion or doubt; of distinguishing where there should be agreement, and where difference; and of making clear what is right and what is wrong. (Legge 1885: 63, translation modified)

Thus, according to the *Liji*, the main function of ritual is to distinguish or separate (*bie* 別) things that are the same (*tong* 同) from those that are different (*yi* 異). Furthermore, this differentiation is essentially hierarchical, inasmuch as ritual effectively ranks entities according to a hierarchy of rights and wrongs: ritual "makes clear what is right and what is wrong" (*ming shi fei ye* 明是非也). An identical understanding of ritual is to be found in the *Bugou* 不苟 ("Nothing Improper") chapter of the *Xunzi*:

> The gentleman examines the Way of the later kings and then discusses events prior to the hundred kings as easily as clasping his hands and debating in court. He extends the controlling influence of ritual and *yi*, marks out the divisions between right and wrong, gathers into hand the crucial affairs of the world, and orders the masses within the four seas, all as though employing a single person. (Hutton 2014: 21)

In the *Xunzi*, just like in the *Liji*, ritual is explained in connection to the establishment of divisions (分). More specifically, ritual "marks out the divisions between right and wrong" (*feng shi fei zhi feng* 分是非之分). That is, it *hierarchically ranks* entities, extending "the controlling influence of ritual and *yi*" and allowing for "the ordering of the masses within the four seas." In this way, ritual's ability to separate things is a prerequisite of its capacity to control (*tong* 統) and order (*zhi* 治) them with exceptional efficacy. Furthermore, according to the *Xunzi*, even cosmic rhythms can be effectively controlled by establishing divisions (*feng* 分) through the practice of rituals: "Thus … they put the four seasons in their proper sequence, bring the myriad things to completion[8] and universally benefit the whole world." (Knoblock 1988: 104, translation modified). The conviction that ritual is capable of orderly arranging (*xu* 序) the timely movement of seasons is extensively developed in the *Yueling* 月令 chapter of the *Liji*. Take the following passage, for example:

If in the first month of spring the governmental proceedings proper to summer were carried out, the rain would fall unseasonably, plants and trees would decay prematurely, and the states would be kept in continual fear. If the proceedings proper to autumn were carried out, there would be great pestilence among the people; boisterous winds would work their violence; rain would descend in torrents; orache, fescue, darnel, and southernwood would grow up together. If the proceedings proper to winter were carried out, pools of water would produce their destructive effects, snow and frost would prove very injurious, and the first sown seeds would not enter the ground. (Legge 1885: 257)

In this passage, ritual is said to *sustain* the normal functioning of the seasons.[9] The possibility of a disruption is seen as occurring not within the operation of cosmic processes themselves, but with respect to the ruler's potential incapacity to cohere with them effectively, by failing to perform the rituals that are appropriate to a specific season. Thus, ritual agency is charged with the responsibility of maintaining the ordered operation of seasonal changes and so of securing the stability and cohesion of the cosmos. Moreover, this cosmological framework applies not only to cosmic rhythms but also to the very vitality and integrity of the land, which were thought to depend on the continued practice of a ritual, as explained in the following passage from the *Jiaotesheng* 郊特牲 chapter of the *Liji*:

At the "altar of the earth" (*she*), they sacrificed to (the spirits of) the land, and on the tablet rested the power of the darker and retiring *qi* (of nature). The ruler stands (in sacrificing) with his face to the south at the foot of the wall on the north, responding to the idea of that influence as coming from the north. A *jia* day is used (for the sacrifice), to employ a commencing day (in the Cycle). The great *She* altar of the son of Heaven was open to receive the hoarfrost, dew, wind, and rain, and allow the *qi* of heaven and earth to have full development upon it. For this reason the *she* altar of a state that had perished was roofed in, so that it was not touched by the brightness and warmth of Heaven. The *boshe* had an opening in the wall on the north, so that the dim and cold (moon) might shine into it. It was by means of the *she* altar that the *dao* of the earth as a spirit was fulfilled. (Legge 1885: 424–5, translation modified)

Consequently, the very existence of the vitality and integrity of the earth, the fulfillment of its *dao* 道, depends on worshipping it in accordance with the rituals that belong to the "altar of the earth" or *she*. It is this "altar" that secures the earth's continued communication with Heaven, filling it with *qi* 氣 (air, vapor, pneuma, energy, etc.) and opening it up to the wind and rain. Thus, although the *qi* comes from Heaven, it only reaches to the earth thanks to the *she*. Just like in the passages reviewed above, the *Jiaotesheng* asserts that the harmonious and ordered operation of cosmic processes relies upon the appropriate practice of rituals, with the following caveat: here the argument that the continued and timely performance of rituals is necessary for the survival of the cosmos takes a more specific form, namely, that the performance of the rituals of the *she* is necessary for the survival of the earth as a pneumatic power. In both cases, however, the cosmic necessity of ritual is asserted. In this way, ritual-centered cosmologies repeatedly defend the necessity of rituals by asserting that they are capable of sustaining the normal operation of cosmic processes and, consequently, maintaining the ordered and harmonious structure of the world. Logically, in these cosmologies cosmic processes do not occur spontaneously, to the extent that their movement depends on ritual agency. At the same time, these cosmologies do not understand the deliberate performance of rituals as hindering the creation of a harmonious cosmos. On the contrary, the primacy of rituals in these cosmologies implies exceptional confidence in the human capacity (1) to determine the provenance of cosmic processes and (2) to guarantee the stability and cohesion of the cosmos by means of ritual. This aplomb is also to be found in the description of the "altar of the earth." But, in reality, speaking of "altar" when referring to the *she* 社 might be misleading. As Roel Sterckx and Kominami Ichiro explain, the *she* was not conceived as a specific building, such as a temple or a shrine. In fact, a *she* was a tree or a group of trees (Kominami 2009: 205; Sterckx 2011: 116).[10] Besides a clump of trees, another shape the *she* could take was that of a mound or a clod of earth (Kominami 2009: 201–2; Sterckx 2011: 116). In fact, according to Kominami, the *she* was often a combination of these two things, as it is regularly "described as several trees tied together with earth spread around it" (Kominami 2009: 205). We find both of these images, copse and clod of earth, in the passage that opens the *Qiwulun* chapter of the *Zhuangzi*. As I will show, this provides an interesting point of comparison with the cosmologies that I have just explained.

The *Dakuai* 大塊 in the *Qiwulun* 齊物論: Doubting of Steering Agencies and Criticism of Hierarchical Differentiations as a Theoretical Precondition for the Articulation of a Self-moving Cosmos

The *Qiwulun* chapter has long been recognized as one of the core sections of the *Zhuangzi*. Most scholars highlight its skeptical (Raphals 1996), relativistic (Hansen 1983), and/or mystical (Roth 2003) character. Yet here I would like to defend the possibility of reading this chapter in a cosmological key. This is not to invalidate the abovementioned readings[11] but to assert that a different reading is equally valid[12] and, in fact, thought-provoking. The first of the "provocations" I propose here is the following: The *dakuai* 大塊 or "Great Clod" can be read as a reversal of the *she* 社. Various indications of this are to be found in the following passage:

> Ziqi said: When the Great Clump belches forth its vital breath (*qi*), we call it the wind. As soon as it arises, raging cries emerge from all the ten thousand hollows. Have you not heard the wind howling and roaring? The towering trees of the mountain forest, a hundred spans around, are riddled with indentations and holes—like noses, mouths, ears; like sockets, enclosures, mortars; like ponds, like puddles. Roarers and whizzers, scolders and sighers, shouters, wailers, boomers,

growlers! One leads with a yeee! Another answers with a yuuu! A light breeze brings a small harmony, while a powerful gale makes for a harmony vast and grand. And once the sharp wind has passed, all these holes return to their silent emptiness. Have you not seen the trees shaking and fluttering?" Ziyou said, "So the piping of the earth means just the sound of these hollows. And the piping of man would be the sound of bamboo panpipes. I dare to ask, what is the piping of Heaven then?" Ziqi said, "It blows through all the ten thousand differences. But if what causes them to blow is their own self-ending and what completes[13] them is their own self-choosing, then who is their rouser?" (Ziporyn 2009: 9–10, translation modified)

In this passage we find various references that resonate with the descriptions of the *she* altar we have reviewed above. First, the very idea of the "Great Clump" (*dakuai*) can be read as a reference to such a concept, inasmuch as one of the defining characteristics of the *she* is the presence of a clump or clod of earth. However, the *Zhuangzi*'s mentioning of a "great clump" can be read as an allusion not only to the *she* altar in particular but also to the earth (*di* 地) and the land (*tu* 土) in general. In fact, Yu Yue 俞樾 (1821–1907) comments that *kuai* 塊 is an alternative form for *kuai* 凷, which means "dirt clod" or, as Scott Cook renders it, a "handful of earth" (Cook 2003: 79 n.10). According to the Qing dynasty commentator, the character is also a reference to the earth (*di*) itself.[14] Now, as we have seen, the *she*, as stated in the *Liji*, is a ritual that indicates the appropriate way of worshiping *di* and securing its continued vitality (*qi*). It is not by chance, I believe, that the occurrence of the *dakuai* here occurs in conjunction with that of *qi*; this, I suggest, is a second indicator of the parallelism between *dakuai* and *she/di/tu*. Third, the image of the trees pervades the entire passage, specifically their sounding/piping. First we read of the "mountain forest" (*shanlin* 山林) and the "big trees" (*damu* 大木), and then we attend to a wonderfully vivid description of their sounds as the breeze flows through them and, assumedly, their moving leaves. Once again, this can also be read as a reference to the *she*, as the most distinctive feature of this "altar" is the tree. Fourth, another important element of the *she* also appears in this passage: the wind. When the *dakuai* gushes out its *qi*, it does so in the manner of a wind (*feng* 風), and thus by blowing (*chui* 吹). As we have seen above, the *she* also manifests its vitality, its enjoyment of *qi*, by remaining open to the wind. Furthermore, the operation of *qi* itself can be understood as a blowing or, more specifically, a breathing: *qi* is not only energy or vitality but also, and most importantly, "breath," "air," or "vapor." Summarily, and in consideration of all of the above, the entire passage can be read as echoing the understanding of the earth's vitality that can be found in the abovementioned description of the *she*.

It is against this cosmological background that, I believe, we should read this whole passage, especially with a view to reassess the nature of Ziqi's answer to Yancheng Ziyou's inquiry. In other words, it appears that this response was formulated with respect to the extraordinary degree of certainty with which the genesis of earthly and heavenly movements is explained in the abovementioned description of the "altar of the earth" and generally in ritual-centered cosmologies. As we have seen in the previous section "Li 禮 and She 社 in Ancient China: Continued Ritual Action as

Guarantor of Cosmic Stability and Cohesion," these cosmologies repeatedly defend the indispensability of rituals by asserting that they are capable of effectively sustaining the orderly succession of cosmic processes and/or the vitality of the earth, thus maintaining the ordered structure of the world. In consideration of this, it is intriguing that the request of Yancheng Ziyou, "I dare to ask, what is the piping of Heaven then?" (*gan wen tian lei* 敢問天籟), finds a provocative answer: "It blows through all the ten thousand differences. But if what causes them to blow is their own self-ending and what completes them is their own self-choosing, then what identity can there be for their rouser?"[15] Ziqi's final remark is literally a question:[16] "Who is the rouser?" (*nu zhe qi shei xie* 怒者其誰邪). He thus admits ignoring the identity of the agent or agency that is assumed to be responsible for this rousing, an admission that can also be interpreted as implicating that to firmly establish a *separate* origin or cause of cosmic processes is impossible and/or unnecessary. Thus, although the passage shares an identical cosmological vocabulary with the *Liji* and other texts, it reworks it for its own subversive purposes.

In fact, Ziqi's admission of ignorance stands in direct contrast to the assurance with which ritual-centered cosmologies determine the provenance and maintenance of cosmic processes. In those cosmologies, in fact, such things are not for debate: (1) Heaven is the origin of cosmic movements and (2) (human) rituals are responsible for their maintenance. The *Qiwulun* effectively subverts the foundations of a cosmology of this type by suggesting that attempting to define a rouser is impossible and, in reality, *unnecessary*. According to this chapter, there is no need to appeal to a rouser or mover to explain the reality of movement and change. If to account for such a reality is our intention, we can do this simply in reference to the "self-ending" (*ziyi* 自已) and "self-choosing" (*ziqu* 自取) nature of cosmic processes, thus sparing ourselves the trouble of having to do this in reference to something that we are in no position to either affirm or deny, that is, a rouser (Graham 1989: 49). Truly speaking, Ziqi's admission of ignorance *does not* amount to a denial of either the ability to explain the movements of the "blowing" (*chui*) or the possibility of establishing a cause or origin for it. To be precise, what Ziqi doubts, and implicitly denies, is the possibility of finding this origin in something that exists *separately* from the very process of blowing. He does this by suggesting the impossibility of asserting the existence of a rouser, which is, by definition, an origin located *outside of* the very mechanisms that already pertain to the blowing process and which thus exists *independently* and separately from them. He suggests that, ultimately, the rouser and the blowing are identical, and that, therefore, the blowing occurs *out of itself*, through a "self-choosing" and a "self-ending." This is, to my knowledge, the Inner Chapter's most consistent and clear articulation of the cosmological view that has come to be known, through the works of Guo Xiang and several other commentators, as *ziran*. If we understand this cosmology as one of self-moving cosmic processes, then, I believe, this is exactly what Ziqi is trying to explain in the passage I have just quoted and analyzed. Now, if we accept this interpretation, the *dakuai* must be a reference to the self-moving nature of the cosmos and thus a subversion of the ritual-dependent world of the *she*: The "Great Clod" does not cause things to blow but *in itself* is a blowing, a piping, a breathing. In fact, while according to the cosmological model of the "altar of the earth," the breathing of the earth depends on the performance of a ritual, in the cosmological model of the "Great Clod," such breathing is the result of the earth's spontaneous propensities. It is in reference to this that I say that the *dakuai* can be read as a reversal of the *she*.

Furthermore, the other main reason Ziqi judges it impossible to account for the reality of change and movement in the way a ritual-centered cosmologist does seems to relate to the chapter's emphatic assertion of important cognitive limitations in a specific type of language, namely, that which relies on *hierarchical distinctions* and which occurs within the context of verbal disputes. This is the topic that the *Qiwulun* addresses right after the passage quoted above, specifically in reference to three major distinctions: (1) "great knowledge" (*dazhi*大知) and "petty knowledge," (*xiaozhi*小知); (2) "great fears" (*dakong*大恐) and "small fears" (*xiaokong*小恐); and (3) "big talk" (*dayan*大言) and "petty talk" (*xiaoyan*小言). This section emphasizes how the making of these hierarchies occurs parallel to the psychological and emotional havoc caused by both our stubborn search for absolute certainty and our constant despair in the face of uncertainty. Apparently, the writer sees our interest in finding causes and creators as part of this obsessive and self-damaging inclination, as indicated by the fact that, after describing this behavior, the text rapidly goes back to the issue of cosmological causation:

> Day and night they alternate each other before us, but no one knows whence they sprout. That is enough! That is enough! Is it from all of this, presented ceaselessly day and night, that things come to exist? Without that there would be no me, to be sure, but then again without me there would be nothing selected out from it all. This is certainly something close to hand, and yet we do not know what makes it so. If there is a real controller behind it all, it is peculiarly devoid of any manifest sign. Its ability to flow and to stop makes its presence plausible, but even then it shows no definite form. That would make it a reality with no definite form."
> (Ziporyn 2009: 10, translation modified)

Uncertainty with respect to the actual cause of things is reiterated in this passage, as it is said that, regarding the succession of day and night, "no one knows whence they sprout" (*mo zhi qi suo meng*莫知其所萌). After being abruptly stopped from this line of questioning (*yi hu yi hu*已乎已乎!), the text inquires, just like in the previous passage, whether the cause for this constant succession is not succession itself: "Is it from all of this, presented ceaselessly day and night, that things come to exist?" The text further develops this idea by turning back to the issue of the theoretical impossibility of a steering agency: "If there is a real controller behind it all, it is peculiarly devoid of any manifest sign. Its ability to flow and to stop makes its presence plausible, but even then it shows no definite form." There "*seems to be*" (*ruo you* 若有) a "real controller" (*zhen zai* 真宰), but its invisibility (*bu jian qi xing*不見其形) is such that all we really know is that is constantly moving and stopping (*ke xing yi xin* 可行已信). And if some conclusion can be drawn from this, it is simply that it lacks a form (*wu xing* 無形), and yet at the same time is undeniably real (*you qing* 有情). The emphasis given to the ability of things to constantly move *even though* they lack a "real controller" and possess "no form" seems to be intended to prove two major things: (1) It is intellectually impossible to determine a specific origin or cause of things *outside* of themselves (i.e., a "real controller") and (2) given this, the only *viable* conclusion we can actually arrive at is that things move *of* themselves. This is, once more, the cosmology that has come to be known as *ziran*.

However, and as explained above, the futility of striving for establishing the steering agency of things with absolute certainty relates not only to the undeniable veracity of the autopoietic nature of the cosmos but also, and most notably, to the inherent limitations and dangers of a specific type of speaking (*yan* 言) and naming (*wei* 謂), namely, verbally quarreling (*shifei* 是非) and disputing (*bian* 辯). As mentioned before, knowing, fearing, and talking all occur within hierarchical distinctions, specifically those between big (*da* 大) and small (*xiao* 小). It is thus suggested that without such distinctions, these potentially damaging activities could never take place. In a different passage, the chapter further describes the type of cognition that occurs within a *shifei* framework:

> The Dao has never had any boundaries, and words have never had any constancy. It is by establishing definitions of what is "this," what is "right," (*shi* 是) that boundaries are made. Let me explain what I mean by boundaries: There are right and left, classes of things and ideas of the proper responses to them, distinctions and disputes, competitions and struggles. Let's call these the Eight Virtues! As for the sage, he may admit that something exists beyond the six limits of the known world, but he does not further discuss it. As for what is within the known world, he will discuss it but not express an opinion on it. As for historical events, he will give an opinion but not debate it. For wherever a distinction is made, something is left undistinguished. Wherever something is debated, something is left undebated. What is it? The sage hides it in his embrace, while the masses of people debate it, trying to demonstrate it to one another. Thus I say that demonstration by debate always leaves something unseen." (Ziporyn 2009: 16, translation modified)

The world of quarrels (*shifei*) and disputations (*bian*) is condemned to always leaving something unseen (*bujian* 不見) and undebated (*bubian* 不辯). Thus, the type of knowledge that debating allows for is highly deficient on account of its inherent partiality. The reason, in turn, for this partiality is the fact that quarreling and disputing rely on distinctions. The world of quarrels is, in fact, a world of boundaries and distinctions as the passage systematically pairs these two together: "there are distinctions and disputes" (*you feng you bian* 有分有辯), it says, suggesting that these two are essentially interrelated. What is more, it then compares distinguishing with disputing: "For wherever a distinction is made, something is left undistinguished. Wherever something is debated, something is left undebated." In other words, to debate is to distinguish, and vice versa, so that the limitations inherent to distinguishing are the same than those inherent to debating: leaving something unnoticed. In this way, to the extent that a debate cannot but take place within distinctions, the type of knowledge that it is capable of attaining is necessarily deficient.[17] In a previous passage, these cognitive deficiencies are squarely attributed to specific individuals:

How could words be so obscured that there could be any question of right or wrong among them? Where can you go without it being a course? What can you say without it being affirmable? The Dao is obscured by the small accomplishments already formed and completed by them. Words are obscured by the ostentatious blossoms of reputation that come with them. *Hence we have* (*gu you* 故有) the rights and wrongs of the Confucians and Mohists, each affirming what the other negates and negating what the other affirms. (Ziporyn 2019: 11, emphasis added)

Like all quarrelers and disputers, Confucians and Mohists also suffer from the limitations imposed by hierarchical distinctions. Furthermore, it is precisely because they actively rely on them that their debates proceed in the manner of an obscuration of the Dao (*gu you ru mo zhi shi fei* 故有儒墨之是非). Thus, this process of occultation is a direct consequence of their adherence to a *shifei* framework that has already obscured the Dao (*dao e* 道惡), a Dao that their own debating/*shifei*-ing thus continues to conceal.[18] The obscuring of the Dao through *shifei* appears to parallel the reference to not seeing it, due to dividing it up through boundaries, in the passage we have just discussed. To obscure and not to see are, in fact, quite similar in nature, as in both something remains hidden, in this case, the Dao. And to say that the *ru* lose sight of the Dao is, in fact, quite a polemic statement, considering that they claimed to have found the key to its understanding. However, such criticism comes as no surprise, as the *Qiwulun* consistently dismantles one of the most fundamental concepts in Confucianism: hierarchical distinctions. As we have seen in the previous section, these are central to the ritual-centered cosmologies favored by the *ru*. In them, ritual agency is understood as capable of enforcing and maintaining hierarchical distinctions and with that, the cohesiveness and stability of the cosmos. By means of *shifei*, ritual effectively steers the cosmos into behaving in an orderly manner. Interestingly enough, and as I hope to have shown, right after doubting the possibility of a steering agency, the *Qiwulun* doubts the cognitive aptness and utility of hierarchical distinctions.

Conclusion

In all, the *Qiwulun* effectively subverts two of the most central notions of ritual-centered cosmologies: steering agencies and hierarchical differentiations. It wastes no time in saying whether these are right or wrong, it simply provides a rigorous demonstration of how the assumptions that they rely on are not only feeble but also, and most notably, damaging to ourselves and others. This critical outlook is expectable, as the cosmology of spontaneity that the chapter adheres to necessarily contravenes ritual-centered cosmologies. In fact, a spontaneous cosmos is in itself subversive of a ritual-dependent cosmos, simply because in the former, the ordered operation of cosmic processes *does not depend* on the performance of rituals but occurs automatically instead. In this way, it is only logical that the articulation of a self-moving cosmos occurs conjointly with the doubting of both steering agencies and hierarchical distinctions, as these are the two main categories behind the efforts of the *ru* to explain cosmic movements as depending on the appropriate performance of rituals. On a different note, there are important political connotations to these disparate ways of explaining the cosmos. On the one hand, ritual-centered cosmologies served to *legitimize* existing political structures and practices, as the claim for the cosmic necessity of ritual action was also, and perhaps most notably, a claim for the cosmic indispensability of political action and political institutions in general.[19] On the other hand, the *Qiwulun*'s self-moving cosmos renders this claim for political legitimacy useless: By asserting that cosmic movements are spontaneous, it also asserts that no ritual, government, or monarch are needed for a cosmos to exist, that is, for the order that defines the world to be sustained.[20]

Notes

1 I am indebted to Hans-Georg Moeller, Brook Ziporyn, Hui-Chieh Loy, Roger Ames, Guoxiang Peng, and Margus Ott for, knowingly or unknowingly, helping me in writing this chapter with their critical suggestions and comments. At the same time, the continuous and thought-provoking exchanges with Nicolas Le Jeune, Daniel Sarafinas, Richard Sage, and Frank Saunders, among other PhD students in Hong Kong and Macau, have been of great help at various stages of development of this chapter. To all of the above, I am sincerely grateful.
2 For the purposes of this chapter, *ziran* refers not to the "spontaneity" or "naturalness" of human actions and/or institutions, but specifically to the spontaneity of *cosmic processes*, that is, the idea that these processes occur *of themselves*.
3 See note 1. By saying that ritual-centered cosmologies should be distinguished from *ziran* cosmology, I do not mean to deny that ritual-centered cosmologies assert that rituals are "natural" or "spontaneous," in the sense of being in a state of continuity and harmony with nature and its processes. Instead, I mean to say that precisely because such continuity is asserted, it is implied that the ordered operation of the cosmos does *not* occur spontaneously, inasmuch as it derives from the continued and appropriate practice of rituals. Logically, if the normal operation of cosmic processes *depends on* ritual agency, then such processes are *not* "of themselves" (*ziran*).
4 Contrarily to what Hall and Ames (1995) argue.
5 Contrarily to what Puett (2002) argues.
6 Thus my argument resonates with Stephen Owen's insightful explanation of *dao* 道 in the *Shijing* 詩經 as proposing "a relation to natural process that is usually *overlooked* in Western formulations of the relation between man and Nature, but one that is pragmatically obvious in the agrarian community … , a different way to think about what human beings do, *neither laissez-faire natural nor artificial*" (Owen 2001: 209-300, emphasis added). Although Owen says this in reference to the feats of Houji 后稷 as described in the *Shengmin* 生民 chapter of the *Shijing*, I believe a similar, if not identical, point can be made with respect to the *Xunzi* and the *Liji*.
7 In this chapter I understand "cosmos" precisely in this way, that is, in its original ancient Greek sense. In fact, scholars agree that the origin of the cosmological use of the term κόσμος relates to an effort to characterize the world in terms of "order" and regularity, which, in turn, runs counter to the idea of a world marked by the *absence of order*—that is, the existence of chaos and disorder—and not the absence of a material realm. See Khan (1960); Cartledge, Millett, and von Reden (2002); and Vlastos (2006).

8   Reading 裁 as 成.
9   A rationale identical to the one behind the *Yueling* is to be found in the *Shize* 時則 ("Seasonal Rules") chapter of the *Huainanzi* 淮南子, the *Xuangong* 玄宮 ("Dark Palace") chapter of the *Guanzi* 管子, and the first twelve chapters of the *Lüshi chunqiu* 呂氏春秋, among several other texts. A concern with the timely performance of activities is also central to another group of texts, namely, the *rishu* 日書 ("daybooks" or "almanacs") of the Warring States period. For a summary review of various ancient Chinese "calendars," see Rickett (2001: 158–63). For the place of daybooks within "astro-calendrical literature" and their relationship with the *yueling* calendars, see Harper (1999).
10 This is exactly how the *Zhuangzi* refers to the *she* at the end of its fourth chapter; and probably at the beginning of its second one as well, as I will explain later.
11 However, it should be mentioned that according to some scholars, to recognize the validity of a specific way of reading the *Zhuangzi* necessarily implies asserting the invalidity of *any* cosmological or metaphysical reading. In their views, to assert the essentially skeptical/relativistic and/or performative character of the *Zhuangzi* necessarily precludes the possibility of asserting its cosmological character (Hansen 1983: 31; Eno 1996: 138; Billeter 2003: 178). I challenge this assumption and argue that the skepticism the *Qiwulun* endorses ought to be read directly in connection with an effort to formulate a cosmology of spontaneity capable of effectively informing the performativity celebrated in the text. Without referring to such cosmology, both the epistemological and performative stances of the text are neither fully understood nor completely appreciated in their full philosophical value.
12 I agree with Moeller and D'Ambrosio when they note that "the multidimensionality of the *Zhuangzi* allows for readings of the same passages in different keys and with different foci of attention" (Moeller and D'Ambrosio 2017: 11).
13 Reading 咸 as 成.
14 Yu Yue's complete comment is the following: 大塊者，地也。塊乃凷之或體 (Guo 2017: 52).
15 A similar translation is offered by David Chai: "When the wind blows, the myriad apertures give off different sounds, using that which *arises of itself*. Ceasing to blow, they also stop of themselves. Taking only what *is for itself*, should there be another that gives rise to them!" (Chai 2008: 72, emphasis added).
16 As indicated by the particle 邪.
17 This, however, is not entirely surprising, as 辯 means not only to dispute and argue but also to distinguish and discriminate. As Brook Ziporyn explains, the character is used in the text as a cognate for homophonous *bian* 辨 (to divide, to distinguish) (Ziporyn 2009: 213).
18 What Ziporyn translates here as "affirming" and "negating" is, in fact, *shi* 是 and *fei* 非, respectively. Thus the *Zhuangzi*'s complaint against these thinkers is, once more, that they also engage in quarrels and distinctions: "*shi*-ing what they *fei*, and *fei*-ing what they *shi*" (以是其所非，而非其所是).
19 Several scholars have noticed the legitimizing function of ritual (Lewis 1997; Pines 2000; Jiang 2006). According to Tao Jiang: "To the kings, the observance of *li* … was the source of political authority, and the appropriate fulfillment of *li* was the springboard of political legitimization" (Jiang 2006: 25).
20 I thus agree with those inclined to read the *Zhuangzi* as a critique of both sociopolitical and religious power. For this view, see Galvany (2012), and Moeller and D'Ambrosio (2017).

References

Billeter, J. (2003), *Cuatro Lecturas sobre Zhuangzi*. Madrid: Siruela.
Boileau, G. (1998), "Some Ritual Elaborations on Cooking and Sacrifice in Late Zhou and Western Han Texts." *Early China* 23: 89–123.
Cartledge, P., P. Millett, and S. von Reden, eds. (2002), *Kosmos: Essays in Order, Conflict and Community in Classical Athens*. Cambridge: Cambridge University Press.
Chai, D. (2008), *Early Zhuangzi Commentaries: On the Sounds and Meanings of the Inner Chapters*. Saarbrucken: VDM Verlag Müller.
Cook, S. (2003), "Harmony and Cacophony in the Panpipes of Heaven." In *Hiding the World in the World: Uneven Discourses on the Zhuangzi*, edited by S. Cook, 64–87. Albany: State University of New York Press.
Eno, R. (1996), "Cook Ding's Dao and the Limits of Philosophy." In *Essays on Skepticism, Relativism, and Ethics in the Zhuangzi*, edited by P. Kjellberg and P. J. Ivanhoe, 127–51. Albany: State University of New York Press.
Galvany, A. (2012), *La palabra transgresora: Cinco ensayos sobre Zhuangzi*. Barcelona: Bellaterra.
Graham, A. C. (1989), *Chuang-Tzu: The Inner Chapters*. Indianapolis: Hackett.
Guo, Q. F. (2017), *Zhuangzi jishi* 莊子集釋. Beijing: Zhonghua shuju.
Hall, D., and Roger Ames (1995), *Anticipating China: Thinking through the Narratives of Chinese and Western Culture*. Albany: State University of New York Press.
Hansen, C. (1983), "A Tao of Tao in Chuang-tzu." In *Experimental Essays on Chuang-tzu*, edited by V. H. Mair, 25–55. Hawaii: University of Hawaii Press.
Harper, D. (1999), "Warring States Natural Philosophy and Occult Thought." In *The Cambridge History of Ancient China: From the Origins of Civilization to 221 BC*, edited by M. Loewe and E. Shaughnessy, 813–84. New York: Cambridge University Press.
Hutton, E. L. (2014), *Xunzi: The Complete Text*. Princeton, NJ: Princeton University Press.
Jiang T. (2006), "Intimate Authority: The Rule of Ritual in Classical Confucian Political Discourse." In *Confucian Cultures of Authority*, edited by P. D. Hershock and R. T. Ames, 21–47. Albany: State University of New York Press.
Kahn, C. H. (1960), *Anaximander and the Origins of Greek Cosmology*. New York: Columbia University Press.
Knoblock, J. (1988), *Xunzi: A Translation and Study of the Complete Works*, vol. 1. Stanford, CA: Stanford University Press.
Kominami, I. (2009), "Rituals for the Earth." In *Early Chinese Religion, Part One: Shang through Han (1250 BC–220 AD)*, edited by J. Lagerwey and M. Kalinowski, 201–34. Leiden: Brill.
Legge, J. (1885), *The Sacred Books of China: The Texts of Confucianism. Part III. The Li Ki, I-IX*. Oxford: Clarendon.
Lewis, M. E. (1997), "Ritual Origins of the Warring States." *Bulletin de l'École française d'Extrême-Orient* 84: 73–98.
Lewis, M. E. (2006), *The Flood Myths of Early China*. Albany: State University of New York Press.
Moeller, H. G., and P. J. D'Ambrosio (2017), *Genuine Pretending: On the Philosophy of the Zhuangzi*. New York: Columbia University Press.
Owen, S. (2001), "Reproduction in the Shijing (Classic of Poetry)." *Harvard Journal of Asiatic Studies* 61(2): 287–315.

Pines, Y. (2000), "Disputers of the 'Li': Breakthroughs in the Concept of Ritual in Preimperial China." *Asia Major* 13(1): 1–41.
Puett, M. J. (2002), *To Become a God: Cosmology, Sacrifice, and Self-divinization in Early China*. Cambridge: Harvard University Press.
Raphals, L. (1996), "Skeptical Strategies in the Zhuangzi and Theaetetus." In *Essays on Skepticism, Relativism, and Ethics in the Zhuangzi*, edited by P. Kjellberg and P. J. Ivanhoe, 26–49. Albany: State University of New York Press.
Rickett, W. A. (2001), *Guanzi: Political, Economic, and Philosophical Essays from Early China*, vol. 1. Princeton, NJ: Princeton University Press.
Roth, H. D. (2003), "Bimodal Mystical Experience in the "Qiwulun" Chapter of Zhuangzi." In *Hiding the World in the World: Uneven Discourses on the Zhuangzi*, edited by S. Cook, 15–32. Albany: State University of New York Press.
Sterckx, R. (2011), *Food, Sacrifice, and Sagehood in Early China*. New York: Cambridge University Press.
Vlastos, G. (2006), *Plato's Universe*. Ann Arbor, MI: Parmenides.
Ziporyn, B. (2009), *Zhuangzi: The Essential Writings: With Selections from Traditional Commentaries*. Indianapolis: Hackett.

14

Dai Zhen's Critique of Song Confucian Ideology

Robert A. Carleo III

In the eighteenth century, the eminent Chinese intellectual Dai Zhen 戴震 (1724–1777) put forth a radical critique of the Song Confucian interpretation of "principle" (*li* 理), a core concept of the reigning Confucian ideology of his time. Dai's criticism consists of three main charges against this concept: the claim that it is historically inaccurate (as an interpretation of classical Confucian teachings), that it is philosophically un-Confucian (as the product of Daoist and Buddhist influence), and that it is socially and morally problematic (in leading to oppression and abuse of power). In making this tripartite argument, Dai attacked the socially and intellectually dominant Confucian orthodoxy, and his criticisms correspond to the particular claims of that ideology. They are thus formulated in line with the standards of that dominant discourse itself: Song Confucianism claimed to present an accurate and authoritative interpretation of the classics, the true teachings of Confucianism, and the proper path to moral and political virtue. In presenting his arguments this way, Dai moved not only against the current of the mainstream, orthodox Confucian teachings of his day, but also against the current of scholarly critique most prevalent in his time, of which he was a leading figure, that of "evidentiary studies" (*kaozhengxue* 考證學). Evidentiary studies limited itself to historical-textual critique and eschewed the kind of philosophical and social arguments through which Dai subverts the teachings of Song Confucianism. From this we may infer that Dai saw particular need for and power in presenting his critique in the historical, philosophical, and moral terms he chose.

Setting the Stage: The Traditional Confucian Use of Tradition

Scholars have noted that Chinese thought has often or generally relied on classical texts and historical narratives, whereas Judeo-Christian and other traditions invoke a Supreme Being. That is to say, within the Chinese tradition, historical authority is "God." This privileged role of history and the classics is commonly drawn on by Chinese scholars to advance certain philosophical positions, and the reinterpretation of and reliance on canonized texts and narratives in these thinkers is a central component of

Confucian tradition (and of course is by no means unique to the Confucian tradition). Confucius himself undertook "rectification" of classical texts and historical narratives, and he was celebrated for having selected and edited existing histories and classics to canonize what might now be seen as mythologized accounts of the tradition, such as stories of earlier sage leaders. In this, he seems to have been epitomizing a practice of the time.

> It is worth a reminder that in the Zhanguo [Warring States] age there was no unified narrative of the past; history was primarily written not by court scribes, as it was during the Chunqiu period, but by rival thinkers who routinely "used the past to serve the present." The degree of manipulation of the past narratives increased enormously during the Zhanguo period, with new heroes, new events, and new interpretations of the past created by almost every contending thinker. (Pines 2009: 78)

As later Confucian tradition developed, a new mythologization and canonization of Confucian teachings began under Han Yu 韓愈 (768–824), who established an orthodox lineage of Confucian thinkers carried forward into present day (*Daotong* 道統). The most influential later Confucian, Zhu Xi 朱熹 (1130–1200), went on to establish the Confucian canon of the Ming dynasty forward, through calculated selection and interpretation of authoritative classics. Zhu likewise proved willing to revise the tradition, both in its historical account as well as in the content of the classics themselves, and did so in highly effective and influential ways—attributing the teachings of the *Great Learning* (*Da Xue* 大學) to Zengzi 曾子 and altering its opening line from advocating affectionate care for the people (*qin min* 親民) to renewal of the people (*xin min* 新民). Indeed, the latter of these supports its own revision, establishing the second of Three Guiding Principles (*san gangling* 三綱領) to emphasize the need for reforms that promote the moral perfection of the people (De Bary 1988: 299), and thus itself provides moral justification for such alteration and innovation. This again seems to have been part of the general trend of the era.

> Reinterpretation of the classics employed a new criticism by which neoclassicism was made to serve the purposes of reform, and a new, abridged and refocused canon was created as the scriptural basis for a new way of life. Even "restoration of the ancient order" found use as a slogan to sanction institutional innovations. (De Bary 1988: 296)

The rise of evidentiary studies (*kaozhengxue* 考證學) in late-dynastic China came to prize critical historical accuracy, especially with regard to the textual integrity and interpretation of the classics. These scholars rejected the robustly interpretive and creative philosophic readings of the classics advocated by Zhu Xi and other Neo-Confucians.[1] What is especially interesting about this movement is that, because the classics retain normative "historical authority," arguments regarding their historical integrity are not merely matters of accurate historical record, but often used to support or debunk normative teachings. Their critical views, accordingly, came to be used by the "school of debate over ancient history" (*gushi bian pai* 古史辨派) in a new attempt to refigure tradition by shifting historical authority, this time seeking to dethrone the classics by calling their historical authenticity into question. Zhang Taiyan 章太炎 (1869–1936) similarly opposed the creative, normative use of the historical authority of the classics, and criticized even Confucius for destroying books in his "editing" process, going so far as to advocate the removal of Confucius from his position as the figurehead of Confucianism (*ru* 儒). The normative use of historical arguments is no less prodigious in contemporary scholarship. Archeological discovery and technological advances have only increased the frequency and intensity of such debates among contemporary scholars.

Because the classics have normative authority, misinterpretation of them is not merely a descriptive, historical matter, but viewed as debunking any theory that deviates from it or even innovates on it. A focused example of this is seen in the work of the great evidentiary studies scholar Dai Zhen 戴震 (1724–1777), a luminary and leading figure of Qing evidentiary studies scholarship, whose arguments against the normative dangers of Zhu Xi's metaphysics are embedded in his charges against the descriptive, historical accuracy of Zhu Xi's reading of the *Mengzi* 孟子. Dai was elevated to great prestige within a school of rigidly critical and empirical historical scholarship that warned against and was largely averse to the philosophical bent of his project; but it is Dai's philosophical contribution, and its role in the narrative of tradition, that is remembered and often celebrated today.

The Motives and Aims of Dai's Arguments

In his *Evidential Commentary on the Meanings of Terms in the Mengzi* (*Mengzi ziyi shuzheng* 孟子字義疏證), Dai Zhen argues that the Neo-Confucian teachings that had become intellectually and socially pervasive in his time, and especially their understanding of moral "principle" (*li* 理), fall short in several ways: they present a philologically and historically inaccurate interpretation of classical teachings, are philosophically problematic, are un-Confucian, and lead to social and political oppression and harm. All of these charges interconnect through dual core problems of the metaphysics and moral psychology of Song Confucianism in conceiving of principle as an independent entity bestowed in the individual heart-mind and as opposed to emotion and desires. He makes clear, however, especially in the preface and conclusion that frame the work, that it is the last set of concerns, regarding social harm, that motivates his arguments. It is noteworthy, then, that he recruits such a wide range of other issues to support the charges.

He may have seen this as necessary in order to be robustly and widely persuasive within the diverse intellectual currents at the time. If his arguments were to resonate with the main current of evidentiary scholarship, they would have to operate through a persuasive philological criticism, showing that these theses about principle were misinterpretations of the teachings presented in the original texts. This would show that they were historically inaccurate. In order to persuade thinkers of a speculative and moral bent still swayed by the metaphysical ideology of Neo-Confucian thought,

Dai would have to demonstrate the philosophical failures of those arguments and views. To connect with the broader establishment of Confucian thought still largely adhering to these views, which continued to exert great influence culturally and politically, one would do well to stress that the above critiques also imply that these views are not properly considered Confucian, since they do not align with the historical authority of the original teachings found in the classics. And, indeed, Dai argues with great emphasis throughout the text that these views are (supposedly) the product of subversive Daoist and Buddhist influence that had distorted the original teachings. A point of interest is that all three of these arguments interconnect with historical authority, especially Dai's choice to present them as an "evidential commentary" on the *Mengzi*. Most interesting is the middle of these arguments, which intersects less directly with historical authority; it proceeds through the premise that the original teachings are of course sagely and thus must be philosophically wise and coherent.

Yet ultimately these arguments based on the normative authority of history and classical texts, and on the proper or pure lineage and interpretation of Confucian teachings, reject Song Confucian teachings for a more fundamental reason: they foster political and social oppression or abuse. Dai here links the historical and philosophical corruption of classical Confucian teachings with such oppression and abuse, arguing that Song teachings support and even cause the oppressive exercise of social power and neglect of the interests of the non-empowered. An accurate understanding of the text of the *Mengzi*, he insists, yields certain philosophical views (his own) that protect against social oppression and promote concern with the interests and basic welfare of the people.

Among the principal means by which Dai forefronts the importance of his political and social concerns is selection of the *Mengzi* as the base from which to launch his criticism. The decision to present his arguments as a commentary on the *Mengzi* is particularly noteworthy, since the substantive arguments given consistently draw on a wide variety of texts, hardly prioritizing the *Mengzi* and consistently grouping Mengzi's teachings with those of Kongzi and the Six Classics. Moreover, several of the eight terms around which Dai organizes his discussion—principle (*li* 理), heavenly way (*tian dao* 天道), intrinsic nature (*xing* 性), ability (*cai* 才), the way (*dao* 道), the four cardinal virtues (*ren yi li zhi* 仁義禮智), sincerity (*cheng* 誠), and discernment (*quan* 權)—appear either infrequently (principle, heavenly way) or not at all (sincerity) as philosophical concepts in the *Mengzi*. Even the concept of principle, the direct subject of the first one-third of the text, occurs as a philosophical concept in the *Mengzi* at most twice, with one of these merely as part of the compound word *tiaoli* 條理 (5B1). Dai's thought, on many accounts, may even have strong affinities with Xunzian rather than Mengzian thought (see Qian 1995: 394–5; Shun 2002). Why, then, did Dai choose to identify his arguments with—and to present the work as an *Evidential Commentary on*—the *Mengzi*?

One factor is presumably the esteemed and influential position of the *Mengzi* in Song Confucianism and in the subsequent pervasiveness of Song Confucian teachings. It had become an authoritative classic, one of the Four Books selected by Zhu Xi as the core Neo-Confucianism texts and on which the imperial examination system centered. Dai is thus drawing on its authority and importance. But in addition to the high status of that text, there is another more direct set of considerations that brought Dai to launch his arguments from the *Mengzi*.

Dai not only identifies his particular philosophical position with Mengzi, arguing that his own conception of principle, and *not* the Song Confucian interpretation, follows from proper understanding of classical teachings; he also identifies the motives and method that drive his arguments with Mengzi. Dai declares that what drove him to author the work and to assign importance to the philosophical position he expresses in it lie in a socially oriented moral mission that corresponds to the motivations Mengzi himself claims for his own teachings: to counteract contemporary social and moral ills resulting from widespread perverse and destructive ideologies (see *Mengzi* 3A5, 3B9, 7A26). Dai frames the text overall in these terms, repeatedly referencing this moral mission in the preface and conclusion of the *Evidential Commentary* (preface/66, §43/172–3),[2] as well as elsewhere in the text (see §7/78, §40/164–6). Dai further identifies with Mengzi in dovetailing this social mission with his philological arguments. He refers repeatedly to Mengzi's emphasis on the idea that properly understanding words and disputing heretical teachings are important because "what arises in the mind will interfere with policy, and what shows itself in policy will interfere with practice" (*Mengzi* 2A2, 3B9; trans. Lau 2003: 63, 143). Drawing on these passages of the *Mengzi* (as well as 7A24), Dai writes in prefacing the *Evidential Commentary*, "Erroneous words do not just end with words; they change and influence the minds of men. A mind that is beclouded must do injury to the conduct of affairs and to government" (preface/66). The closing lines of the *Evidential Commentary* as a whole read:

> Alas! If the doctrines of these men did not do injury to men's practice and to their policy and result in great harm to the people, I would honor them. Why would I dislike them? I dislike them because I fear for the heart-minds of the people. (§43/176)

The conclusions of both the preface and the entirety of the *Evidential Commentary* assert that Dai, in the spirit of Mengzi himself, has been impelled to author the *Evidential Commentary* by a moral mission to redress false teachings and the social ills that result from them. Dai thus draws on the historical authority of Mengzi to emphasize that although fostering political and social ills is hardly his only argument against Song Confucian principle, it is fundamental to his arguments and drives them.

The *Mengzi*, then, is a fitting foil for Dai's combined philological, philosophical, and social project in several dimensions, including the contemporary influence of the *Mengzi* and reverence for it, its status as an authoritative Confucian text, and the way in which the idolized figure of Mengzi is recorded as presenting his own critical project in opposition to heretical or corrupting teachings of his time. Of course, the speculative Neo-Confucian philosophies that Dai targets with his criticisms also identify closely with Mengzi, and are even largely the source of the authority and esteem of that text. The problems with these interpretations of Mengzi's teachings lie principally in the dual qualities they ascribe to moral principle identified above, in light of the social harms that they produce.

Dai's Philosophical Sentimentalism

One count on which Dai indicts the Neo-Confucian conception of moral principle is that it is supposedly embedded "as if it were a thing" (*ru you wu* 如有物) in subjective conscience (§5, §10, §13, §14, §21, §27, §33, §40, §41, §43). Dai argues:

> [Neo-Confucian teachings] have made it customary for people to think of principle as if it were a thing acquired from heaven and endowed in the heart-mind, and as a result, personal opinions are taken to be principle. … As a result [of relying on personal opinion], others frequently suffer an injustice without the person ever realizing his mistake. (§5/74)

Dai sees such a conception of principle as *necessarily* leading people to substitute biased moral opinion for moral principle, and thus thwarting even the most well-intentioned subjects (§5/74, §10/82, §40/166, §43/172). Indeed, "Whenever reliance is placed on personal opinions, misfortune will always result for the people" (§5/76; see also §40/165).

Comparable harms result as well from the second dimension of the Neo-Confucian conception of principle that Dai targets with his animosity, its separation from and opposition to desires. He concludes the *Evidential Commentary* with the climactic refrain:

> This distinction of principle from desire leaves superior persons with no way to perfect their conduct. This is the harm that it creates.
>
> …
>
> This distinction of principle from desires is apt to become an instrument for a cruel form of killing. This again is the harm that it creates.
>
> …
>
> This distinction of principle from desires is apt to turn all people of the world into shams and hypocrites. How can one describe the harm that it creates?
> (§43/174; Ewell 1990: 421)

What is wrong with the opposition of moral principle to desire? Certainly, desires do indeed often lead people to act against moral principle. Dai's philosophical charge against this opposition is that it leads people to overlook the emotional constitution of moral principle. Here enters Dai's own positive conception of principle, which he proposes as the proper reading of the *Mengzi* and classical Confucianism generally.

Against Song doctrine, Dai argues for his own ethical theory in which principle is never an object independent of the things it governs, but rather a perfected state of things and affairs themselves. Dai emphasizes principle's constitution in, rather than opposition to, emotion and desire, and is quite explicit that "principle is to be found in desires" (§10/82; cf. §3/72, §6/76, §11/86). This view matches what is natural to things (*ziran* 自然) to what is necessary, or ethically imperative, to them (*biran* 必然). Principles governing human affairs, then, consist in the proper patterning within affairs of the desires and emotions arising from human nature. We correspondingly achieve this principle by referencing our own essential emotions to guide action toward others:

> When I gauge the response of others by my own [responses], principles will become clear. ... The principle that is differentiated on the basis of what is natural means this: gauging the feelings of others by one's own so that there is fairness in every action. (§2/70)

Since the essential emotions are rooted in a common human nature, each person is capable of recognizing and according with emotionally (empathetically) recognized moral standards, which by virtue of their universality (being rooted in uniform human nature) can then be extended "to all the world" and made "a standard for all" (based in *Mengzi* 4A2; §13/331). Principle, then, is precisely what all people can "affirm in common" through their essential emotions (based on *Mengzi* 6A7; §5/325).

Here we also see the connection back to Dai's other main charge against the Neo-Confucian conception of principle. Proper understanding of principle thus recognizes that we justify action through "balancing emotions" rather than by arbitrary appeal to some sort of supposed subjective access to principle:

> It is only when one gauges his own feelings by the feelings of others that he can deal with affairs without settling each matter on the basis of his personal opinion. If the feelings of others are disregarded when one is seeking for a principle, what he calls principle will not be anything other than his personal opinion. (§5/75)

The philosophical charge against opposition between principle and desires thus connects back with the motivating social concern. Song teachings conceive of principle in a way that leads people to substitute their personal opinions for principle, which leads to social and political harm. But it adds an important further dimension to this. What is being overlooked in the Song conception, on both counts, is the need to determine right and wrong by reference to the emotional condition of others in human affairs. Most importantly, this means recognizing the moral importance of people's suffering.

The fundamental role Dai gives to emotions is thus no accident. Dai's motivating concern is inattention to the suffering of the people. This suffering is easily or necessarily overlooked when the Song Confucian conception of principle is adopted. The aim of both of Dai's core charges against the Song Confucian conception of principle is to show that morality consists in, or at least must prioritize considerations of, sensitivity to suffering.

> When they see people crying out of hunger and cold, men and women wailing because of the injustice done to them, and even those on the verge of death still desperately hoping to live, they claim these are no more than human desires, point blankly to a thing [that is, pseudo moral principle] devoid of feelings and desires, and claim that this is the original state of heavenly principle. ... Of those who

believe "principle dwells in the mind" and "what does not emanate from desires emanates from principle," there are none who do not take their own opinions as principle and thus cause the world to suffer. (§40/165)

Opposing moral principle to desires pushes subjects to discount the importance of people's suffering in their moral evaluation, and bestowing principle as a thing in the subject's conscience reinforces that there is no need to take heed of that suffering, since one must merely act in accordance with the moral knowledge one possesses within.

Although he does not emphasize the point, this is not unlike Mengzi's description of human rulers and ideal government as not being unfeeling toward, or unwilling to bear, the suffering of the people (*bu ren ren* 不忍人).

[The ancient kings] had governments that did not bear the suffering of people. Carrying out government that does not bear the suffering of people with a heart that does not bear the suffering of people, ordering the empire can turn on the palm of one's hand. (*Mengzi* 2A6; cf. 4A1, 7B31)

Dai Zhen's emphasis on emotion and empathy led Liang Qichao 梁啟超 (1873–1929) to characterize his thought as a "philosophy of emotion" (*qinggan zhexue* 情感哲學) intended precisely to replace the Song Confucian "philosophy of reason" (*lixing zhexue* 理性哲學) (Liang 1985: 35; Wu 2015: 4, 6). Liang further describes Dai as advocating sentimentalist (*qingganzhuyi* 情欲主義) views in order to promote government's consideration of the desires or basic interests of the people and connects this with Mengzi's teachings (Liang 1994: 368).

We see then that Dai's two integrated charges against Song Confucian principle—rejecting its subjective internality and rejecting its opposition to desires—together target a deeper, underlying concern: the inevitability of *arbitrary* assertions of moral principle, which falsely legitimize and even induce harmful social and political uses of power. This is further attested to in Dai's personal correspondence regarding the work. Dai writes to Duan Yucai 段玉裁 (1735–1815), "People today, whether good or bad, all wrongly refer to their personal opinions as principle, which thereby harms the people; I therefore had no choice but to write the *Evidential Commentary*" (quoted in Yu 1996: 109–10). Concern for social harm motivates Dai's robust metaphysical and epistemological arguments against Neo-Confucian orthodoxy.

Of particular note here are Dai's decisions to argue against the established Song Confucian doctrine and to present largely philosophical rather than philological charges. The first decision is significant because it is not obvious that Song teachings are actually greatly at odds with Dai's views. Many scholars have noted the inaccuracy and unfairness of Dai's attribution of a basic opposition between principle and desires to Song Confucianism. Liu Shu-hsien, for example, argues that Dai's claims substantively attack only Buddhism and are not properly applicable to Song-Ming Neo-Confucians, who never denied human desires, but, like Dai, merely distinguished proper desires from improper desires (Liu 2000: 88, 97). Dai was, moreover, originally sympathetic to Neo-Confucian thought, and only in his later work, culminating in the *Evidential Commentary*, did he shift gradually toward increasing hostility to Neo-Confucian teachings (Yu 2016: 41–3). But the important point is that there was no definite need for that hostility, and some scholars have correspondingly identified Dai's true target not as Song Confucianism itself but rather, as Zhang Xuecheng argued, the people in political power in his time (see Qian 1995: 396). Yet still, arguing from a basis of orthodoxy rather than against it seems an easier sell to those Dai aims to persuade. The second noteworthy decision is to make the argument largely in philosophical terms. As a leading philologist, Dai could have focused instead on showing that Song teachings were simply not what the classical texts said. This would have, on most accounts, been much better received within the contemporary intellectual culture, in which evidentiary studies held pride of place and speculative philosophy was generally besmirched.

Dai as Intellectualist

In stark contrast to this emphasis on emotion, identification with Mengzi, and opposition to Song Confucian teachings, much formidable scholarship reads Dai as intellectualist and rationalist, substantively Xunzian, and closely aligned with the thought of Zhu Xi. These arguments have at least two relatively firm bases. The first is Dai's prioritization of study of the Confucian classics, which he sees as essential grounds for proper moral views. Second is Dai's prioritization of learning and wisdom over empathy and moral emotions within his moral theory. Together, these seem to support reading Dai as a Xunzian rationalist and in line with Song Confucianism rather than at odds with it.

To this end, Yu Yingshi identifies Dai as a pioneer of the tradition of Confucian intellectualism (*Rujia zhishi zhuyi* 儒家智識主義), in contrast to the anti-intellectualist trend that had come to predominate Neo-Confucian thought by the Ming era (Yu 2016: 21). In Yu's analysis, Confucian intellectualism develops Kongzi's original emphasis on learning and reflective speculative thinking (*xue* 學 and *si* 思, respectively), and is seen in certain strands of early Neo-Confucian thought that are "more 'inquiry and study' oriented" and "tended to assign a greater role to knowledge," such as with Zhu Xi (Yu 2016: 3–4). In contrast, the anti-intellectualism of other Neo-Confucian thinkers, as represented by Zhu's intellectual rival Lu Xiangshan, emphasized an intuitive connection with innate moral nature and gave a less prominent role to "acquisition of knowledge" and study of the classics (Yu 2016: 5). Elsewhere, Yu describes these not as contrasting emphases on knowledge and nature but rather as prioritizing two different forms of knowledge, intellectual and intuitive, the distinction between which begins with Zhang Zai and Cheng Yi (Yu 1996: 21; 2016: 6).[3] Neo-Confucian thinkers following Zhu Xi, however, later developed away from Zhu's emphasis on intellectual knowing, thus leaving the true "rise of Confucian intellectualism" to the Qing period (Yu 2016: 6). Yu argues, following Zhang Xuecheng, that Dai Zhen is actually properly seen as the "intellectual heir" to Zhu Xi's School of Principle thought, emphasizing "inquiry and study" (*dao wenxue* 道問學), which "deals with the whole territory of what we call objective knowledge," over the Lu-Wang School of Heart-Mind's emphasis on "honoring moral nature" (*zun dexing* 尊德性), which is closer to moral intuition or "revealed truth" (Yu 1996: 55; 2016: 4, 10–11, 41–3). (Yu draws this terminology from the Neo-Confucian thinkers themselves.)

Yu further notes scholarly consensus that Qing scholarship and earlier Song-Ming Neo-Confucian scholarship constitute "two entirely different types of intellectual discipline, each of which must be pursued according to its own rules": the latter establishes moral principles through metaphysical speculation, and the former examines the (textual) grounds of those principles through philological study (Yu 2016: 8).[4] Dai seems to belong, first and foremost, at least, to the latter. He argues that the Confucian classics embody the teachings of the sages and are thus the source of proper moral views. Exegetical correction of the classical texts is therefore prerequisite to moral learning. Dai writes, "only if etymology is clear, can the ancient classics be understood, and only if the classics are understood, can the sages' philosophical ideas be grasped" (quoted in Yu 2016: 9, which cites Dai 1974: 11.168; see also Yu 1996: 104, 112; Cheng 2009: 231, 322). Dai also intends this statement as a repudiation of Song Confucian metaphysical speculation. Yu quotes Dai's personal correspondence:

> If the so-called philosophical ideas (of the sages) can be obtained by sheer speculation apart from the classics, then anyone is able to grasp them out of emptiness. If that is so, what do we need classical learning for? It is precisely because sheer speculation cannot lead one to the ancient sages' philosophical ideas that one has to seek them from the ancient classics. (quoted in Yu 2016: 9)

The classical texts have moral authority, and correct reading of them is necessary to correct philosophical and moral views. There is no sense, then, in philosophical moral speculation; we ought merely to clarify, through textual analysis, the teachings of the sages embodied in the classics.[5] As long as one accepts the first premise of moral authority—as a good Confucian ought to—the rest of the argument seems valid. It is also a distinctly Xunzian rather than Mengzian view, asserting a reliance on the teachings of the sages as the source of moral authority, rather than reflection on our innate moral feelings.

If this position is obviously intellectualist rather than intuitivist, it is also classicalist rather than rationalist. It constitutes a "philological claim to independence and orthodoxy" that rejects philosophical speculation, and thereby "led followers of Dai Zhen, if not Dai himself, to believe that Dai's Neo-Classicism had completely demolished Neo-Confucian Rationalism" (Yu 2016: 10; summarizing Zhang 1956: 58–9 and 368–70). Yet Dai Zhen's intellectualism was neither a thoroughgoing affirmation of classicism nor an outright rejection of philosophical speculation, which distinguished him sharply from the textualism (*wenxianzhuyi* 文獻主義) predominant among philologists of his time (Yu 1996: 2). As "intellectual heir" to Zhu Xi, Dai distinguishes himself from Qing textualism on the one hand and from Neo-Confucian moral intuitionism on the other.

Correspondingly, scholarship has largely located Dai's moral philosophy within debates over whether moral cultivation is a matter of learning or of intuition, and over whether proper moral doctrine is established through studying classics or philosophical speculation. Classical Confucianism seems to support all of these positions—and a balance among them. Confucius advocates both intellectual learning and reflective critical thought, and Mengzi advocates a doctrine of innate moral emotions while stressing the crucial importance of correct moral doctrines; and he gives rational and intellectual arguments to help rulers identify, and identify with, their moral emotions. Likewise,

> For Dai, the possibility is ruled out that there is a kind of innate moral knowledge independent of intellectual knowledge. As one acquires knowledge from constant inquiry and study, he believes, one's moral nature will be substantiated day by day. (Yu 2016: 45)

Such a view remains potentially open to compatibilism between intellectual learning and moral intuitivism. But Yu Yingshi rejects viewing Dai as a compatibilist in this way; he concludes rather that Dai Zhen "intellectualized moral nature to such a point that it was conceived as an epiphenomenon of study and inquiry. ... He transformed the moral-intellectual dualism in the Cheng-Zhu tradition into an intellectual monism" (2016: 46).

Conclusion

While the characterizations of Dai as an intellectual monist and as an ethical sentimentalist are not natural bedfellows, I do not mean to suggest that the powerful empathetic philosophy of the *Evidential Commentary* and Dai's classicalist intellectualism deeply conflict. I do not think they do, although we lack space to address the issue here. At the very least, Dai rests the former on the latter, claiming that his philosophy is in fact the correct reading of the classical texts and understanding of Confucian moral theory. This is a noteworthy facet of Dai's legacy in itself, reflecting the broader use of historical authority of the classics in Confucian tradition. But the two intersect in richer and potentially more fascinating pragmatic ways, as well.

What explains the passion with which this renowned philologist pursued an increasingly philosophical and increasingly vitriolic line of attack on Song Confucianism, from a position originally sympathetic to Song Confucian thought, and at a time when such philosophical arguments were decidedly out of favor? Could it be in part related to the historical confluence of antipathy for Neo-Confucian teachings among early Qing evidentiary studies scholars, on the one hand, with the continued establishment of orthodox Neo-Confucian teachings, on the other? Dai seems to situate himself awkwardly between these opposed camps, so that while he is at odds in some manner with each, he also, as noted above, connects in substantive ways with both. The two groups leverage the normativity of historical authority differently—one relying on empirically historical and textual arguments about early texts and the other on speculative moral arguments of a later but more established canon—to support views at odds with one another. To speak to one inherently distanced the other. For this era of late-imperial Chinese intelligentsia, critique and subversion in Chinese philosophy had become less straightforward than in previous eras.

To address sociopolitical concerns, Dai argues against Neo-Confucian orthodoxy on its own philosophical terms while also aligning with the contemporary current of antipathy toward that and all such abstract speculation generally. The philosophical arguments hit their mark. Scholars such as Liang Qichao, Tang Junyi, and Hu Shi have celebrated Dai's core argument that the Song conception of principle as bestowed in subjective conscience leads people to commit harmful acts in the name of (arbitrary and false assertions of) principle, even while these scholars find other dimensions of Dai's theory problematic. But Dai also presents his philosophical and practical critique in the manner of an evidentiary study, although its content hardly is. He thereby subverted both the orthodox Confucian doctrine of his time as well as the orthodox method of scholarship of his time, and made a lasting contribution to Confucian ethical and political theory in so doing.

Notes

1 Wing-Tsit Chan describes the movement generally as "characterized philosophically by a revolt against [Zhu Xi], and methodologically by objective, inductive, and critical methods" (Chan 1963: 709).
2 Citations to the *Evidential Commentary* give the article number followed by the page number of Ann-Ping Chin and Mansfield Freeman's translation (Chin and Freeman 1990). The translations themselves are modified at the discretion of the author, following primarily Chin and Freeman's work and with reference to Ewell (1990) and Mao (1992).
3 Under this distinction, moral knowledge (*dexing zhi zhi* 德性之知) "differs categorically from all other knowledge," all other knowledge being "intellectual knowledge" (*wenjian zhizhi* 聞見之知) (Yu 2016: 6, citing Chan 1963: 570).
4 Zhang Xuecheng argues, however, that this distinction between emphases on intellectual and moral knowledge is best seen not as marking the difference between Song-Ming and Qing thought, but rather as two schools or approaches that belong to both periods, although their application shifts from Song-Ming moral speculation to Qing intellectual philology (see Yu 2016: 11). Zhang thereby sees Dai as the Qing-era representative of Cheng-Zhu learning, and himself as the Qing representative of Lu-Wang views.
5 For a review of Zhang Xuecheng's criticism of Dai on this point, see Cheng (2009: 323); for an original criticism, see Cheng (2009: 231–5, 323).

References

Chan W. T. (1963), *A Source Book in Chinese Philosophy*. Princeton, NJ: Princeton University Press.
Cheng C. Y. 鄭宗義 (2009), *Ming-Qing Ruxue zhuanxing tanxi:* 明清儒學轉型探析 ——從劉蕺山到戴東原 (The Transformation of Confucianism between the Ming and Qing Dynasties: From Liu Jishan to Dai Dongyuan), rev. edn. Hong Kong: Chinese University Press.

Chin A. P., and M. Freeman (1990), *Tai Chen on Mencius: Explorations in Words and Meaning*. New Haven, CT: Yale University Press.

Dai Z. 戴震 (1961), *Mengzi ziyi shuzheng* 孟子字義疏證 (Evidential Commentary on the Meanings of Terms in the Mengzi). Beijing: Zhonghua shuju.

Dai Z. (1974), *Dai Zhen wenji* 戴震文集 (Collected Writings of Dai Zhen). Beijing: Zhonghua.

Dai Z. (1994), *Dai Zhen quanshu* 戴震全書 (Complete Works of Dai Zhen), edited by Zhang Dainian 張岱年. Hefei: Huangshan shushe.

De Bary, W. T. (1988), "Neoconfucianism as Traditional and Modern." In *Interpreting Across Boundaries: New Essays in Comparative Philosophy*, edited by G. J. Larson and E. Deutsch, 294–309. Princeton, NJ: Princeton University Press.

Ewell, Jr., J. W. (1990), *Re-Inventing the Way: Dai Zhen's "Evidential Commentary on the Meanings of Terms in Mencius" (1777)*. PhD. diss. Berkeley: University of California,.

Lau, D. C., trans., (2003), *Mencius: A Bilingual Edition*, rev. ed. Hong Kong: Chinese University of Hong Kong Press.

Liang Q. C. (1985), "Qingdai xueshu gailun" 清代學術概論 (Outline of Qing Dynasty Scholarship). In *Liang Qichao lun Qingxue shi er zhong* 梁启超论清学史二种 (Liang Qichao on the Two Histories of Qing Studies), edited by Zhu W. Z. 朱维铮. Shanghai: Fudan daxue chubanshe.

Liang Q. C. (1994), "Dai Dongyuan zhexue" 戴東原哲學 (Dai Dongyuan's Philosophy). In *Dai Zhen* (1994): 353–79.

Liu S. H. 劉述先 (2000), *Rujia sixiang yihan zhi xiandai chanshi lunji* 儒家思想意涵之現代闡釋論集 (Collected Papers on Modern Explication of the Meaning of Confucian Thought). Taipei: Taiwan Central Research Academy, Center for Studies in Chinese Literature and Philosophy [台灣中研院中國文哲研究所].

Mao H. X. 冒懷辛, trans. (1992), *Mengzi ziyi shuzheng quan yi* 孟子字義疏證全譯 (Complete Translation of the Evidential Commentary on Meanings and Terms in the Mengzi). Chengdu: Bashu shushe.

Pines, Y. (2009), *Envisioning Eternal Empire: Chinese Political Thought of the Warring States Era*. Honolulu: University of Hawaii Press.

Qian M. 錢穆 (1995), *Zhongguo jin san bai nian xueshu shi* 中國近三百年學術史 (History of the Last Three Centuries of Chinese Scholarship). Taipei: Taiwan shangwu yinshuguan.

Shun, K. L. (2002), "Mencius, Xunzi, and Dai Zhen: A Study of the *Mengzi ziyi shuzheng*." In *Mencius: Contexts and Interpretations*, edited by A. K. L. Chan, 216–41. Honolulu: University of Hawai'i Press.

Wu G. Y. et al, eds., (2015), *Dai Zhen Qian-Jia xueshu yu Zhongguo wenhua* 戴震乾嘉學術與中國文化 (Dai Zhen Qian-Jia Scholarship and Chinese Culture). Fuzhou: Fujian jiaoyu chubanshe.

Yü Y. S. (1996), *Lun Dai Zhen yu Zhang Xuecheng: Qingdai zhongqi xueshu sixiangshi yanjiu* 論戴震與章學誠: 清代中期學術思想史研究 (On Dai Zhen and Zhang Xuecheng: A Study of Scholarly Intellectual History in the Mid-Qing Dynasty). Hong Kong: Longmen shudian.

Yü Y. S. (2016), *Chinese History and Culture: Seventeenth Century through Twentieth Century*, edited by Josephine Chiu-Duke and Michael S. Duke. New York: Columbia University Press.

Zhang X. C. (1956), *Wenshi tongyi* 文史通義. Beijing: Guji chubanshe.

15

What Is Critique and What Does It Subvert? Epistemic Intransparency in the Critique of Modern Society

Ady Van den Stock

What Is Critique ...

Any attempt to outline and clarify the semantic and conceptual range of the notion of "critique" (for an example with a refreshing focus on everyday discourse instead of philosophical language, see Irandoust 2006) is immediately complicated by the considerable historical baggage of this term. It has become such an integral part of the self-understanding of modern societies and the self-appointed mission of post-Enlightenment philosophers, and hence so broad in scope and varied in content, that we would lapse into indeterminacy if we simply treated it as a known quantity that allows us to analyze (and indeed, in some sense, to transform or pave the way toward the transformation of) other social phenomena. In its ubiquity, "critique" becomes "increasingly vague and ambiguous" and even risks turning into "a liability and a caricature of itself" (Raffnsøe 2015: 3). Additionally, in assuming "critique" to be a self-evident concept, we would perhaps already be violating the first basic requirement of the critical endeavor, that is to say, the demand to be reflexive. The practice of critique is something from which we (not unreasonably) expect a considerable amount of self-awareness, an unconscious critique being a contradiction in terms. No form of critique, it would seem, is complete without the ability to call its own conditions of possibility into question. This already raises the possibility that the critical enterprise can become self-undermining and, in a sense, that critique cannot but (at least rhetorically) welcome this possibility as consistent with and reflective of its own basic outlook and attitude.

Kant's *Critique of Pure Reason* from 1781 probably counts as the most famous philosophical testament to this demand for reflexivity, and it is often seen as marking the beginning of a turn toward the subject as a transcendental source of epistemological spontaneity (reason as the "lawgiver of nature") as well as of normative autonomy. Ironically, the post-Kantian development of German Idealism eventually steered thinkers away from subjectivity as the privileged locus of the transcendental (for the peculiar example of Schelling, see Habermas 1963). Attempts to safeguard the self-grounding status of the subject while at the same time preserving a space for the facticity of the world as non-reducible to thought or consciousness (Fichte, Hegel) came to be seen as largely unsuccessful, and these attempts were criticized for having overinflated the conditioning (subject) at the expense of the conditioned (object) and effectively imploding the latter into the former. A "worldless" (in Heidegger's words) condition of possibility cannot make the world (or, for that matter, any world) possible. It merely ends up putting itself in the world's place, as its much-impoverished substitute.

By contrast, the novel and revolutionary focus, during the late nineteenth and early twentieth centuries, on the determining influence of factors such as labor, language, civilization/culture, and the unconscious, categories which do not fit easily within the convenient subject-object scheme, opened up a space that Foucault famously described by means of the (in his own words) "barbarous" term, "*historical a priori*" (italics in original; Foucault 2002: 143). Interestingly enough, these historically fluid categories would come to be seen, to a considerable extent, as structurally independent from human beings, analytically, and factually subject to them. As such, there was no longer a necessary overlap between reflexivity and human autonomy (see "The Reflexivity of Critique"). Marx's critique of industrial capitalism, for instance, was grounded precisely in an analysis of the historically specific conditions in which capital can come to subsume the concreteness of human labor within the operations of a self-valorizing form of exchange value that progressively strives to liberate itself from any dependence on actual use value (see Postone 1993). In more general and positive terms, within the space described by such "historical *a priori*" as the pair capital/labor, the conceptual powerhouse that is reflexivity could be dislodged from the problematic figure of a self-constituting (human) subject fatally severed from the world; for the status and condition of the latter is precisely what is at stake in practicing the "patient labor" (to quote Hegel) of critique. The conditions of the possibility for criticizing the world coincide with the conditions of the social world itself. As such, they can only be understood through a radically immanent and self-implicative analysis. Any claim to take up a "critical" position outside of the observable world opens itself to the accusation of being predicated on an ideologically motivated withdrawal from the urgent sublunary concerns of the here and now. Or as Marx put it more memorably: "the criticism of religion is the prerequisite of all criticism" (Marx 1844 [no pagination]).

... and What Does It Subvert?

Perhaps the preceding paragraphs have already led us too far away from the rich and evocative quality of the word "critique" in more straightforward forms of everyday communication by reproducing a potted summary of relatively well-trodden paths in the history of Western philosophy. Another and potentially more productive way to proceed would be to depart from the contingent (if not entirely coincidental, let alone random) fact that the notion of critique is aligned with the equally suggestive and loaded word "subversion," which appears in the title of the current volume. Whatever critique may be, and however we choose to characterize the historically specific conditions for its emergence and enactment, it seems clear that it is not all that uncommon for us today to expect it to subvert and be subversive. Having a closer look in the following section at the closely related idea of "subversion" will, I believe, help us further clarify the notion of critique in a more determinate manner.

For one thing, in academic as well as popular discourse, terms such as "subvert," "disrupt," "interrupt," "destabilize," "transgress," and "upset" have increasingly taken on a positive, commendable, appealing, and indeed urgent and imperative quality. The need or the call to subvert can be found in contexts as diverse as that of aesthetic production, economic theory, and social criticism. These examples were not chosen entirely at random. Indeed, according to Boltanski and Chiapello's by-now classic study, the post-May '68 revolution in managerial discourse (and more broadly speaking, in social analysis), which accompanied the birth of what they call the "new spirit of capitalism," was grounded in the incorporation and cooptation (we could also say "subversion") of "aesthetic" (as opposed to "social") critiques of capitalist society in its Fordist guise (Boltanski and Chiapello 2006). In this sense, the continuing preference in political rhetoric for reassuring promises of continuity, order, predictability, security, and control, in societies that are economically dependent on a considerable amount of instability and volatility ("flexibility"), is the exception that proves the rule: we have "resigned" ourselves (in a manner of speaking) not only to living and coping with the contingency and fluidity of what Zygmunt Bauman has called "liquid modernity," but also to upholding and celebrating it as a normative expectation, aesthetic criterion, measure of behavioral competency, and so on. While politicians are the rare species that is generally still rewarded for promoting instead of subverting stability (which of course can paradoxically enough only be provided for by means of continuous "growth" and "reform"), it seems that most other domains of society and forms of social activity have found ways to ideologically accommodate the idea and practice of subversion. Academics must subvert established research paradigms, artists are expected to subvert existing styles and genres, couples can subvert inherited modes for living their social and gender roles (a lot of empirical ifs and buts are at work at this instance), teachers should subvert conventional pedagogical methods, "modern" CEOs willingly subvert established hierarchical boundaries, entrepreneurs performatively subvert institutional and professional identities (at least according to Bureau 2013, as well as Kauppinen and Daskalaki 2015), and so on.

Dismissing such phenomena as a mere matter of hollow rhetoric (which may be accurate enough in specific cases) would miss the point that the way we communicate about our activities and responsibilities in society is hardly extrinsic or inconsequential to the way we enact, experience, and assess our social roles. To be sure, we cannot all be subversive all of the time, either logically speaking or in practical terms. To begin with, this would involve the counterfactual and unrealistic assumption that our everyday activities are carried out with a constant and paralyzing sense of reflexive awareness. A person should be allowed to eat a steak in peace without having to worry about raising a political storm, although this example is probably poorly chosen (after all, why not opt for a plant-based alternative instead?). There are obviously also domains of society such as religion and the legal system where "subversion" usually designates only a negative value, something to be excluded, prevented, or counteracted (then again, see Myles 2016 on the fetishization of the notion of subversion in the unlikely domain of research about the historical Jesus). That being said, while certain forms of behavior or speech may not "really" be subversive at all (this requires a prior determination of precisely what is being subverted and what qualifies as a subversive act or observation), it is significant enough in itself that they are often valued positively simply for being perceived or presented (I am tempted to say "marketed") as subversive. In Luhmann's words, "the production of deviating ideas gains a certain regularity, an almost businesslike nature" (Luhmann 2012-13: vol. 1, 275). In any case, the most straightforward candidate for occupying the other side of the category of subversion, that is to say, "conformism," is hardly ever openly embraced as a commendable attitude or course of action. To give an example from politics, conservatives too will be inclined to perceive and communicate about their political stance as challenging and "subverting" the liberal/progressive dogma. The indeterminacy of the category of what qualifies as subversive or critical implies that we cannot approach these notions in ontological terms, but are always forced to ask, as the sociologist Niklas Luhmann never tired of repeating: "who says so?" (e.g., see Luhmann 2013: 99–100 and Esposito 2017: 21). I will address Luhmann's constructivist position, which I am drawing on throughout this chapter, in somewhat more detail in the next section.

Just as is the case with "critique," "subversion" is an interesting case of a politically hazardous term that has acquired a predominantly positive moral connotation instead of (exclusively) invoking images of political and military conflict, social turmoil, or physical violence. However, an important difference between the notions of "critique" and "subversion" would seem to be that whereas the former is marked by a more militant, ambitious, and demanding outlook in aiming for a transformation of a given state of affairs that has been identified as in some sense problematic and in need of critique, "subversion" appears more open-ended and ambiguous in its (often unstated) goals. Like critique, subversion cannot but be "concerned with the position of the proponent relative to [a given] reality" (Irandoust 2006: 133), but insofar as "subversiveness" is merely approached as the quality of an action or observation made by a subject, it does not necessarily include a determination about whether or not the act or observation in question effects (or prepares for the effectuation of) a positive transformation in the subverted object. In short, "subversive" subjects can, in principle, remain relatively indifferent to the clarion call of Marx's eleventh thesis on Feuerbach, according to which we should not merely interpret, but also change the world. Instead they can remain content with adopting the posture of someone who knows it ought to be changed and profiting from the cultural capital this affords them. Moreover, if subversiveness as an attitude or stance is restrictively situated within a predetermined domain of social activity or mode of action that in itself is left unquestioned (such as when entrepreneurs are treated as skilled subverters of the economic "game"), the capacity for subversion to genuinely undermine and change what it purports to reject or distance itself from risks being severely compromised.

As such, in abstract terms at least, the idea of "subversion" is perfectly compatible with the acceptance of a high degree of structural stability in pregiven relations of power and domination (see Grindon 2011: 868–9), although it remains to be determined whether the same might be said about "critique" as well. The question thus becomes to what extent it is possible to truly subvert something (e.g., a gender role, a hierarchy, a discourse) without also in a more radical sense deconstructing or dismantling it. After all, when approached in a generalizing and depoliticized fashion, "to subvert" does not so much mean to reject, abolish or overcome, but rather comes to resemble a perverted version of the Hegelian notion of "sublation" (*Aufhebung*) in seeking to "preserve while/by overcoming" (or the other way around).

We would in all likelihood be going too far in claiming that subversion is a covert or more subtle form of reactionary conformism, and that any attempt to subvert existing models or procedures of thought or action is doomed to failure because "the system" already includes its own critique within itself as a diabolical means of structurally precluding any challenges to its existence. In doing so, we would effectively be further blurring the distinction between the position of the critic and that of the conspiracy theorist, as one famous critic of critique has observed (see Latour 2004: 228–30). That being said, the above observations indicate that we should be wary of treating "subversion" as a capacity that is first and foremost expressive of the creative potential and the indomitable spirit of human subjectivity. The phenomenon and discourse of subversion is conditioned by larger social and cultural developments that transcend the individuals usually assumed to be the ultimate agents of subversion. No one, I suspect, could have anticipated that the idea of subversion would become so culturally and institutionally entrenched in everyday behavior and discourse as to begin to appear as a sign of social conformity. While the very term "subversion" is often closely aligned with the ability of individual agents to modify or repurpose their conditions of existence, it is precisely these conditions themselves which have, in modern society at least, become marked by a structural and systemic form of "subversion." In a sense, it is systems such as the capitalist economy that are the real subverters of social life. By contrast, individual human beings can easily come to feel that their attempts at critique and subversion amount to little more than an inconsequential form of moral posturing, a situation that the late Mark Fisher described as leading to a self-reinforcing sense of "reflexive impotence" (Fisher 2009: 21). At the very least, we should not take for granted the presumed capacity of human beings to emancipate themselves through the reflexivity we tend to associate with the transformative activities of critique and subversion.

The Reflexivity of Critique: Epistemic Intransparency in Modern Society

Unlike subversion, the idea of critique retains a close and decisive connection to that of reflexivity. It would not sound all that far-fetched (anymore) to claim that "dance subverts movement" or "jokes subvert language," which suggests that no reflexive self-awareness need be involved in subversion, as something that may occur as an event without being carried out as a conscious practice. As such, whereas subversion can apparently happen in a quasi-unconscious and spontaneous manner, the same cannot be said for critique. If the subject of critique is to maintain an edge over its object of critique, it must not only know what it is doing, but also take this (self-)knowledge into account in its analysis. At the same time, however, the central position accorded to reflexivity in our contemporary understanding of (the quintessentially modern notion of) critique poses considerable difficulties for critique as a practice aimed toward the transformation of (particular aspects of) modern society in all its structural complexity (see Esposito 2017). As I will try to explain in what follows, this complexity casts doubt on its hallowed status as part of the Enlightenment's "double deity Reason and Critique" (Luhmann 2012-13: vol. 1, 5; compare with vol. 1, 109). Due to limitations of space as well as the tentative nature of my own research, my discussion will mostly remain on a relatively abstract, epistemological level.

Let me proceed by focusing on what at first sight may very well appear to be a completely trivial observation, although one that has considerable consequences at a deeper level of analysis: critique is not concerned with *states of affairs* at a first-order level, but rather with *observations* or *representations*. What we normally understand by a critique cannot be directly targeted at a given state of affairs that, for one reason or another, is seen as problematic, undesirable, or condemnable. Critique functions on the level of representation, not on that of the immediacy of reality as such (even if, from a constructivist epistemological perspective at least, the categories of "immediacy" and "reality" are not so easy to reconcile). Otherwise, it would be indistinguishable from mere condemnation. One cannot "criticize" a hurricane or an earthquake, or even "man-made" phenomena such as global warming. Let us take the more straightforward example of poverty. Of course, a critique of poverty must depart from the commonsensical observation that poverty is a bad thing and that it would be good if it were somehow abolished or overcome in the future (even if treating the problem in moral terms is not necessarily a "good thing," *pace* Moeller 2009). In this sense, agents of critique remain firmly anchored in the pregiven social reality that they intend to address, reconceptualize, and possibly even change for the better. But as soon as we imagine what a critique of poverty as a factual state of affairs would look like, it is fairly easy to see that the critic in question would almost immediately proceed by concentrating their critical energies on tackling certain *representations* of poverty. A critic might argue, for example, that poverty is not the result of a natural order or divine ordinance, of "laziness" or a lack of entrepreneurship, but rather of structural social conditions such as systemic class discrimination or racial bias. He or she would deal with prevalent or neglected views of poverty and adopt a position with respect to what others have said and are saying. In some cases, this might involve the prior labor of convincing another observer of the existence of the state of affairs in question (think of global warming), or, alternatively, of its problematic nature.

Hence, a critic is forced to join the ranks of other observers and make a specific intervention in a preexisting discourse concerning the state of affairs he or she is criticizing. Just as importantly, a critique must be articulated in such a way as to be communicatively productive; that is to say, it must have the potential to become the topic of and usher in new communication. Representations of states of affairs, critical ones perhaps even more so than others, are forced to invest a considerable amount of time and energy in representing themselves, that is to say, in making sure they are seen and heard (and are perceived as "critical" to begin with). In any case, critique cannot function without communication, and it is an inherently social category.

This also expresses itself in the expectation that critique will reflexively situate both its object and itself in a broader discursive as well as societal context. As Irandoust notes in drawing a distinction between "critique" and mere "criticism": "criticism ... is understood to remain content with passing judgement upon an object in a way which reifies the object, isolating it from its real and concrete relations with other objects" (Irandoust 2006: 134). Among other concerns, this implies that, ideally at least, critique does not concern itself so much with targeting the specific enunciators of a certain representation as individual people, but rather with these representations themselves, insofar as they are part of a broader social problem or ideological discourse. In other words, "critique can only apply to products, and never to individuals" (Irandoust 2006: 135).

The fact that critique deals with representations and not with states of affairs undergirds and reinforces its status as inherently reflexive, but also complicates it. Critique observes, but primarily observes other observations, and will in turn be observed in ways it cannot always foresee, and must try to take this inevitable self-exposure into account lest it consign itself to irrelevance. Reflexivity thus creates a certain distance between the subject and object of critique, a distance that can in turn be presented or experienced as pathological, as a sign of disengagement or even indifference. Critique is the archetypal Kantian stance that refuses to deal with "things in themselves." In modern societies in particular, the endeavor of critique is expected to internalize and bear out, in a more radical and consistent fashion, the general pervasiveness of reflexivity that is institutionalized in procedures of self-examination and self-assessment. Michael Power's notion that we are currently living in an "audit society" pervaded by "rituals of verification" is worth invoking here (quoted in Raffnsøe 2015: 5). This also affects our personal sense of self-identity and the possibilities on offer to identify with our social roles (see Moeller 2017: 37–41). As Luhmann put it, "an individual in the modern sense of the term is someone who can observe his or her own observing" (Luhmann 1998: 7). In more general terms, Luhmann claims that the prevalence of second-order observation (the observation of observers, including self-observation and self-description) is a structural feature of modern society that characterizes and defines all its functionally differentiated subsystems. Each of these systems (law, politics, economy, art, the mass media, etc.) operates "rationally" in its own manner; that is to say, each "autopoietically" constructs (its own) reality according to a certain code that is not grounded in an external, self-sufficient foundation (e.g., in the case of the legal system, legal/illegal). However, there is no overarching "meta-rationality" with the ability to authoritatively represent, let alone steer, society as a whole (e.g., see Luhmann 2012–13: vol. 2, 87–108 and Moeller 2017: 30–7). From this "polycontextural" and "postontological" perspective, "suppositions of reality are needed ... only in order to accept a multiplicity of incommensurable constructions and, when needed, to move from one of them to another" (Luhmann 2002: 52). What is "rational" depends very much on the functional subsystem and type of rationality involved (see Luhmann 1998: 22–43).

For our present purposes, it is perhaps enough to elaborate a bit more on the relatively straightforward observation that critical thought is expected to be aware of its own position in relation to what it critiques. In criticizing a certain state of affairs, a critique must at the same time try to monitor its own position vis-à-vis the reality in question and gauge its ability to intervene and modify its object, if only by means of an altered representation. As such, critique involves a "capacity to reflexively incorporate the sociohistorical conditions and contexts of its own emergence," which in turn presupposes a "heightened awareness of time" (Kompridis 2006: 18). Critique is thus anything but a view from nowhere, but rather "a thing of this world" (Boland 2014). This implies that agents of critique have to be cognizant of the fact that their observations will in turn be observed by other observers and that any critique will be assessed both according to its own stated goals (in internal critiques) as well as in terms of how well it supposedly presents and/or transforms (or allows for the transformation of) the object of critique (in an external critique, which starts out by offering up an alternative representation of the object in question and assessing the first critique's representation in comparison to this alternative). To again quote Luhmann: "in self-description, description is always part of what it describes and changes what it describes simply by appearing and exposing itself to observation" (Luhmann 2012–13: vol. 2, 178, compare with 327–8). Consequently, we can no longer expect to see without being seen or to know without being known. The first casualty in critique is the critic.

Hence, we should not so much or exclusively expect a critique to pass judgment on the content of a certain representation, but also, and perhaps above all, on the way it represents its own position over and against what it constructs (for that is what it must do) as its immediate object of critique. To phrase it in a Luhmannian style: how does critique see itself in seeing what it sees (and what others do not see)? One of the most important implications here is that if we want to formulate a concept of ideology (still the most likely target of contemporary critiques) that does not already presuppose the acceptance of a specific political position (so that anything opposed to that position can simply be rejected as "ideological," and thus wrong and dangerous), one way to proceed would be to approach it in a more formalistic manner, by conceiving it in terms of how it (implicitly or explicitly) portrays the relation to its own social context (see Van den Stock 2016: 16–19). Ideological distortion not only operates on the level of representation but also on the more reflexive level of how representations are presented in relation to the reality they make accessible.

Consequently, we have to look at how certain modes of observation observe their own observations. This is not an easy task, but there are no convincing shortcuts on offer which would allow us to directly see things as they really are. The epistemic intransparency of society, as the ultimate "object" of any critique, and of our own observational position, as well as the unforeseeable effects of our observations in a social world where rationality is, to use Luhmann's preferred phrasing, "discharged" by function systems, complicates the desire to be done with the complexities of critique and return to "things themselves." Lacking a determinate understanding of how the societies in which we currently live are structured and how they function, critique always risks deteriorating into a dogmatic replication of one's preferred political positions, and hence reproducing a predetermined set of questions that can be answered by ticking the right boxes. By contrast, as Judith Butler has rightly cautioned, the historical specificity of the critical endeavor forces us to pay attention to "certain kinds of questions [which] *cannot* be posed or, rather, can only be framed and posed by breaking through a certain prohibition that functions to condition and circumscribe the domain of the speakable" (Butler 2009: 777).

To be sure, the question remains whether we can realistically continue to expect the reflexivity of critique to serve, if not as a guarantee, then at least an enabling condition, for arriving at the affirmative moment expected of it. In the prevalent understanding, critique is supposed not merely to reject but also to indicate how things could be different and how to make the leap from the "is" to the "ought." To paraphrase Žižek, what do we do on the "morning after," when critique has scored its final victory over what it set out to expose and dismantle? Do we have no other choice than to learn to enjoy the ensuing hangover in the proverbial "desert of the real"? But isn't the notion of critique always grounded in an audacious hope that what it critiques can be positively changed by unearthing or exposing the ideological fabrications that prevent other observers from seeing through it and coming to terms with what it really is? Additionally, doesn't the very idea of critique presuppose something like an overlap or continuity between the epistemic reflexivity we have explored above, and a more positive and concrete form of normative autonomy?[1]

Building on the preceding observations, it seems that such expectations have become increasingly unlikely and untenable. Reflexivity cannot function as the "lifeboat" Bruno Latour accuses critique of always looking for; for this presupposes an "ascetic" and "thrifty" division of the world into "two packs, a little one that is sure and certain, the immense rest which is simply believed and in dire need of being criticized, founded, re-educated, straightened up" (Latour 1987: 85). One of the most often-voiced complaints against the concept of critique is that it tends to assume a privileged position vis-à-vis the normal or "uncritical" attitude it distinguishes itself from (see Raffnsøe 2015: 5). It can thus observe social reality and those "duped" by ideological representations of social order from a safe distance, a distance without which it cannot function or even begin. Like a complicit and complacent subverter, critique postures as a form of thought that can pass judgment on society without implicating itself in what it criticizes.

In highly simplistic terms, the critic appears as a figure who *knows better*, *makes better*, and thus in some sense, *is better*. This is, it seems to me, precisely the sort of attitude and outlook critique must learn to set itself apart from within the specific conditions of modernity. We do not necessarily know better because we are aware of being seen and have learned to modify our cognitive habits accordingly or because we know that our observations take place within conditions that already determine the modes of observation and action at our disposal. Such conditions can, in turn, only be observed by drawing specific distinctions (which always exclude and hide something else) without ever yielding a transparent object or allowing the observer to bask in the radiance of self-transparency. As Luhmann nicely put it in a different context, "the mirror itself is opaque" (Luhmann 2012–13: vol. 2, 318). The state of epistemic intransparency in which the observed world is placed when one particular distinction is chosen over another, out of a potentially infinite number of others, applies just as much to the observer; and even an observer who knows that this is so has no a priori strategic advantage over other, first-order observers who appear as more "naïve" by contrast. Even if this were so, the question would remain what greater potential for action a full, reflexive knowledge of the object of a critique would have. After all, the truth will not necessarily set us free, but might just as likely have a paralyzing effect, or, less dramatically, may turn out to be rather boring. As Mahāyāna Buddhist thinkers have long known, the "ontological significance of our epistemic stance to the world" places the world in a state of "ontological indeterminacy" (Kantor 2006: 135). But does all of this mean we can wallow in this intransparency as a superior form of ignorance? To continue on a Buddhist note, such "resignation" (which critical theorists such as Adorno have always struggled with) would only be morally justifiable if there were no suffering in the world and if compassion would not force us to act, instead of waiting for a moment of complete insight that will never arrive without compassion in the first place. That being said, I suspect no one is eagerly waiting for philosophers to take on the role of Bodhisattvas and enlighten those who often know all too well how socially determined they are and do not need someone to instruct them in the extent of their "conditioned arising" and "ignorance." "Ignorance" is not only a diagnosis by someone equipped with the cure, but before all else, a basic source of solidarity. As such, it seems that we must, contra Bob Dylan, find ways to criticize what we can't understand.

Note

1 Max Horkheimer's famous text "Traditional and Critical Theory" from 1937 is interesting to consider in this context, particularly since Horkheimer's name is more often associated with the overtly bleak analysis of the prospects for social emancipation put forward in *Dialectics of Enlightenment* from 1944, coauthored with Adorno, while both Frankfurter Schule luminaries were exiled in California. In this earlier text, Horkheimer still claimed that "in the transition from the present form of society to a future one, mankind will for the first time be a conscious subject and actively determine its own way of life" (Horkheimer [1937] 2002: 233). As is the case in Lukács's *History and Class Consciousness* from 1923, the epistemological relation between subject (humanity) and object (society) is at the same time conceived of in emancipatory terms here, with reflexive self-consciousness being presented as in some sense coinciding with normative self-determination and human autonomy. That being said, Horkheimer already had a highly distinctive understanding of reflexivity. In the course of his text, Horkheimer makes it clear that he sees the critical attitude as to some extent overlapping with the ability of observers to see themselves as situated within a broader social context. In contrast to "traditional theory," critical theory does not understand itself as confined to a specialized role in society and does not lay claim to a form of false self-sufficiency that Horkheimer condemns as amounting to a "hypostatization of Logos" (199). Rather, critical theory recognizes itself as part of and conditioned by larger social and historical processes (197–200). As he puts it pointedly, "the insistence that thinking is a fixed vocation, a self-enclosed realm within society as a whole, betrays the very essence of thought" (243). Horkheimer believes that the reflexive awareness he expects of critical as opposed to traditional theory is foreshadowed in an idealist form in the philosophy of Kant and its transcendental turn toward the subject. He reads such an outlook as an abstract blueprint for a real process of emancipation, in which human beings will come to recognize society as their own product (200–11). Kant's Copernican revolution thus becomes the logical precondition

for social emancipation. What transcendentalism formulates as the subjective foundation of objectivity will be practically realized as social autonomy in a future society. As Horkheimer writes: "in genuinely critical thought explanation signifies not only a logical process but a concrete historical one as well. In the course of it, both the social structure as a whole and the relation of the theoretician to society are altered, that is, both the subject and the role of thought are changed" (211).

References

Boland, Tom (2014), "Critique Is a Thing of This World: Towards a Genealogy of Critique." *History of the Human Sciences* 27(1): 108–23.

Boltanski, Luc, and Eve Chiapello ([1999] 2006), *The New Spirit of Capitalism*. London: Verso.

Bureau, Sylvain (2013), "Entrepreneurship as Subversive Activity: How Can Entrepreneurs Destroy in the Process of Creative Destruction?" *M@n@gement* 16(3): 204–37.

Butler, Judith (2009), "Critique, Dissent, Disciplinarity." *Critical Inquiry* 35: 773–95.

Esposito, Elena (2017), "Critique without Crisis: Systems Theory as a Critical Sociology." *Thesis Eleven* 143(1): 18–27.

Fisher, Mark (2009), *Capitalist Realism. Is There no Alternative?* London: Zero Books.

Foucault, Michel (2002), *The Archaeology of Knowledge*. London: Routledge.

Grindon, Gavin (2011), "Subversion." In *The Encyclopedia of Literary and Cultural Theory. Volume II. Literary Theory from 1966 to the Present: A–Z*, edited by Michael Ryan, 867–9. Hoboken: Wiley.

Habermas, Jürgen (1963), "Dialektischer Idealismus im Übergang zum Materialismus— Geschichtsphilosophische Folgerungen aus Schellings Idee einer Contraction Gottes." In *Theorie und Praxis: Sozialphilosophische Studien*, 172–227. Neuwied: Luchterhand.

Horkheimer, Max ([1937] 2002), "Traditional and Critical Theory." In *Critical Theory: Selected Essays*, 188–243. New York: Continuum.

Irandoust, Hengameh (2006), "The Logic of Critique." *Argumentation* 20: 133–48.

Kantor, Hans-Rudolf (2006), "Emptiness of Transcendence: The Inconceivable and Invisible in Chinese Buddhist Thought." In *Transcendence, Immanence, and Intercultural Philosophy*, edited by Nahum Brown and William Franke, 125–52. New York: Palgrave Macmillan.

Kauppinen, Antti, and Maria Daskalaki (2015), "'Becoming Other': Entrepreneuring as Subversive Organizing." *Ephemera: Theory & Politics in Organization* 15(3): 601–20.

Kompridis, Nikolas (2006), *Critique and Disclosure: Critical Theory between Past and Future*. Cambridge, MA: MIT Press.

Latour, Bruno (1987), "The Enlightenment without the Critique: A Word on Michel Serres' Philosophy." *Royal Institute of Philosophy Supplements* 21: 83–97.

Latour, Bruno (2004), "Why Has Critique Run out of Steam? From Matters of Fact to Matters of Concern." *Critical Inquiry* 30: 225–48.

Luhmann, Niklas (1998), *Observations on Modernity*. Stanford, CA: Stanford University Press.

Luhmann, Niklas (2002), *Theories of Distinction: Redescribing the Descriptions of Modernity*. Stanford, CA: Stanford University Press.

Luhmann, Niklas (2012–13), *Theory of Society*, 2 vols. Stanford, CA: Stanford University Press.

Luhmann, Niklas (2013), *Introduction to Systems Theory*. Cambridge: Polity Press.
Marx, Karl (1844), "A Contribution to the Critique of Hegel's Philosophy of Right." https://www.marxists.org/archive/marx/works/1843/critique-hpr/intro.htm, accessed June 2, 2020.
Moeller, Hans-Georg (2009), *The Moral Fool: A Case for Amorality*. New York: Columbia University Press.
Moeller, Hans-Georg (2017), "On Second-Order Observation and Genuine Pretending: Coming to Terms with Society." *Thesis Eleven* 143(1): 28–43.
Myles, Robert J. (2016), "The Fetish for a Subversive Jesus." *Journal for the Study of the Historical Jesus* 14(1): 52–70.
Postone, Moishe (1993), *Time, Labor and Social Domination. A Reinterpretation of Marx's Critical Theory*. Cambridge: Cambridge University Press.
Raffnsøe, Sverre (2015), "What Is Critique? The Critical State of Critique in the Age of Criticism." *MPP Working Paper* 1: 1–26.
Van den Stock, Ady (2016), *The Horizon of Modernity: Subjectivity and Social Structure in New Confucian Philosophy*. Leiden: Brill.

Contributors

Dimitra Amarantidou (易冬蘭) is a PhD candidate in the Department of Chinese Philosophy at East China Normal University (ECNU, Shanghai). Her research focuses on irony and paradox in early Confucian thought. For the past three years, she has taught Chinese philosophy courses at ECNU and has been working both individually and collaboratively on several translation projects, including Chen Guying's 陳鼓應 *Annotated Critical Laozi*, Guo Qiyong's 郭齊勇 *Contemporary Studies of Chinese Philosophy, 1949–2009*, and Yang Guorong's 楊國榮 *Twenty Discourses on Chinese Philosophy*, as well as the latter's *Zhuangzi's World of Thought*.

Rudi Capra completed his BA in philosophy and classical studies at Siena University in 2011 and his MA in philosophy and aesthetics in 2013 at Paris-Sorbonne University. He was awarded his PhD in comparative philosophy east-west at University College Cork in 2019, with a doctoral fellowship from the Irish Research Council. His research focuses on the role of irony in the *Blue Cliff Record* (*biyan lu* 碧巖錄) and Chinese Buddhism. His scholarly interests are Buddhism; Chinese, Japanese, and Greek philosophies; and philosophy of film.

Robert A. Carleo III, holds an MPhil in Chinese Philosophy from Fudan University, and a PhD in Philosophy from the Chinese University of Hong Kong. He works principally on comparative and Chinese philosophy, specializing in Confucian and liberal moral and political theory.

Paul J. D'Ambrosio is Associate Professor of Chinese Philosophy at East China Normal University (ECNU) in Shanghai, Fellow of the Institute of Modern Chinese Thought and Culture, Dean of the Center for Intercultural Research, and Program Coordinator for ECNU's English-language MA and PhD programs. He is the author of 真假之间 (*Between Truth and Falsity*), co-author (with Hans-Georg Moeller) of *Genuine Pretending*, editor (with Michael Sandel) of *Encountering China*. Additionally, he has authored over seventy articles, chapters, and reviews, and is translator of over a dozen books on Chinese philosophy.

Ting-mien Lee is Assistant Professor in the Philosophy and Religious Studies Programme at University of Macau. She received her BA in Chinese literature from National Taiwan University and MA in philosophy from University of Leuven. She completed her PhD in sinology at University of Leuven. Lee's main research interest lies in the area of classical Chinese philosophy, with a specific focus on the interaction of language, power-struggle strategies, and moral theories in pre-Han and early Han China. She also conducts research in the history of Mohist studies.

Hans-Georg Moeller is Professor of Philosophy at the University of Macau. His research focuses on Chinese and comparative philosophy, and on social and political thought. He is the author of *Genuine Pretending: On the Philosophy of the Zhuangzi* (with Paul D'Ambrosio), *The Radical Luhmann*, *The Philosophy of the Daodejing*, and *The Moral Fool: A Case for Amorality*.

Manuel Rivera Espinoza holds a PhD in comparative and Chinese philosophy from the University of Macau. He completed his BA in History at the Universidad de Chile and his MA in History at the University of Arkansas-Fayetteville. His research centers on the interplay of cosmology, philosophy, and religiopolitical institutions in early China. He also has an interest in Latin American philosophy.

Jana S. Rošker studied sinology and obtained her PhD at Vienna University in Austria. She is a Professor of Sinology with expertise in Chinese philosophy. Professor Rošker is a founding member of the Department of Asian Studies at the Faculty of Arts, University of Ljubljana, Slovenia. She is Chief Editor of the journal *Asian studies* and founder, first president, and honorary member of the European Association for Chinese philosophy (EACP). Rošker is the author of numerous influential works on Chinese philosophy, including *Following His Own Path: Li Zehou and Contemporary Chinese Thought*.

Daniel Sarafinas, originally from Pembroke, Massachusetts, is currently a doctoral candidate in philosophy at the University of Macau, where he works primarily on classical Chinese texts, particularly in the field of Lao-Zhuang thought, and critical philosophy. Over the past several years he has also translated many works in contemporary Chinese philosophy.

Geir Sigurðsson is Professor of Chinese Studies in the School of Humanities, University of Iceland. His research focuses on Chinese philosophy and particularly on its hermeneutic value for the contemporary world. His recent publications are *Confucian Propriety and Ritual Learning: A Philosophical Interpretation* and an annotated Icelandic translation of Sunzi's *Art of War*. He received a PhD in philosophy from University of Hawaii.

Ady Van den Stock is a postdoctoral researcher at the Department of Languages and Cultures at Ghent University in Belgium. His research focuses on modern Chinese intellectual history, philosophy, and religion, specifically Sino-Islamic traditions of thought and new Confucianism. He has published a monograph devoted to the latter topic entitled *The Horizon of Modernity: Subjectivity and Social Structure in New Confucian Philosophy* and has translated the work of Chinese thinkers such as Li Zehou, Yang Guorong, Feng Qi, Ge Zhaoguang, and Tang Wenming. He currently serves as executive director of the Académie du Midi Philosophical Association and as a board member of the European Association for Chinese Philosophy.

Robin R. Wang is the Robert H. Taylor Chair Professor in Philosophy at Loyola Marymount University, Los Angeles, and the Berggruen fellow (2016–17) at the Center for Advanced Study in the Behavioral Sciences (CASBS), Stanford University.

Her teaching and research center on Chinese and comparative philosophy, particularly on Daoist philosophy, and women and gender in Chinese culture and tradition. She is the author of *Yinyang: The Way of Heaven and Earth in Chinese Thought and Culture* and editor of *Chinese Philosophy in an Era of Globalization*, and *Images of Women in Chinese Thought and Culture: Writings from the Pre-Qin Period to the Song Dynasty*. She was a credited cultural consultant for the movie *Karate Kid*, 2010.

Andrew K. Whitehead is Associate Professor of Philosophy at Kennesaw State University in the United States. He specializes in east-west comparative philosophy, particularly Japanese and Chinese philosophies, and the German and French traditions of phenomenology and existentialism. He is the President of the Académie du Midi Philosophical Association, an Associate Editor of the journal *Comparative and Continental Philosophy*, an Executive Officer of the Comparative and Continental Philosophy Circle, and a Guest Professor for the Higher Institute of Philosophy (HIW) at KU Leuven in Belgium. He has co-edited several books, including *Wisdom and Philosophy: Contemporary and Comparative Approaches* and *Imagination: Cross-Cultural Philosophical Analyses*.

Ellen Y. Zhang holds a PhD in philosophy of religion from Rice University. She is currently an Associate Professor and Head of the Department of Religion and Philosophy at Hong Kong Baptist University (HKBU). She is also the Associate Director of the Center for Applied Ethics at HKBU and Editor of the *International Journal of Chinese and Comparative Philosophy of Medicine*. Her research relates to Chinese philosophy, ethics, and comparative studies.

Brook Ziporyn is a philosopher, sinologist, buddhologist, and comparativist whose work is internationally known for its rare combination of philologically and historically rigorous work on ancient Chinese texts. He received his BA in east Asian languages and civilizations from the University of Chicago and his PhD from the University of Michigan. He has taught at the University of Michigan, Harvard University, Northwestern University, and National University of Singapore. He is currently Professor of Chinese Religion, Philosophy and Comparative Thought at the Divinity School of the University of Chicago and a member of the fundamentals faculty. Ziporyn specializes in Chinese Tiantai and Chan Buddhism, Daoist philosophy and literature, and comparative philosophy. He also publishes on Confucianism and issues in the history of European metaphysics. He is the author of *Evil and/or/as the Good: Omnicentric Holism, Intersubjectivity and Value Paradox in Tiantai Buddhist Thought*; *The Penumbra Unbound: The Neo-Taoist Philosophy of Guo Xiang*; *Being and Ambiguity: Philosophical Experiments with Tiantai Buddhism*; *Zhuangzi: The Essential Writings with Selections from Traditional Commentaries*; *Ironies of Oneness and Difference: Coherence in Early Chinese Thought*; *Prolegomena to the Study of Li*; *Beyond Oneness and Difference: Li and Coherence in Chinese Buddhist Thought and Its Antecedent*; and *Emptiness and Omnipresence: An Essential Introduction to Tiantai Buddhism*. Translations of his work and his own writings in Chinese have also been published in both the People's Republic of China and the Republic of China on Taiwan. His complete annotated critical translation of the *Zhuangzi* (*Zhuangzi: The Complete Writings*) will be published by Hackett in 2020.

Index

aesthetics 123, 193
  Marxist 116, 117
agency 131, 150, 153, 155, 156, 158, 159, 160, 161, 162
altar of the earth (*she*) 155–8
Ames, Roger 58, 59, 65, 66, 67, 133, 135, 162, 164
animals 27–30, 101, 106, 107, 116, 124
anthropomorphism 39, 40, 46
appropriateness (see *yi*) 14
a priori 2, 22, 24, 116
  historical 182
argument, alternative forms of 15, 19, 70, 74
  by relegation v, 4, 5, 69–75
atheism 43–6, 51, 54
  apophatic 51, 54
atheist(ic) 4, 36, 37, 39, 40, 42, 44, 45
aufhebung (sublation) 185
authority 4, 27, 58, 62, 65, 70, 73, 92, 93, 95, 96, 114, 134, 140–3, 146, 147, 163, 164
  normative authority of history 167–71, 176, 177
autonomy 11, 12, 114, 116, 143, 151, 181, 189, 191
  human 182, 190

barbarians 99–100, 102, 104, 106, 108, 109, 146
  barbarian sages 100, 104
Blue Cliff Record v, 4, 77–8, 80–6, 193
body 25, 28–9, 37–42, 45–7, 105, 126, 128, 129, 130, 139–44, 147, 150
Book of Changes (*Yijing*) 128, 133
Buddhism v, 1, 2, 3, 4, 69–73, 75, 77, 79, 83, 85, 86

Cao Wenyi 128, 132
capitalism 182–3
Chan Buddhism v, 3, 4, 69–75, 77, 79, 85, 86

change(s) 1, 4, 13–15, 17, 19, 24, 28, 35, 45, 57, 60–2, 66, 119, 121, 129, 133, 155, 158–9, 184, 186, 191
  and constancy 60–1
chaos 37, 52–3, 162
China 1, 2, 9, 19, 79, 103, 116, 117, 123, 128, 133, 135, 139, 148, 164, 168, 193
  ancient 12, 83, 89, 98, 100, 139, 140–1, 150, 151, 153, 157, 164, 165, 193, 194
  modern, modernization of, 1, 3, 5, 19, 114, 150, 151, 195
civil society 107
civilization 2, 4, 5, 122, 125, 164, 182, 195
  civilization project 9, 99–109, 111, 117
class struggle v, 1, 113–14, 118, 121
classics 86, 129, 167–70, 175–7
cognition 22–5, 33, 160
collapse 4, 9, 21, 24, 25, 91, 92
communication 62, 134, 155, 182, 186
conformism 184, 185
Confucian 1, 2, 3, 9–12, 14–16, 18, 19, 20, 57–61, 63, 90, 96, 100, 105, 108, 111, 115, 131, 139, 167–8, 179, 193
  ideal of womanhood, v, 5, 125, 131–2
  ideology vi, 5, 9, 107, 167
  orthodoxy 59, 167
  philosophy of education 10–11, 14, 19, 108
  rites and rituals 105–6, 146, 164, 194
  roles 133–5
  sage 101, 103
  social structure 143, 144, 146, 161, 194
Confucianism 1, 2, 3, 9, 90, 105, 125, 143, 147, 148, 150, 161, 164, 178, 194, 195
  critical elements in 3, 10–11, 17–19
  Song Dynasty 167–9, 170–8
  as a state ideology 9, 139
consciousness 2, 24, 26, 38, 43, 48, 73, 78, 83, 101, 182, 190
  karmic 78
contingency 30, 31, 109, 133, 183

convention(al) 13, 27, 29, 32, 35, 42, 62, 63, 65, 69, 71–4, 82, 106, 129, 146, 183
  conventional world 69, 70, 72–3
correlationalism 70–1, 73, 74
cosmology vi, 5, 13, 19, 153–65
  ritual-centered 153, 161
cosmos 63, 127, 133, 155–62
  self-moving 156, 158, 161
creation 14, 156
  as transformation (*zaohua*) 38–40
creator 37, 39–48
crisis v, 3, 4, 21, 23–9, 31, 71, 75, 92, 131, 143, 191
critical attitude 3, 11, 12, 14, 15, 16, 109, 113, 190
critical method 4, 12, 22, 26, 178
critical thinking 2, 11–16, 19, 23
critique
  contextual 16, 18
  self 2, 3, 58, 60, 63, 64
  self-subversive 11
Cultural Revolution 113, 117, 121

Dai Zhen vi, 167–79
dakuai ("Great Clump, Clod") 40, 156–9
Daodejing 5, 49, 52, 101, 102, 125–9, 132, 134
Daoism 1, 2, 3, 31, 59, 90, 125, 128, 135, 139, 147
Daoist(s)
  classics and texts 1, 100, 129
  and Confucians 1, 146
  critique v, 4, 99, 146
  female v, 3, 4, 5, 102, 125–35
  influence of 167, 170
  master or sage 26, 98, 107, 128
  philosophy 5, 27, 49, 84, 130, 135, 139, 143, 146, 150, 195
  practice 128, 130, 132, 134
  self-cultivation 130
  themes and motifs 38, 129
  tradition 3, 115
death 3, 21, 25, 27, 29, 31, 35, 37, 38, 39, 41–6, 47, 50, 51, 81, 95, 107, 135, 173
deconstruction, deconstructionism 29, 81, 83
desire 40, 62, 96, 103, 140, 141, 143, 145, 169, 172–4, 188
dharma 73, 74, 78, 80, 81

dialectic(al), 2, 28, 29, 77, 190
  materialism 1, 3, 117
  relation 28, 29
  self-negating 4, 77, 80
Diaoling 4, 26–7, 31–2
disputes 31, 32, 159, 160
distinctions 43, 47, 105, 107–9, 111, 130, 140, 153–4, 159–61, 163, 189
Dogen 71
dogma (tic) (tism) 2, 9, 10, 11, 16, 18, 21–6, 28, 30, 31, 57, 60, 62, 63, 65, 66, 69, 70, 103, 105, 109, 147, 148, 184, 188
Du (solitude) 132

earth 15, 27, 38, 40–7, 80, 103, 105, 106, 126, 127, 128, 132, 136, 155–9, 164, 195
education 3, 10, 11, 14, 19, 78, 103, 108
emotion(al)(s) 27, 35, 58, 62, 114, 130, 159, 169, 172, 173, 174, 175
empathy 17, 174, 175
emptiness 53, 54, 69, 72, 73, 74, 83, 84, 126, 132, 141, 157
enlightenment philosophy 9, 11, 100, 181, 186, 190, 191
ethical theory 172
Evidential Commentary 169–72, 174, 177–9
evidentiary studies (*kaozhengxue*) 167, 168, 169, 175, 177
experience, experiences 4, 17, 21, 24, 26, 28, 35, 48, 57–60, 62, 69, 73, 80–3, 101, 102, 109, 116, 119, 128, 131, 133, 134, 144, 165, 183

female v, 4, 5, 52, 102, 125–36
feminine values 101
feminism 135, 136
  feminist critique 3, 128, 135, 136
form 40, 44, 45, 46, 49, 82, 83, 116, 130, 159
Foucault 100, 102, 111, 182, 191
Froese, Katrin 59, 63. 66, 67
Fu, Peirong 61, 63, 64, 67

gender(ed) 46, 125, 127–8, 134, 136, 183, 185, 195
generation (*sheng*) 30, 31, 48, 54, 127, 130, 153
German Idealism 181, 191
Genuine Persons 47, 52

God(s) v, 24, 35, 36, 39, 40, 47, 129, 165, 167
gongans 79
Great Clump (*dakuai*) 38, 40, 156–7
Guthrie, William K. C. 57–8, 67

Hall, David 4, 59, 67, 164
Harbsmeier, Chris 58–9, 66, 67
harmony 1, 2, 41, 134, 157, 162
heaven (*tian*) v, 15, 27, 30, 37, 38, 41–55, 80, 89, 90–7, 102, 103, 126, 127, 128, 130, 132, 135, 136, 141, 144, 145, 155, 157, 158, 164, 170, 172, 173, 195
Hegel(ian) 2, 5, 21, 24–6, 29, 32, 115, 116, 118, 121, 182, 192
hermeneutics 81
  subversive v, 4, 77–85
hierarchical
  distinctions 5, 153, 154, 156, 159–61
  structures 78, 144
hierarchy 73, 106, 135, 154, 185
Huaxia civilization 4, 5, 99–112
human(s)
  body 129
  civilization 125
  Confucius as 58–9, 63, 66
  cultivation, transformation 54, 125, 131
  form 38–41
  knowing not-knowing 44–5, 48, 49–51, 53
  labor 118, 120
  mind 114, 116, 119
  and nature 19, 125, 162
  nature and condition 11, 12, 17, 35, 45, 51, 58, 116, 129, 130, 134, 139, 143, 146, 149, 150, 173–4, 153, 182, 185, 190
  potential 38, 46, 122, 129, 133–4, 156
  purpose, responsibility 13, 15, 16, 18, 24, 35, 41, 43, 51, 107, 129, 142, 158
  society, interaction 29, 30, 42, 43, 72, 92, 108, 132, 190
  subject, subjectivity 115, 116, 117, 122, 182, 185
  virtue 128
Hume, David 21, 22
humility 15, 64
humor, humorous 27, 58–9, 66, 67, 109
Husserl 3, 70, 71, 72, 75

ideology vi, 1, 5, 9, 10, 11, 14, 83, 100, 102, 105, 107, 108, 109, 110, 121, 139, 167–79, 188
individuality 11, 12, 132
inner-outer (*neiwai*) distinction 99, 103
intellectual monism 177
intellectualism, intellectualist 175–6, 177
interdependent origination 71
intransparency, epistemic vi, 181, 185, 188–90
inward turn 24–5, 28, 29, 30
irony 57–67, 80, 111, 193

jing (patterns) 57, 60, 61

Kant, Immanuel, Kantian v, 2, 3, 5, 21, 22–6, 32, 33, 75, 100, 113–17, 119, 122, 123, 134, 181, 187, 190
Kasulis, Thomas 72, 75
King of All Under Heaven v, 89, 91, 94–6
King Wu 93, 95, 96
knowing 4, 16, 25, 35–6, 42, 45, 47–54, 65, 128, 135, 160, 175
knowledge v, 2, 11, 12, 15, 16, 24, 35–7, 39, 41, 43, 45–53, 55, 63
Kukai 71
Kundao v, 5, 101, 102, 125, 128, 130–5

labor 49, 118–21, 182, 192
language 12, 39, 43, 59, 62, 71, 73, 111, 116, 119, 148, 159, 181, 182, 185, 193
Laozi 27, 32, 100, 136, 141
learning 3, 10, 14–19, 24, 61, 64–5, 67, 78, 82, 168, 175–8, 194
li (principle) 15, 167, 169, 170, 195
li (ritual propriety) 14, 15, 59, 61, 63, 66, 67, 105–6, 153–4, 157, 163–5, 170
li (taking a stand) 57, 60, 66
Li Zehou v, 4, 5, 61, 63, 67, 113–24
  "subjectality" (*zhutixing*) 114
Liji 154–5, 157–8, 162
Lin Yutang 58, 59, 63, 66, 67
Lingyuan Dadaoge (Song of the Ultimate Source of the Dao) 129, 135
Luhmann, Niklas 5, 23, 32, 33, 184, 186–9

Mao Zedong 114, 117, 121, 123
Mazu Daoyi 3, 73–4
Marx, marxism, marxist v, 1, 2, 3, 5, 10, 113–23, 124, 182, 184, 192

aesthetics 116–17
economic theories 116, 118–19,
    120–1, 182
Sinicization of 115, 117, 121
Mengzi, Mencius v, 4, 14, 19, 89–98, 139,
    140, 141–51, 169–79
Merleau-Ponty 70, 71
metaphysics, metaphysical 21–5, 29, 33, 37,
    80, 109, 143, 163, 169, 174, 176
mind 2, 22–4, 30, 35, 36, 40, 44, 45, 49, 50,
    52, 78, 79, 80, 114, 116, 129–30, 132,
    147, 169, 171, 172, 174, 175
Ming Dynasty 10, 103, 168, 174, 175,
    176, 178
ming (fate) 110, 129, 138
ming (life force) 130
mirror v, 4, 35, 52, 53–4, 59, 74, 129, 189
Mohists 30, 31, 161
monkey, monkeys 53, 107
moral principle 144, 146, 171, 172,
    173–4, 176
mother (*mu*) 44, 47, 51, 125, 126–7,
    129, 131
mourning rituals 44, 46, 51, 105
Mozi 90, 97, 98, 139, 141, 148
mysticism 4, 37, 42, 54
    apophatic 37

nature 12, 15, 19, 27, 29, 73, 78, 80, 84,
    125, 126, 127, 133, 134, 153, 155, 162,
    175, 181
    human 139, 173
    inner or intrinsic 129, 130, 141, 143, 145,
        146, 147, 149, 170
    moral 175, 177
neiwai (inner-outer) distinction 99
Neo-Confucianism 58, 63, 168, 170
    philosophy 169, 171–6, 178
    teachings 169, 172, 177
no-self doctrine 72
non-knowing 35–6, 40, 44–7, 50–1, 53–4
nothing 36, 38, 39, 41, 45
nothingness 37, 38, 40, 42, 45, 46

observation 23, 30, 184, 186, 187, 188, 189
    second-order 23, 25, 30, 187, 188, 192
openness 15, 16, 17, 46–7, 51, 55, 69,
    73, 74, 82
origin 127, 158, 160

orthodoxy 135, 175, 176
    Confucian 167, 174, 178

paradoxicality 4, 57, 60, 66
patterns 15, 57, 60, 61, 62, 127, 130, 148
pedagogical self-subversion v, 3, 9,
    15–16, 18
pedagogy 4, 77
performance 62, 71, 82, 106, 155, 156, 159,
    161, 163
performative showing 71
perspective 4, 22, 24, 25, 26, 28–31, 43, 45,
    48, 51–4, 101–2, 107, 134, 140, 145–7
perspectivism 30, 37, 43, 44
planetary humanity 133–4
Plato 2, 3, 11, 15, 19, 50, 58
    Republic 2, 6
practice 3, 10, 17, 24, 69, 70–4, 77, 78,
    80–3, 121, 125, 128, 132–3, 134, 135,
    171, 181, 183, 185, 186
    of rituals 153–4, 155, 162
praxis 59, 77, 78, 136, 191
principle 5, 13, 17, 22, 25, 60, 82, 90–2, 116,
    119, 130, 139, 140, 141–2, 143, 144–5,
    146, 147, 168, 171–4, 176, 178
    as *li* 167, 169–71
punishment 96, 104, 105, 110, 111
purpose, purposiveness 35–7, 39, 41, 42,
    43, 45, 47, 52, 53, 74, 77, 78

qi (vital energy) v, 43, 44, 45, 129, 130, 155,
    156, 157
Qi (state of) 92, 93–5, 96
Qiwulun 153, 156, 158, 159, 161, 162,
    163, 165
quan (weighing things) 57, 60, 61, 170
Qulishang 154

reason 2, 11, 12, 15, 22, 23, 24, 32, 48, 65,
    115, 116, 117, 119, 123, 128, 174, 181
reciprocity 17
ren 12, 14, 15, 98, 116, 170
representation(s) 5, 53, 186, 187–9
right-wrong (*shi-fei*) distinctions 107,
    111, 160–1
ritual vi, 5, 13, 14, 15, 19, 41–2, 46, 146,
    153–65, 187, 194
roles 13, 17, 72, 128, 131–3, 134, 183, 187
    Confucian 131, 133, 144

sage-king(s) 92, 93, 96
seasons 154–5
self
  abnegation 102, 131
  concept of 5, 139
  consciousness 24, 25, 190
  contradiction 35, 51, 97
  critical attitude, critique 2, 3, 11, 15, 16, 18, 57, 58–64, 65, 66, 69
  cultivation 16, 130, 141, 144
  desecration 80, 83
  erasure 83
  manifestation 28, 29, 30
  movement 153, 156, 161, 162
  natural, 133
  negation 4, 25
  overcoming, 18
  realization 125
  transformative 134
  undermining 4, 70, 77
  understanding 181
self-subversion v, 9, 15, 16, 17, 18, 78
  pedagogical 3, 15, 16
  self-subversive critique 11
she (shrine) 132, 153, 155–7, 158, 159, 163
skillful means 72, 82
society
  capitalist 183
  Chinese 114, 121, 128, 143
  civil 107
  civilized 105
  Confucian 133, 134
  critique of vi, 5, 29, 101, 188, 189, 190–1, 192
  huaxia 105
  hypocrisy in 149
  and identity 29
  impact of 130
  and individual 11, 145, 185, 187
  modern 5, 181, 185–7
  obligations to, 142, 183
  retirement from 146
  and selfhood 29
  subversion in 131, 183
  and trust 12
Socrates 2, 3, 11, 15, 18, 57–8, 67
solitude 17, 18, 19, 26, 132
Son of Heaven 90–1, 92, 93, 96, 97, 155

Song of the Ultimate Source of the Dao (Lingyuan Dadaoge) 129, 135
Speculation 48, 80, 118, 176, 178
speech, Confucian distrust of 12, 14
spontaneity (*ziran*) 110, 148, 153, 161, 162, 163, 181
Spring and Autumn Period 99
stability 9, 14, 42, 57, 60, 78, 106, 153, 155, 156, 158, 161, 183, 184
strategic manuals 89, 98
strategist(s) 4, 89 ff., 90, 91, 93, 95, 97
subject-object 182
sublation (aufhebung) 110, 185
subversion iii, v, vi, 12, 57, 60, 62, 66, 69, 70, 72, 73, 74, 75, 77, 78, 82, 91, 113, 114, 125, 139, 140–1, 142, 143, 144, 146, 148, 149, 150, 154, 158, 177, 182–91
  self- 3, 9 ff, 15, 16–18, 78
  socio-political iii, 3, 4, 5, 87
  strategic 4
  regime 4, 89, 91, 93, 95, 97
supplement 82, 85

theist(ic) 37, 40, 43, 46
tian (Heaven) 37, 91, 94, 102, 103, 126, 143, 144, 149, 158, 170, 185
Tiananmen 113
tools and human development 113, 114, 116, 118, 119
tradition
  Chan Buddhist 69, 77, 78, 79, 80, 83, 86
  Chinese 2, 3, 115, 140, 143, 167, 195
  Confucian 11, 16, 20, 58, 59, 96, 134, 139, 167–9, 175, 177
transcendental 24, 25, 71, 75, 115, 116, 119, 190, 191
  illusion v, 5, 113, 114, 115, 117, 118–19
transformation 18, 27, 38–42, 43, 44, 45, 46–7, 52, 54, 60, 108, 127, 129, 131, 147, 178, 181, 184, 186, 188
  of things 27–9
trust (*xin*) 12, 14, 48, 111
truth 12, 13, 14, 16, 17, 22, 24, 25, 47, 50, 62, 72, 74, 77, 78, 134, 136, 176, 190, 193

uncertainty 85, 133, 159
unconscious 181, 182, 185

unity of three teachings (*sanjiao heyie*) 1, 2, 6

Warring States 12, 89, 92, 102, 108, 139, 163, 164, 168, 179
Way 5, 14–15, 24, 25, 36, 57, 59, 61, 65, 67, 73, 81, 82, 83, 102, 117, 123, 125, 128, 136, 143, 146, 154, 168, 170, 179, 181, 195
Westernization 115
wisdom (*zhi*) ii, 16, 49, 50, 61, 101, 108, 109, 175, 195
woman(hood) v, 5, 80, 102, 125, 126, 127, 128, 129, 131, 132
   ideal of 125, 131, 133, 134
   social construction of 127, 131, 134
wuwei 46, 52

xin (trust) 12, 13
xing (inner nature) 32, 129–30, 141, 143, 144, 170

Xunzi, Xunzi(ian) 14–15, 16, 17, 18, 20, 37, 47, 54, 55, 90, 143, 151, 154, 162, 164, 175, 176, 179

Yang Zhu vi, 5, 139–51
yi (appropriateness) 14–15, 110, 154
Yijing 128, 133
yin and *yang* 19, 37, 38, 39, 126, 195

zhi (wisdom) 50, 159, 178
Zhou Dynasty 90, 92, 93, 96
Zhuangzi, Zhuangzi v, vi, 3–5, 21, 23, 25, 26, 27, 29, 30, 31, 32, 33, 35–55, 59, 84, 85, 86, 100–11, 129, 132–3, 135, 136, 139, 140, 141, 143, 144, 146, 147–8, 150, 151, 153, 156–7, 163, 164, 165, 193, 194, 195
ziran (spontaneity) 141, 144, 153, 158, 160, 162, 172

www.ingramcontent.com/pod-product-compliance
Lightning Source LLC
Chambersburg PA
CBHW072237290426
44111CB00012B/2129